The Stances of e-Government

Policies, Processes and Technologies

The Stances of e-Government

Policies, Processes and Technologies

Edited by
Puneet Kumar, Vinod Kumar Jain, and
Kumar Sambhav Pareek

CRC Press
Taylor & Francis Group
Boca Raton London New York

CRC Press is an imprint of the
Taylor & Francis Group, an **informa** business

CRC Press
Taylor & Francis Group
6000 Broken Sound Parkway NW, Suite 300
Boca Raton, FL 33487-2742

Printed on acid-free paper

International Standard Book Number-13: 978-1-138-30490-1 (Hardback)
International Standard Book Number-13: 978-0-203-73145-1 (eBook)

Library of Congress Cataloging-in-Publication Data

Names: Kumar, Puneet (Assistant professor), editor. | Pareek, Kumar Sambhav, editor. | Jain, Vinod Kumar, editor.
Title: The stances of e-government : policies, processes and technologies / editors: Puneet Kumar, Kumar Sambhav Pareek, Vinod Kumar Jain.
Description: Boca Raton, FL : CRC Press, 2019. | Includes bibliographical references and index.
Identifiers: LCCN 2018028402| ISBN 9781138304901 (hardback : alk. paper) | ISBN 9780203731451 (ebook)
Subjects: LCSH: Internet in public administration.
Classification: LCC JF1525.A8 S835 2019 | DDC 352.3/802854678--dc23
LC record available at https://lccn.loc.gov/2018028402

Visit the Taylor & Francis Web site at
http://www.taylorandfrancis.com

and the CRC Press Web site at
http://www.crcpress.com

Contents

Foreword

Electronic governance, or e-governance, is the leveraging of Information Communication Technology (ICT) by governments to provide services, exchange information, communicate and transact business with their citizens. e-Governance has come a long way in transforming the way government works and digitally empowers its citizens.

By employing e-governance, governments retain a strong citizen-centric focus, for universal access, participation, transparency and accountability to the citizens. Thus, governments not only became more efficient but also increase their accountability and transparency in delivery of services to the citizens in an efficient and effective manner and a shorter timeframe.

The Government of India's ambitious 'Digital India' programme with the vision to transform India into a digitally empowered society and knowledge economy covers initiatives in several sectors such as agriculture, banking, education and health, among others. Some noteworthy initiatives are MyGov, Direct Benefit Transfer (DBT), Digital Locker, GEM and so forth. In the field of education, nowadays, ICT is being used widely for developing Massive Open Online Courses (MOOCs) for enhancing the penetration of education. The dissemination of the MOOCs is through the Government of India platform SWAYAM, National Academic Depository, National Programme on Technology Enhanced Learning (NPTEL) and National Scholarship Portal, among others.

New emerging technologies like Artificial Intelligence, Big Data, Block Chain technology and Machine Learning are now being employed globally for collecting organised data and automate processes.

At this juncture, this research book *The Stances of e-Government: Policies, Processes and Technologies* is timely and will play a vital role, as it is a fusion of multiple tributaries *viz* political science, economics, electronics and computer science. The book not only provides political insights about the government's policies but also discusses the handling and analysis of huge amounts of unstructured data, i.e. Big Data, being produced by e-government applications. It provides readers with an insight into the economic impact of e-governance on the livelihood of a common man. The book also discusses the legal framework for e-government and utility of wireless sensor network for the common man and governments at large. While nations across the globe are vying with each other in a blind race of technological upgradations, they have to keep in mind any adverse or inadvertent impact on climate such technological advancements may have. The book also shows a very serious concern about electronic waste.

Overall the book has some insightful data covered in its eighteen chapters which will be immensely beneficial to researchers, academic fraternity and ICT enthusiasts.

The efforts of the editors of the book, Prof. V. K. Jain, Dr. Puneet Kumar and Dr. Kumar Sambhav Pareek, are indeed laudable.

I wish the book a great success.

Prof. Rajnish Jain
Secretary, University Grants Commission,
New Delhi, India

Foreword

Preface

"If the people cannot trust their government to do the job for which it exists—to protect them and to promote their common welfare—all else is lost," said Barack Obama, former President of the United States of America.* The single point agenda of the transformation from traditional governance to electronic governance is to empower the public in terms of social, political, economic, and technological development. The whole world is witnessing the transcendental growth of information and communication technology (ICT) in the last two decades. As per the general perception, our conventional systems have been replaced with smart systems, whether it is by machine or the *modus operandi* of the traditional governance system. In the current era, ICT has become the backbone of IT enabled governance, whereas data is like its bone marrow. Napoleon Bonaparte once said, *"I am sometimes a fox and sometimes a lion. The whole secret of government lies in knowing when to be the one or the other."*† Hence, while infusing ICT into the governance process, a nation has to be clever like a fox in order to rule like a lion.

The Global Information Technology Report by the World Economic Forum reflects deep insights about the performance of countries toward adoption of e-government. Countries such as Singapore, Luxembourg, Hong Kong, and Sweden have an average Internet bandwidth more than 500 kbps, whereas developing countries such as India, Bangladesh, China, and Pakistan have less than 10 kbps. Many countries such as Armenia, Israel, and Italy have 100 per cent mobile network coverage, whereas most developing and developed nations have more than 86 per cent coverage, and a few countries, for example, Burundi and Mali, have less than 50 per cent coverage. But the global community is facing a serious concern about the security of Internet servers; for example, the highly ranked country Iceland is able to secure 3214.4 servers per million population, whereas 50 per cent of countries have only 40–50 secure servers per million population.

This book is an attempt to envisage current scenarios of e-government across the globe in terms of technological, economic, and political aspects. The Prime Minister of India, Mr. Narendra Modi, has said, *"E-Governance can bring minimum government and maximum governance. It is easy, effective and economic governance. It brings empowerment, equity, and efficiency of the economy. It is a very useful field that can be the greatest problem solver of the people."*‡ In this attempt, we have tried to throw a spotlight on current e-government practices, technological solutions to cope with future demands, the economic impact on the livelihoods of the public, and the inadvertent impact of digitalization on the global community. We hope this book will open new avenues for further research and will be beneficial for all stakeholders of society.

Editors

---

* https://www.brainyquote.com/quotes/barack_obama_409130
† https://www.brainyquote.com/quotes/napoleon_bonaparte_166656
‡ http://gujaratindia.com/printpreview.aspx?id=163&lg=en&NewsID=fYbNyLflZMz0n50gjPmc7g==

The MathWorks, Inc.
3 Apple Hill Drive
Natick, MA 01760-2098 USA
Tel: 508 647 7000
Fax: 508-647-7001
E-mail: info@mathworks.com
Web: www.mathworks.com

Editors

Dr. Puneet Kumar is currently working as an Assistant Professor in the Department of Computer Science and Engineering and Coordinator of Research and Development Cell, College of Engineering and Technology, Mody University of Science and Technology, India. Although he earned his master's and PhD degrees in computer science, he believes in the philosophy of interdisciplinary research. He has also completed a certificate course on intellectual property rights from WIPO Academy, Geneva. Dr. Kumar has more than 15 years of teaching, research, and industrial experience. His major research interests are e-government, the semantic web, and ontologies. He has published various research papers and articles in national and international journals, and his papers are widely cited by various stakeholders across the world. He is also the recipient of a software copyright on his software from the Ministry of Human Resource and Development, Government of India. Apart from this, in 2016 he published a book on e-governance titled *E-Governance in India: Problems, Prototypes and Prospects*. He is also a Life Member of CSI (Computer Society of India), IAENG (International Association of Engineers) and a Professional Member of ACM (Association for Computing Machinery).

Dr. Vinod Kumar Jain earned an MBA, an MTech (CS), and a PhD in computer science and engineering from Devi Ahilya University, Indore. He has been involved in teaching, training, research, and administration for the past 22 years, which includes his 12 years of experience as director/dean in various institutions/universities of repute in India. He has rich experiences in autonomy implementation at ABET (Accreditation Board for Engineering and Technology), United States; NBA (National Board of Accreditation), India; and NAAC (National Assessment and Accreditation Council), India accreditations. He is a recipient of Rashtriya Shiksha Gaurav Puruskar-2016 by Center for Education Growth and Research (CEGR), New Delhi and an accredited management teacher by AIMA (All India Management Association), New Delhi.

There are more than 200 publications to his credit, including books, monographs, cases, research papers, popular articles, and so on. Dr. Jain has organized many conferences/seminars/QIPs and delivered more than 50 keynote/expert lectures. He is actively associated with professional and social organizations such as IEEE (Institute of Electrical and Electronics Engineers), ICSA (International Science Community Association), CSI (Computer Society of India), ISTD (Indian Society for Training and Development), ISTE (Indian Society for Technical Education), IEI (Institution of Engineers (India)), AIMA (All India Management Association), AIMS (Association of Indian Management Schools), GLOGIFT (Global Conference on Flexible Systems Management), QCFI (Quality Circle Forum of India), and BVP (Bharat Vikas Parishad). He is a PhD supervisor at Devi Ahilya University, Indore, and Mody University, Lakshmangarh, and has guided 12 PhD scholars.

His areas of interest include IT enabled supply chain management, service quality in technical education, research methodology, AI (Artificial Intelligence) and Big Data analytics, and ERP (Enterprise Resource Planning), RFID (Radio Frequency Identification), and EDI (Electronic Data Interchange) technologies.

Dr. Kumar Sambhav Pareek is a renowned academic in the realm of political science. He has more than 11 years of teaching and prolific research experience. He is a keen observer of not only the Indian political system but also the systems of other developing and developed nations. His professional associations include Life Member of the Indian Political Science Association, Life Member of the Rajasthan Political Science Association, and Life Member of the Indian Society for Gandhian Studies. Apart from various research publications, Dr. Pareek has authored one book on the primary unit of the Indian political system, i.e., "Zila Parishad."

List of Contributors

Himanshu Aggarwal
Department of Computer Engineering
Punjabi University
Patiala, India

Jyoti Anand
College of Engineering and Technology
Mody University of Science and Technology
Lakshmangarh, India

Bhaskar Arora
School of Business and Commerce
Manipal University Jaipur
Jaipur, India

Minali Banerjee
Department of Economics
Faculty of Arts and Law
Manipal University
Jaipur, India

Vandana Bhatia
Department of Computer Science and Engineering
Thapar Institute of Engineering and Technology
Patiala, India

Partha Pratim Bhattacharya
College of Engineering and Technology
Mody University of Science and Technology
Lakshmangarh, India

Bhartendu Kumar Chaturvedi
Department of Economics
School of Business, University of Petroleum and Energy Studies
Dehradun, India

Deepa
KIET School of Management
KIET Group of Institutions
Ghaziabad, India

Geetanjali Dutta
Entrepreneurship Development Institute of India (EDII)
Ahmedabad, India

Akanksha Gupta
Department of Computer Science
Swami Shraddhanand College, Delhi University
New Delhi, India

Prateek Gupta
KIET School of Management
KIET Group of Institutions
Ghaziabad, India

Siddharth Jaidka
Department of Information Technology
Manipal University
Jaipur, India

Monika Jain
Department of Information Technology
Manipal University
Jaipur, India

Minakshi Kalra
Department of Computer Science
Government College
Hisar, India

Vijay Kumar
Computer Science and Engineering Department
Thapar Institute of Engineering and Technology
Patiala, India

Jatinder Manhas
Department of Computer Science and IT
University of Jammu
Jammu, India

Ishaya Martins
Department of Jurisprudence and International Law, Faculty of Law
National Open University of Nigeria
Lagos, Nigeria

Raunak Monir
Department of Electronics and Communications
College of Engineering and Technology, Mody University of Science and Technology
Lakshmangarh, India

Sanjay Kumar Pradhan
School of Liberal Studies
Pandit Deendayal Petroleum University
Gandhinagar, India

Sushil Kumar Rai
Department of Economics
School of Business, University of Petroleum and Energy Studies
Dehradun, India

Rinkle Rani
Department of Computer Science and Engineering
Thapar Institute of Engineering and Technology
Patiala, India

Vishalakshi Rituraj
Department of Mathematics
Magadh University
Bodhgaya, India

Ravi Sankar Sangam
Department of Computer Science and Engineering
VIT AP University
Amaravathi, India

Abid Sarwar
Department of Computer Science and IT
University of Jammu
Jammu, India

Rahul Saxena
Department of Information Technology
Manipal University
Jaipur, India

Deepak Sethi
Department of Computer Science and Engineering, ASET
AMITY University
Uttar Pradesh, India

Vinod Sharma
Department of Computer Science and IT
University of Jammu
Jammu, India

Manju Singh
Department of Humanities and Social Sciences
Malaviya National Institute of Technology
Jaipur, India

Rajeev Srivastava
Department of Decision Sciences
University of Petroleum and Energy Studies
Dehradun, India

Satyajee Srivastava
School of Computer Science and Engineering
Galgotias University
Greater Noida, India

Ranjana Thalore
Department of Electronics and Communications
College of Engineering and Technology, Mody University of Science and Technology
Lakshmangarh, India

Meena Thangaraj
Department of Computer Science and Engineering
VIT AP University
Amaravathi, India

Umang
Department of Information Technology
Institute of Technology and Science
Ghaziabad, India

Dilbag Singh
Department of Computer Science and Engineering
Thapar Institute of Engineering and Technology
Patiala, India

1

Making of e-India through the "Digital India" e-Governance Plan: Impact and Challenges

Vishalakshi Rituraj

CONTENTS

1.1 Introduction

The core element behind the development of a country is its citizens because they directly participate in the democratic processes of selecting and running the government successfully. With growing computerization in each and every field of life, people are becoming more aware of their rights and duties. Today, there are many social media platforms like Twitter, Facebook, WhatsApp, YouTube, and so on, where people put their points loudly, either supporting or opposing the government, and they cannot be fooled in any way. This technological revolution demands the government to be transparent to its citizens so that they can have active participation in making a state democratic in a real sense.

e-Governance is a system of using electronic media and information technology, such as the Internet and mobile networks, to properly and effectively connect people and the authoritative bodies so that there could be a better and quicker delivery of government services to benefit its citizens. e-Governance is gaining popularity in today's world as a digital media of communication between the government and the masses for conveying policies and services. In fact, it is an electronic version of government that uses information and communications technology (ICT) to make a state capable of standing firmly in the race of digitization. There are several benefits of e-governance over conventional governance methods, some of them are as follows:

1. All the policies and services are only a click away from people, making it more transparent and trustful.

2. It is smooth and fast because it takes less time to accomplish a service.
3. It saves people's time and money in wandering around different offices, ensuring less corruption, which leads to cost reduction and better revenue growth.
4. Electronically accessed services require less paper, thus it is more environmentally friendly.

India is a country with a vast population, and democracy is the soul of it. Handling such a big population with diverse cultures and languages is quite a cumbersome task for any government. The target of e-governance in India is to make government accessible even in remote rural areas. One of the milestone initiatives of Indian government is the *Digital India Program*. The Digital India Program is a flagship program of the Government of India with a vision to transform India into a digitally empowered society and knowledge economy ("About Digital India," 2018). It is a transformative dream for all Indians that is changing people's livelihood as well as their mindset, which is going to be a real development.

1.2 e-Governance in India

With emerging technology, India is one of the fastest growing economies in the world. Information technology has brought awareness to the masses, which has resulted in the active participation of people in democracy. Prime Minister Sri Narendra Modi addressed the nation on 10 May 2017 to state that "e-governance stands for easy, effective, economical, and environment-friendly governance. Technology has the power to transform our economic potential as well. *IT + IT = IT. This means 'Information Technology + Indian Talent = India Tomorrow.'*"

The beginning of e-governance was started in 1977 with the foundation of the National Informatics Centre (NIC) by the Department of Electronics and Information Technology, Government of India. NIC has played a major role in deploying ICT-based communication systems to connect the central government, state government, union-territory administrations, district headquarters, and other government or autonomous bodies by computerizing the entire system.

The National e-Governance Plan (NeGP) takes a holistic view of e-governance initiatives across the country, integrating them into a collective vision, a shared cause. Around this idea, a massive countrywide infrastructure reaching down to the remotest of villages is evolving, and large-scale digitization of records is taking place to enable easy, reliable access to the Internet. The ultimate objective is to bring public services closer to citizens, as articulated in the vision statement of NeGP (National e-Governance Plan, 2018).

1.2.1 Types of e-Governance

1. *Government to Government (G2G)*: G2G e-governance takes place only within the government entities, such as interaction among different government agencies, between national, provincial, and local government agencies, and as a communication between different levels within an organization.
2. *Government to Citizen (G2C)*: G2C involves the interaction between the government and citizens. Its main focus is to provide accessibility to government schemes and

services for each citizen, with the aim of making the government approachable for every citizen. Some examples of G2C are online income tax filing, online retrieval of birth/death or other certificates, and computerization of land records.

3. *Government to Business (G2B)*: G2B is an interaction between the government and business in order to make a more transparent and efficient business environment. It includes services like online registration, permits, licensing, tax payments, and many others.
4. *Government to Employees (G2E)*: This mode of governance provides communication between the government and its employees for an easy execution of policies. Examples of G2E are online conferencing or training of employees.

1.3 Digital India Project

The Digital India project, a dream of every Indian, was launched by Prime Minister Mr. Narendra Modi on 1 July 2015. It is coordinated by the Department of Electronics and Information Technology (DeitY), India, with the co-operation of various government and non-government departments as well as the state government.

The prime aim of this scheme is to boost e-governance and to make India a digital nation. The world acknowledged the caliber of twenty-first-century India and its futuristic project during Prime Minister Modi's visit to Silicon Valley. Mr. Sundar Pichai (Google's CEO), Mr. Satya Nadal (Microsoft's CEO), Mr. Tim Cook (Apple's CEO), and other technology titans showed interest and stepped ahead to be a part of the digital transformation of India. Furthermore, this initiative became popular and started trending as an Internet sensation when, after meeting Indian Prime Minister, Mark Zuckerberg (the CEO of Facebook) changed his Facebook profile picture to a tricolor supporting the Digital India Campaign (Facebook, 2015).

As soon as the post went viral, people from teenagers upwards started changing their profile picture to support the campaign, the word "Digital India" was on everyone's lips, and this was the desired step toward being a part of Digital India.

Digital India is an ambitious step toward implementing e-governance in the country in order to fulfill the gap between the government and its citizens by connecting rural areas with high-speed Internet connections. This will make the government and its services digitally available to each citizen with a click. In a layman's term, this project encourages use of computers, mobile phones, and other ICT-based methods to interact with the government or private services, for example, online tax payments, money transfers, mobile recharging, shopping, e-registration, e-certificates, and many more. For the successful implementation of e-governance, the government are putting in a large amount of effort. One such major and basic step is the Unique Identification (UID) project, which provides a digital identification to each citizen that is publicly known as the "Aadhar card" of an individual. The Aadhar card is a person's digital biometric identity, which is beneficial in terms of availing of government schemes.

The Digital India project gained lots of support at the national and international level as soon as it was launched. Some of the major corporate supports for this project are:

1. Google announced the provision of free and high-speed Wi-Fi access to over 400 railway stations in India with the collaboration of RailTel (Dhapola, 2015).

2. Intel has announced three innovative initiatives to strengthen its support for the Digital India program. These projects are aimed at accelerating digital literacy at the grassroots level (Bokil, 2016).
3. The Microsoft CEO, Mr. Satya Nadella, supported the Digital India initiative in a video message at the launch of Digital India week and promised to help the government in efforts to "transform" the country through technological innovations (Press Trust of India, 2015).
4. Top business tycoons of India committed investments of 45 trillion Indian rupees for Digital India initiatives, promising to create about 1.8 million jobs in the country in the next 5–10 years (Bhargava, 2015).
5. Reliance Industries Chief Mukesh Ambani committed an investment of 250,000 crore Indian rupees on the initiative, which will create over 500,000 direct and indirect jobs (The Hindu, 2015).

1.3.1 Vision of Digital India

The Government of India initiated the Digital India project to achieve smooth e-governance. It has the following visions for this dream project (Vision of Digital India, 2018):

1. *Digital infrastructure as a utility to every citizen*: The first step of digitization focuses on the availability of a high-speed Internet connection as a backbone. BharatNet is one of the pillars of the Digital India scheme, which provides broadband connectivity using optical fiber. Under phase-1 of BharatNet, 1 lakh gram panchayats have been provided with high-speed broadband connectivity. On 8 January 2018, Telecom Secretary Aruna Sundararajan said that the second phase of the project has been initiated for connecting the remaining 1.5 lakh gram panchayats for the high-speed broadband network by December 2018 (Press Trust of India, 2018).

   The DigiLocker service of the government enables citizens to use digital certificates and documents with digital signatures, which are sharable electronically among agencies that ensures authenticity, security, and safety in the cyber world. The government is focusing on cashless financial transaction by promoting Internet banking and other mobile applications for easy money transfers and to move toward paperless governance.
2. *Governance and services on demand*: There will be an integration of all departments of central and state government and the digitized information will be available and accessible for all citizens. This will facilitate people with services on demand by a single click. Digital financial transactions will be easy for doing online business, which is an initiation toward a cashless economy.
3. *Digital empowerment of citizens*: Digital literacy is one of the key issue through which all the other visions of government can be achieved. Under this vision, there will be an availability of online educational resources, documents, forms, and so on, which will encourage people to be technically aware and to educate themselves without being physically present in any institution.

1.3.2 Projects under the "Digital India" Initiative

1. *Aadhar*: Aadhar is an identification system for citizens of India based on biometrics, which makes it unique. The government focused on having an Aadhar identity so that people can be benefit from government welfare schemes in social or financial sectors by eliminating fraud with duplicate identities. It has been one of the effective tools of the Digital India campaign.
2. *DigiLocker*: DigiLocker is an initiative under Digital India that eliminates the need of carrying physical documents by providing people with a dedicated digital space for storing their documents and certificates electronically. The DigiLocker of a person is linked and accessible via the Aadhar number of that person.
3. *MyGov.in*: This is an online platform hosted by NIC for Indian citizens to directly participate in their governance. Through this portal, people can discuss ideas and put their views and suggestions on various projects such as Skill India, Clean Ganga, Digital India, or any other government schemes.
4. *e-Hospital*: e-Hospital is an ICT-based hospital management system designed to provide a complete solution in the health sector such as registration, enquiries about blood banks, laboratories, operation theatres, electronic billing, and other services of a hospital. It saves people's time and effort in moving from one hospital to another.
5. *Gramin Digital Saksharata Abhiyan (GDISHA)*: GDISHA is a project under "Skill India" under which the government's vision is to provide digital knowledge to people in rural areas to make them capable of using computers, smartphones, or other gadgets to access knowledge and information. On 8 February 2017, the Prime Minister, Mr. Narendra Modi, approved *Pradhan Mantri Digital Saksharta Abhiyan (PMGDISHA)*. The budget for this project is Rs 2,351.38 crore to use for digital literacy in rural India until March 2019. This project is expected to be one of the biggest projects of the world in order to make 6 crore Indian houses digitally literate (Information Bureau, 2017).
6. *Farmer portal*: Farmers directly contribute in a country's gross domestic product (GDP). So, a farmer portal has been launched for Indian farmers that serves to provide farmers with relevant and detailed information of weather, soil fertility, crop, seed, fertilizers, market price, and stock, as well as training, insurance, and other government schemes for their welfare. This portal provides almost all types of assistance to farmers in order to boost agriculture.
7. *Start up India portal*: On 15 August 2015, Prime Minister Mr. Narendra Modi introduced the Start Up India project, which was unveiled on 16 January 2015 (India Today, 2016). Through this portal, the government aims to boost the economy by attracting and helping young, innovative entrepreneurs to start up in India. This project provides a simple and user-friendly approach as well as guidelines for investing and doing business in India, allowing opportunities for employment to be maximized.
8. *National scholarship portal*: The government of India initiated the National Scholarships Portal under NeGP. This initiative aims to provide a simplified and transparent scholarship program that assures a timely and accurate distribution of financial help to meritorious and needy students.

9. *e-Visa*: The e-Tourist Visa enables prospective visitors to apply for an Indian visa from his/her home country online without visiting the Indian Mission and also pay the visa fee online (eVISA, 2018).
10. *e-Panchayat*: The e-Panchayat project is an initiation of the Ministry of Panchayati Raj (MoPR), the Government of India, to strengthen e-governance by automating day-to-day functioning in gram panchayats, block panchayats, and zila panchayats. This scheme has resulted in a better delivery of government services at Panchayat level and thus changing people's livelihood in villages.
11. *Jeevan Pramaan*: Prime Minister Sri Narendra Modi launched "Jeevan Pramaan," an "Aadhar-based Digital Life Certificate" on 10 November 2014 for pensioners, which could eventually benefit over a crore pensioners (PMINDIA, 2014). This scheme has made the entire process of verification, authentication, and pension disbursement simpler thus making the retirement phase hassle free.
12. *Swachh Bharat Mission Mobile App*: This is a mobile application for the Swachh Bharat Mission campaign initiated by the Government of India. People can download this application, click images of waste/dirty areas, and send the image with its geographical location to the Swachh Bharat National Server. This is the way we can claim our active participation in the cleanliness mission anywhere in the country.
13. *BHIM (Bharat Interface for Money) App*: This is a digital application supported by all Indian banks for direct money transactions using UPI (Unified Payment Interface). This is an easy, secure, and quick e-payments service launched by the Government of India for its citizens to encourage cashless transactions.

1.3.3 Impact of the Digital India Scheme at Grass Roots

1. The Digital India scheme provides ICT equipped infrastructure and the modernization of agriculture, education, health, industry, and other sectors as catalysts for the economy. According to Mr. K.J. Alphons, Minister of State for Electronics and IT, the Digital India program has the potential to provide an incremental 20 per cent to 30 per cent increase in India's GDP by 2025, owing to the significant progress made under the scheme since its inception in July 2015 (ASSOCHAM India, 2017).
2. India is the second largest country in the world and has a huge number of Internet users, with 34.4 per cent Internet penetration in the world (Internet World Stats, 2018). According to Mr. Amitabh Kant (CEO of Niti Aayog), India has ranked in the top position in the world for mobile data usage and its mobile data consumption is higher than the United States and China's mobile data consumption put together (Times of India, 2017). Reliance Jio's digital services have boosted the Indian digital market across the world.
3. The ICT-based Skill India project has increased digital literacy among people residing in rural areas by facilitating technology-based training to farmers through smart and virtual classrooms. The government is installing free Wi-Fi hotspot at public places for universal access to the Internet. The Digital India scheme targets the maximization of employment opportunities by providing IT training to people.
4. In order to move the masses toward technology, the government has started to provide applications in Hindi and other regional languages to ensure people's maximum participation in e-governance. Rajasthan is the first state in the country

to launch free email addresses in Hindi for people who are not comfortable with English e-mail ids. The facility will be available at name@rajasthan.bharat (in Devanagari script) (Ahuja, 2017).

5. Aadhar-based digital identity has simplified almost all types of financial transactions and tax payments, availing subsidy from government that has provided a road for new startups in the country. This electronic modernization has led to an improved socio-economic status of the populous.
6. To initiate mobile governance, the Government of India has launched UMANG (Unified Mobile Application for New-age Government) (Chakraborty, 2017), which can help people in a number of ways. It enables citizens to get information about EPF (Employee Provident Fund), passports, women's safety, healthcare, and so on; one can apply for his/her PAN (Permanent Account Number) and have hundreds of services in 12 languages.
7. Online availability of government schemes, documents, results, and other public records, as well as the online RTI facility, have strengthened people's faith in the government, resulting in their active participation. This is the core element of a real democracy.
8. Digitization of sectors like banking, railways, aviation, universities, healthcare, business industries such as e-commerce, and other day-to-day activities from a simple mobile recharge to a big business deal, is only one click away from our doors with quick responses and fast delivery of services.
9. The Digital India program has boosted India's digital market by promoting and advertising the government's vision, schemes, or services extensively on social media platforms for a global reach. Social media has been a weapon for people and even for ministers and government officials to utilize Facebook, Twitter, and so on, to receive complaints and feedback from citizens for quality service delivery.
10. The Reliance India chief, Mr. Mukesh Ambani, has come forward to support the Digital India scheme by launching the 4G network plan Reliance JIO on 5 September 2016 in India. It started a revolution in the telecom industry by offering free 4G Internet service along with a 4G handset. This free scheme made the Internet affordable for the masses even in the remotest area of the country and at the same time it initiated a competition in the Indian telecom industry to offer cheap and affordable Internet and voice data in order to lock in customers.
11. The Digital India scheme aims to reduce the corruption rate by a direct service delivery to the individual instead of bribing an intermediary agent and moving around different offices. Thus, it saves people's time, effort, and money.
12. Digital India is an environmental friendly approach as it involves less paper consumption, hence, contributing to the achievement of a Green India.

1.3.4 Challenges in Implementing Digital India

There are some challenges that the Digital India project has to face in its implementation and for its accomplishment.

1. *Population*: India has the second largest population in the world (Worldometers, 2017), so handling such a huge population and implementing e-governance in rural and remote villages, where people are struggling for the fundamental needs

of life, requires a lot of effort and patience. Moving this vast population to the mainstream as well as integrating people with diverse cultures, languages, and education levels toward digitization is not an easy task.

2. *Lack of management*: For implementing this project at the ground level, proper channelization and coordination among departments of central and state government, district headquarters, Gram Panchayat, and other agencies are essential. Execution of the project at village level and to guarantee service delivery to each citizen is possible by overcoming hurdles like bureaucracy, lack of will power, corruption, and a proper infrastructure for digitization.
3. *Digital literacy*: Success of the Digital India program completely depends on the awareness of the people, and if possible, the information can be reached for everyone. Digital literacy is one of the important needs of the Digital India program, that is why government has initiated Skill India, PMKVY (Pradhanmantri Kaushal Vikash Yojna), and other schemes in this direction so that people can be able to handle electronic gadgets. But before achieving this goal, the government needs to address the illiteracy that is the biggest obstacle in the adoption of any scheme. Efforts should be made in rural areas to provide ICT-based training to poor and illiterate people so that digitization may not be only a dream for them.
4. *Cost*: The Government of India aims to connect all panchayats with high-speed broadband and to provide free Wi-Fi facilities to railway stations, schools, universities, and public places for universal access of information by 2019. Implementation of such a big project requires more investment in establishing appropriate infrastructure, Wi-Fi centers and hotspots, and fully equipped data centers for better execution of services.
5. *Security*: Security of the personal records of billions of citizens is a crucial task as tampering with such data may lead to a risk of national security. People hesitate to use digital media for financial transactions over traditional methods due to increasing fraud. So, the government should make a strict policy to deal with cybercrime and ensure confidentiality of citizens' personal information.
6. *Internet and speed*: India ranks third in the world for Internet users and Reliance's Jio Telecom service has played a vital role in making the Internet available everywhere. But according to a survey of Ookla Speedtest Global Index, India ranks in 109th position in the world with 8.80Mbps mobile data networks (The Economic Times Bureau, 2017). Slow Internet speed is a major challenge in achieving digitization.

1.4 Conclusion

With increasing technological evolution and Internet penetration, the need of e-governance in India has grown because true democracy demands transparency in governance. Digital India has lit the path of e-governance in India by integrating the people through technology and making governance easy, reliable, cost-effective, and corruption free. Today, people from every age group spend time on social media to be in touch with their dearest ones. So, the goal of Digital India is not only to change the infrastructure but to actually change the perception of the individual toward technology and changing people's way of thinking. The government will have to come through a number of instances of resistance in implementing e-governance due to poverty, illiteracy, and other issues in India.

In spite of this, Digital India is going to be a milestone achievement in the making of an e-India.

References

"About Digital India" [available online: www.digitalindia.gov.in/content/about-programme]. Retrieved: 5 March 2018.

Ahuja, Manoj, Hindustan Times, 11 December 2017 [available online: www.hindustantimes.com/jaipur/rajasthan-becomes-first-in-country-to-offer-e-mail-ids-in-hindi/story-J9EmC7qfXX3OZczrLbJQJI.html]. Retrieved: 23 December 2017.

"ASSOCHAM India," 12 October 2017 [available online: http://assocham.org/newsdetail.php?id=6528]. Retrieved: 6 March 2018.

Bhargava, Yuthika, The Hindu, 1 July 2015, "Top corporates back Digital India" [available online: www.thehindu.com/news/national/top-corporates-pledge-support-to-prime-minister-narendra-modis-digital-india-project/article7375540.ece]. Retrieved: 13 April 2018.

Bokil, Sneha, Fonearena [available online: www.fonearena.com/blog/186200/intel-india-announces-three-new-digital-india-initiatives.html]. Retrieved: 26 May 2016.

Chakraborty, Sumit, Financial Express, 23 November 2017 [available online: www.financialexpress.com/industry/technology/what-is-umang-app-how-to-download-and-use-pm-modis-e-governance-app-for-aadhaar-other-government-services/944813/]. Retrieved: 11 March 2018.

Dhapola, Shruti, The Indian Express [available online: http://indianexpress.com/article/technology/tech-news-technology/explained-what-is-googles-wifi-at-railway-station-project-and-how-will-it-work/]. Retrieved: 17 December, 2015.

"eVISA" [available online: www.digitalindia.gov.in/content/evisa]. Retrieved: 18 February 2018.

Facebook profile pictures of Sri Narendra Modi (PM, India), Mr. Mark Zuckerberg (CEO, Facebook) [available online: www.facebook.com/supprtdigitalIndia/]. Retrieved: 27 September 2015.

India Today, "Start Up India, Stand Up India," 18 January 2016 [available online: www.indiatoday.in/education-today/gk-current-affairs/story/start-up-india-stand-up-india-304315-2016-01-18]. Retrieved: 16 February 2018.

Internet World Stats, "Top 20 countries with the highest number of internet users," [available online: www.internetworldstats.com/top20.htm]. Retrieved: 6 March 2018.

"National e-Governance Plan" [available online: http://meity.gov.in/divisions/national-e-governance-plan]. Retrieved: 12 January 2018.

PMINDIA, 10 November 2014 [available online: www.pmindia.gov.in/en/news_updates/pm-launches-jeevan-pramaan-digital-life-certificate-for-pensioners/]. Retrieved: 6 March 2018.

"Press Information Bureau Government of India Cabinet," 8 February 2017 [available online: http://pib.nic.in/newsite/PrintRelease.aspx?relid=158292]. Retrieved: 16 February 2018.

Press Trust of India, 1 July 2015 [available online: www.ndtv.com/india-news/digital-india-microsoft-to-focus-on-rural-internet-cloud-solutions-777277]. Retrieved: 3 March 2018.

PTI, 8 January 2018 [available online: www.moneycontrol.com/news/india/bharat-net-phase-2-may-be-completed-by-december-2478057.html]. Retrieved: 10 February 2018.

The Economic Times Bureau, 12 December 2017 [available online: https://economictimes.indiatimes.com/tech/internet/india-ranks-109th-in-mobile-internet-speed-and-76th-in-fixed-broadband/articleshow/62033640.cms]. Retrieved: 23 January 2018.

The Hindu, 1 July 2015 [available online: www.thehindu.com/business/Industry/mukesh-ambani-commits-rs-25-lakh-crore-for-digital-india/article7375158.ece]. Retrieved: 12 April 2018.

Times of India, 22 December 2017 [available online: https://timesofindia.indiatimes.com/business/india-business/india-top-ranked-country-in-mobile-data-consumption-amitabh-kant/articleshow/62203927.cms]. Retrieved: 6 March 2018.

"Vision of Digital India" [available online: www.digitalindia.gov.in/content/vision-and-vision-areas]. Retrieved: 10 February 2018.

Worldometers, "Countries in the world by population (2017)" [available online: www.worldometers.info/world-population/population-by-country/]. Retrieved: 26 December 2017.

2

Role of e-Media in Good Governance and Support to Democracy: A Review of Political Communication in Ghana

Geetanjali Dutta

CONTENTS

2.1 Introduction

Good governance is essential for the good life of every citizen. This good life is sustained when the government, political parties, parliament, the judiciary and the media all work in a comprehensive and systematic manner. Ultimately, this justifies good governance, which means responsive and effective governance. This effective and responsive governance is characterised by efficient policy making and implementation through the correct and best possible decisions. It also creates an environment where the public, political leaders and various government machineries work in a cooperative manner to sustain changes and bring development (DFID, 2008). Therefore, according to the UN Commission for Human Rights, transparency, accountability and participation are the most important features of good governance. Similarly, the United Nations Economic and Social Commission for Asia and the Pacific (UNESCAP) acknowledged that participatory, consensus-oriented, accountable, transparent, responsive, effective and efficient, equitable and inclusive features are some of the important attributes of good governance (Adetoye and Omilusi, 2016). Equally, the World Bank also emphasises that good governance always favours enlightened policy making, effective action and accountable government; the dynamic and visionary professional ethos of bureaucrats; and a strong civil society participating in public affairs; all are expected to behave under the rule of law (Today, 2015).

Like good governance, democracy is also an arena where people have rights and freedom to participate in elections, choose the candidates who will govern them and reject or disapprove the candidates if they are not satisfied with who already holds public office. Both good governance and democracy promote advanced and sustainable human development. Robert Dahl, the famous political theorist, defined democracy as a process that follows the policy of procedural electoral process, with regular, free and fair elections, universal suffrage and unbiased choice among alternatives (Albritton and Bureekul, 2009). A former president of the United States also stated that "Democracy is a government of the people, for the people and by the people". Thus, these two definitions justify democracy as a forum based on the equality of freedom of choice and opportunities, where all the citizens have equal rights to participate and play a significant role in the political process (Praveen, 2014).

Thus, good governance and democracy, although not always compatible with each other and not always on the same track, have aims and objectives that are more or less the same. For example, Albritton and Bureekul (2009) viewed a contradiction between democracy and good governance. They revealed that there are the instances of non-democratic countries having very good governance and some democratic countries that have instances of poor governance. For example, the military regimes in Pakistan embrace some components of good governance, but those do not have any rule of law, or there is no government transparency, free media or any free, fair and regular elections. But they exhibit the most responsive, efficient and effective governance for the betterment of their public. On the other hand, India, although one of the largest and successful democracies, is characterised by poor governance.

Despite these tensions and incompatibility, there are some studies that justify good governance as the basic pillar of democracy. Good governance is always visible in a successful democracy because both possess more or less similar characteristics and both aim for the good life of citizens of a country. Therefore, political philosophers like Thomas Hobbes, John Locke and J. J. Rousseau have emphasised the necessity of good governance in their social contract theories of the origin of the state. Hence, the father of political science, Aristotle, also stated that "the state came into existence for the sake of mere life, but continued for the sake of good life" (Ashraf, 2014). Here, good life is ultimately dependent on good governance and good governance enumerates large-scale success for democracy.

The democratic system, as enunciated by Robert Putman, is a participatory political system and governance becomes good and target-oriented when there is wide participation and there is communication between the masses and the government in various political processes. However, this participation and communication in political process is impossible without people being informed about the various issues. Ultimately, to make active participation of the citizen, various types of media, both the print media as well as new media, have engaged citizens in the political process by informing, educating and mobilising the public. As a platform for information and communication, social media has been playing a major role for some time. While the print media gained wide popularity in the past, electronic media particularly television, radio, Internet, fax, CD-ROMs, DVDs and so on, and the new media like Facebook, YouTube, Twitter and so on have been achieving more popularity in spreading and disseminating information. Among all these, Facebook, which was launched in 2004, and Twitter which was launched in 2006, are the fastest growing social network sites and they are very easy to use. Social media helps people to open free accounts, and through these accounts they can communicate messages with each other easily by using short text messages or "tweets" with a maximum of 140 characters (now 280 characters) (Khasawneh and Abu-Shanab, 2013).

In Ghanaian democracy, the advent of the Internet has exposed the majority of Ghanaians to different interactive platforms on which a different kind of information is exchanged that might have a significant impact on human behaviour, decisions and judgement. Hence, personal communication via social media brings politicians and political parties in Ghana closer to the voters. It also allows politicians to communicate faster and reach citizens in a more targeted manner and vice versa. In fact, e-media plays a prominent role in political communication of Ghana. With the release of frequent information, many political leaders, parties and organisations find that the media is helpful in reaching their target. This also became clear from the statement of one communication official of the New Patriotic Party, who once revealed that their party adopted a writing style that was suitable for social media in its messaging and through this channel, their leaders were able to be closer to a larger number of voters and supporters. Further, the National Democratic Congress also praised social media for its interactive nature, which in fact facilitated the incorporation of feedback from voters into the party's decision-making processes.

Taking into all these accounts, this chapter will examine the role of e-media in promoting good governance and democracy in Ghana. It also tries to find out the role of e-media in political communication and political socialisation by educating and developing the political consciousness among Ghanaians.

2.2 e-Media's Role in Shaping Good Governance and Democracy

Mass media is communication – whether written, broadcast or spoken – that reaches a large audience. It is a source of information; therefore, it has a fundamental role in the functioning of a democratic society and good governance (Ashraf, 2014). For that reason, Pandit Jawaharlal Nehru said media is "the *watchdog of our democracy*" (Praveen, 2014). Not only Pandit Jawaharlal Nehru, but also Gandhiji also emphasised the importance of the media in upholding freedom, expanding education, promoting social reforms and change (Yazav, 2001) (Role, 2018). In fact, these are the essential dimensions of good governance and democracy.

Furthermore, media also functions as a civic forum for political debate, facilitating informed electoral choices and actions, and acts as an agenda setter for policy makers – strengthening government responsiveness to social problems and exclusion (Ashraf, 2014). People also become capable of taking the right decisions in the participation of democracy when they are well informed about the various political issues and problems. In that place, e-media acts as a platform to communicate messages with larger groups within a short span of time, in an easy, cost saving way. It also guides people to think and judge rationally and to take the right decisions and actions that will be beneficial for them. It also helps in promoting the values of pluralism and socialise people to develop the spirit of brotherhood. It makes public services more responsive and strengthens the culture of democracy. In many cases, e-media improves government responses by giving a voice to the vulnerable (Today, 2015).

The media also plays the role of intermediary between the executive, the legislative and the judiciary, which are the main three bodies of the democratic system. Even though electronic media is not a direct institutional branch, it forms part of any successful political set up that can be described as a good democracy. During elections, e-media plays a key role in mobilising masses and thereby affecting voting behaviour. Not only does e-media provide information about political parties, candidates and party manifestoes, but it also offers a platform through which voters and interested individuals across geographical divides can interact with them (GSMIR, 2016).

The illiterate and rural masses learn political knowledge and take decisions in political life through e-media. The dialogue and image of a political leader influences the masses and strengthens the culture of democracy. As a result, people mobilise and participate in the political process and give their views through feedback, which provides inputs for new and target-oriented policy making and for the review and adjustment of policy design, as well as the implementation of policies that will help the needy and socially excluded section of society. The media keeps a close eye on the functioning of the government. It informs the government about the plight of the people. The citizens learn about politics and the government primarily from television and newspapers. Similarly, it also allows people to know the operation of the government (www.cssforum.com). Apart from these, the media acts as a watchdog that helps in promoting transparency and accountability. In many cases, it spreads the news of corruption in the judiciary, the maladministration of public officials, any policy failures of the government and so on. It also communicates critical information about the government, governance and political behaviour between the citizen and the government. In this way, media brings the news to the public and helps in making public services more responsive and effective (Ashraf, 2014).

2.3 e-Media and Political Communication in Ghana

In the twenty-first century, the use of e-media in elections, for example, in campaigning, accessing information relating to politics and communicating political messages, has significantly intensified. Facebook, Twitter, YouTube and so on are becoming innovators and influencers as opinion creators in the political discourse. People are getting information online without the constraints of space and time. In fact, e-media is becoming a cost-effective way for politicians to reach their constituents and to provide insights into political dynamics. They provide a forum for citizens, politicians and civil society organisations to engage in an open discussion and debate, which is essential for the enrichment of democratic values and aspirations. They not only carry a strong and influential voice, but also provide an opportunity for direct interaction and feedback with the target audience. Social media allows users to create, share and search for information without having to login to any specific portal destination.

Over the years, as social media has gained increased prominence in political discourse all over the world, Ghana has not been an exception. Ghanaian politics extensively uses new media in political communication, which has a significant impact on political mobilisation, decision making and judgements. It has been observed by many studies that throughout the political history of Ghana, the media, particularly e-media, has played a vital role in the process of political communication. In political campaigning and marketing, its role is highly recognised in the Ghanaian political sphere (Political Campaigning, 2018). It acts as a channel through which politicians get the opportunity to disseminate political messages to target groups (Dankwah, 2016). With this record, Ghana is ranked as one of the first countries in Sub-Saharan Africa to have Internet access after connection in 1989 to 1990 (GSMIR, 2016).

Since 1992, Ghana has achieved a positive record in conducting successive general elections. When multiparty democracy came to power, and Jerry John Rawlings became the president, the policy of the liberalisation of industry allowed extensive freedom to the media (Kalyango and Adu-Kumi, 2013). Since that time, in every election in Ghana, e-media has been responsible for making democracy more transparent and civic participation more possible. Moreover, e-media has a record in monitoring and checking irregularities in elections and is successful in mobilising people to choose their most efficient leader without any bias for any particular candidate (Treisman, 2016). Therefore, many leaders in Ghana, like elsewhere in the world, take advantage of social media in setting the agenda for civic discussions and political campaigns. With a larger share, Twitter, Facebook and YouTube have given the opportunity to various candidates to reach target groups within a short span of time and free of cost (Penplusbytes, 2018). Some political parties in Ghana, for example, the National Democratic Congress, say the interactive nature of social media facilitates incorporating feedback from voters into the party's decision-making processes (UKEssays, 2013).

2.4 Role of e-Media in Voter Registration and Political Participation

Some studies have revealed that there is a positive and significant relationship between social media and political communication. Social media helps to engage citizens in various political activities such as rallies, protests, demonstrations, virtual or physical meetings and so on (Kalyango and Adu-Kumi, 2013). Social media platforms have not only become important channels for distributing news but they have also remained a central part of how well the news is communicated. Due to the media's intervention, since Ghana's independence (1957), about 66 per cent of its citizens have successfully voted in elections and it is assumed that these e-technologies will help to increase this figure in future (Treisman, 2016). The implementation of the first-ever biometric voter registration in Ghana in 2012 helped to verify identity and streamline the voter registration process in the general election of 2012 (Paul, 2012).

In the 2012 general election, Ghana saw a substantial record in using social media to check fraud and other election-related violence and issues. For example, at that time, many young Ghanaians were encouraged to register their name in the voter list and to cast their vote in the 2012 general election by fun campaigns through using hashtags #iRegistered and "Our Vote, Our Voice" – #OVOV (Treisman, 2016). Observing the limited number of voter registrations exercised between April 28 to May 2016, Ghana Decides, a Blogging Ghana Election Project launched the online #iRegistered campaign to get eligible Ghanaians to register their name in the voter list and increase their number in the 2016 elections (Penplusbytes, 2017). In 2012, during the starting of the voter registration process on March 24, the organisers of Ghana Decides had used Facebook, Twitter, YouTube and so on to put the spotlight on the voter registration process (Paul, 2012). These technologies are so flexible that through SMS, using a short code established by Ghana's Electoral Commission, the citizens can check their registration details.

Apart from that, the website – *Ghana Decides* – also collects various election-related news about various elections conducted in Ghana. They are also able to mobilise fellow citizens in making informed decisions by creating and sharing important information about the election in real time. In the 2012 general election, expecting to conduct free, fair and safe elections for a better-informed electorate through using social media tools, the nonpartisan Ghana Decides was launched on March 24, 2012 (Paul, 2012). At that time, major initiatives were taken in using new electronic media tools in political processes and political communication. For example, fingerprint scanning technology was used for potential voters and to verify identities, which ensured a fair electoral process. Moreover, through *Odekro,* a parliamentary monitoring site, the citizens of Ghana are able to access information of various debates, discussions and the vision of their leaders (Treisman, 2016). In this way, e-media is helping citizens to access various live interviews with MPs, participate in polls, find out information of election results and so on.

2.5 Involvement of e-Media in Political Campaigning

Election campaign through e-media plays a crucial role in the electoral victory of candidates and political parties. In the past, politicians relied on traditional methods including the use of newspapers, radio and television (TV) advertisements, mounting of political billboards, posters and branding of vehicles with party logos and symbols, among a host of others. However, today in Ghana, the use of social media platforms has emerged, which has had an impact in reaching out to a large proportion of the electorate (www.ghanapoliticsonline.com). For example, during the 2012 Ghana elections, new digital technologies were applied by all stakeholders in the election continuum, from the electoral management body, political parties and electoral observers, down to the level of individual voters.

Moreover, in December 2008, in the Ghanaian presidential election, the extensive use of digital media and mobile phones was found in election campaigning by the political workers of both presidential candidates – John Atta Mills and Nana Akufo-Addo (Penplusbytes, 2017). By establishing separate websites for each party, they used their own site to spread their election campaign messages and for the collection of funds, and used mobile phones for network connections and monitoring of the election process. For the first time, extensive use of the media service in the Ghanaian political field, where through a larger SMS-based system of election campaign and the use of Twitter and Facebook by both candidates, gave the best result in the election. More interestingly, John Atta Mills, who was defeated two times in the earlier election, won the presidential race. Both parties accepted the results because of the monitoring of the electoral process by international NGOs and observers through the SMS services (Riaz, 2010).

e-Media also plays a very significant role in spreading every type of information – positive or negative – related to government action, effort, behaviour and so on. For example, in 2015, *Odekro* spread news of high absenteeism of MPs, which revealed that about 50 per cent of MPs in Ghana remained absent in parliamentary meetings and sessions, which is against the law of the Ghanaian Constitution (Treisman, 2016; MyJoyOnline.com, 2016). Apart from that, *Penplusbytes,* a civic tech organisation, has developed several platforms to supports free and fair elections in Ghana. It collects data through social media site and SMS reports to track election irregularities, fraud and outbreaks of violence. It also creates short videos that can be easily shared on social media and WhatsApp to encourage youths to vote. Moreover, through Facebook, which is the most popular social network, where Ghana's position is 37th in the world, and having about 1,436,560 Facebook users, they express their support and opposite views about various important national issues (UKEssays, 2013).

There are also some Civil Service Organisations (CSOs) such as the Center for Democratic Development (CDD) Ghana and the Institute of Economic Affairs (IEA), which operate in Ghana, that explored the importance and usefulness of new medias during the 2012 general election. Acknowledging the importance of new media, they used Twitter and

Facebook in order to communicate their demands to the political parties during the 2012 election campaigning, which ultimately grabbed the attention of both political parties as well as the public (Oxfam, 2013). Furthermore, in the same election, Dr Paa Kwesi Nduom, the presidential candidate for the PPP (Progressive People's Party), had requested more than 10,551 Facebook followers to participate in an online chat with him, which finally provided an opportunity to engage with his supporters and gave them the chances to ask questions and make comments (Fridausu, 2012). Ras Mubarak, one of the youngest parliamentary candidates in the 2012 election, connected with around 2,000 public subscriptions on his Facebook account and constantly updated his campaign activities. By doing this, he was able to reach out to many people by providing them with the opportunity to be informed about his decisions and his ideas, and he replied to public queries, views and comments (Fridausu, 2012).

Even after coming to power, most political parties and even governments in Ghana, publicise their achievements, objectives and policy perspectives through social media. For example, after coming to power, the National Democratic Congress (NDC) have been using social media since 2016, especially Facebook, to show video adverts to inform Ghanaians about government achievements. The president also used this medium to entreat prospective voters to register during the 2016 election (GSMIR, 2016). Further, in the 2016 election period, social media reached its highest point in highlighting the issues of internal wrangling of the largest opposition party, the judicial scandal and violence during voter registration that led to limited voter registration (Penplusbytes, 2017). Noticing limited voter registration in 2016, domestic election observers (CODEO) also used social media to educate the public to register their name to vote and other related issues (Penplusbytes, 2017). Even the New Patriotic Party (NPP), the largest opposition political party, used social media to critique the sitting government and to provide policy alternatives. Through social media, the party engaged youths and solicited their votes with the promise of economic emancipation in the coming years if they won the election (GSMIR, 2016).

The below picture reflects the celebration of the supporters of Ghana's New Patriotic Party on the streets of Kasoa, Ghana, on December 1, 2012.

2.6 e-Media's Importance in Controlling Election-Related Violence

In some elections across the world, violence is a common occurrent. So, Ghana is not an exception to it. During elections, although the violence in Ghana is comparatively less than in many other countries in the continent of Africa, still, it is difficult to ascertain the details about election-related violence in Ghana. Hence, many media reports and research on election-related violence have revealed that, since 1992, violence often occurs during and after elections in certain parts of Ghana.

Violence is seen among various sections of people; it may be between supporters and opponents, during the election or after the election. Sometimes, there is a direct clash between opposing parties; sometimes, some people are forced to cast a vote for a particular party or candidate; or sometimes, there is the capture of ballot boxes forcefully and so on (Aning and Danso, 2012). In many elections, this type of incident is responsible for violent activities and an unhealthy atmosphere, which creates fear among many Ghanaians. The pre-electoral period conflicts are often connected to voter registration processes. Further, the ethnic issue in many cases generates political violence and politicians are accused of exploiting ethnic minorities by using them in violent activities for their vote bank policies.

Observing this chaotic situation during and after various elections in Ghana, many researchers have highlighted the importance of the media. They hold the view that mobile phones, radio stations and social network sites, like Facebook and other social networking platforms, have helped to check the violence and control violent situations. It speeds the delivery of the message in such a way that communities, individuals and groups take various preventive actions. For example, just before the elections of 1996 in Ghana, the media helped to spread the issue of expected violence in a very precise and comprehensive manner (Stremlau and Price, 2009). As the news spread throughout Ghana, politicians very strategically handled the issue and controlled the situation. Finally, the public took the right decision to choose their candidate in the 1996 election.

During the 2016 election, when the government asked to shut down most of the media, Penplusbytes, a non-governmental organisation, was committed to using new media to strengthen the governance of Ghanaian democracy. By using software programmed with keywords to track what Ghanaians were posting online during the polling, Penplusbytes aimed to pick up on problems on the ground and get them resolved quickly. As Ghana had already experienced violent incident in the 2008 election, Penplusbytes took major initiatives to check this violence further, starting from the voter registration process to the declaration of the election result in the 2016 election in Ghana. Even in the 2012 election, when Penplusbytes used the software for the first time, it logged nearly 350 incidents of misinformation and false news that were rife at sensitive periods during the election (Hairsine, 2016).

Similarly, in the 2016 general election, to check these types of vandalism, Penplusbytes played a very important role through tracking Twitter, Facebook and RSS feeds, as well as collecting different types of irregularities and misconduct related to voting through a dedicated SMS short code. It also analysed and visualised keyword trends, which can be grouped into topics – such as voting logistics (Is the polling station open on time? Are there enough ballot papers?), violence, political parties or specific locations with a history of trouble. Moreover, to get the reliable information in a short span of time, the police of Ghana also started using social media and a Twitter account in October 2016. They also used the hashtag #safeballot to campaign for peace during the Ghana 2016 elections (Hairsine, 2016).

2.7 e-Media's Role in Good Governance

Good governance encompasses accountability, transparency, responsiveness, equitable and inclusive growth, effective and efficient administration, rule of law, participatory democracy and a consensus-oriented system. In 2005, UNESCO highlighted that for good governance, the participation of citizens is essential in the decision-making process, as it allows greater transparency and democratic legitimacy (Dunu, 2013). In the present day, this participation of citizens in governance is enhanced due to the intervention of various social media platforms. As good governance implies, maintaining accountability, transparency and efficiency in all aspects of governmental and administrative machineries, the role of the media in this regard cannot be ruled out (Dunu, 2013). In the United Kingdom, a "Survey of Policy Opinion on Governance and the Media", published by the BBC (2009), examines that although the emphasis on good governance in the development agenda is questionable, there seems to be increasing recognition of the media's role in governance in the development community. Moreover, in democracy, the media also helps citizens to gain knowledge relating to politics and their rights and responsibilities as a citizen, which ultimately helps in strengthening the culture of democracy.

In Ghana, the media are empowered to lead the crusade against corruption, underdevelopment and the promotion of democracy and human rights. In promoting these ideals, it plays a watchdog role (Stapenhurst, 2000). This watchdog role of the media in fact contributes to the promotion of free, fair, transparent and competitive elections in Ghana. To promote good governance and to make public service better, the Media Foundation for West Africa (MFWA) has been taking various initiatives in Ghana. It has provided training to 40 young and vibrant community citizens from four metropolitan, municipal and district assemblies (MMDAs) in Ghana (MFWA, 2017).

It gives training to actively participate in governance processes at the local level through the effective use of the media and other governance dialogue platforms. It also assists the participant in creating blogs and Facebook and Twitter accounts to effectively utilise them and to participate in governance processes. These help in the accountability of the management and utilisation of public resources in their local assemblies. In this way, the media in Ghana are more independent and professional, and significantly contribute to democracy and development in the region.

There are many instances in Ghana where the masses, through the local language, use social media and can express their views and opinion. In consequence, it solves many problems through fruitful discussion that affects society. To prevent corruption, social media has a dual role: first, report incidences of corruption in a professional and ethical manner; second, raise public awareness about corruption and investigate the issues (Stapenhurst, 2000). According to the World Bank Good Governance Report 2007, Ghana improved its civil freedoms, government effectiveness and political stability and had made extraordinary progress on corruption over the past decade due to the free and professional media in Ghana (GhanaWeb, 2009). Further, in 1992, the Constitution of Ghana allowed for a free media without any restriction.

2.8 Conclusion

Independent and free media provides a solid foundation for good governance, development and peace. Good governance can check corruption, promote the free flow of information, strengthen accountability for decisions and encourage greater participation in the decision-making process. Accurate and professional reporting is often the only recourse to combat corruption and ensure good governance of a society. Therefore, United Nations member states, through the Millennium Declaration, expressed their strong, unanimous and explicit support for democratic and participatory governance and came to the conclusion that free and open media is one of the best tools necessary to achieve this goal.

Therefore, in recent years, the government of Ghana has invested more in the telecommunication infrastructure to bring forward socioeconomic development of society. Due to this initiative in policy, there has been a considerable improvement in Internet connectivity throughout Ghana. In spite of this development, some studies found that it is helpful only to the business community. Further, the data reveals that the extent of use of the new media technology among Ghanaians is very limited, where only 30 per cent of Ghana's population are online and only 13 per cent subscribe to Facebook. In addition, very few numbers of Ghanaians are skilled enough to use the Internet and social media sites. Some reports claim that only a substantial section of users use this to reduce poverty by connecting with the Western world. On the other hand, for the purpose of politics, only well acquainted and politically aware people use the Internet and other digital media. Apart from that, the media was under the control of various governments during various periods. For example, during Ghana's post-independence history, the government of Ghana has controlled the media.

Although the media has played a positive role in the political communication of Ghana, it has a record of destabilising social as well as political harmony. Sometimes, the media also propagates political news that is not genuine. Therefore, to a certain extent, free media should be limited in its views and expressions for a constructive purpose. Moreover, journalists should be trained enough to publicise the genuine issue of politics and prepare fair, accurate and balanced reports.

References

Adetoye, D. and Omilusi, M.O. (2016), "The symmetrical relationship between good Governance and Development", *International Journal of Economics, Commerece and Management*, IV (3), 572–581.

Albritton, R.B. and Bureekul T. (2009), "A comparative survey of Democracy, Governance and Development", Working paper Series: 47, Taipei: Global Barometer.

Aning, K. and Danso, K. (2012), "Managing election- related violence for democratic stability in Ghana", www.fesghana.org/.../ Managing_ Election Related_Violence.pdf (Accessed on 2nd January 2017).

Ashraf, P. (2014), "The role of media in good Governance: Paid news culture of media and the challenges to Indian Democracy", *International Research Journal of Social Sciences*, 3(3), 41–43.

Dankwah, J.B. (2016), "Political marketing in Ghana: The role of social media", http://ugspace.ug.edu.gh/handle/123456789/21806 (Accessed on December 21, 2017).

Department for International Development (DFID) (2008), "Media and good governance", A DFID practice paper, www.gsdrc.org/document-library/media-and-good-governance-a-dfid-practice-paper/ (Accessed on December 12, 2017).

Dunu, I. (2013), "Good governance in Nigeria: What role for the media", *European Scientific Journal*, 9(32), 178–197.

Fridausu, M. (2012), "Social media is playing a role in Ghana's election 2012", www.modernghana.com/news/388773/1/social-media-is-playing-a-role-in-ghanas-election-.html (Accessed on December 22, 2017).

GhanaWeb (2009), "Ghana Rated High For Good Governance", https://www.ghanaweb.com/GhanaHomePage/NewsArchive/Ghana-Rated-High-For-Good-Governance-165533 (Accessed on September 19, 2018).

Governance Social Media Index, Report (GSMIR) (2016), Ghana, www.newsghana.com.gh/wp-content/uploads/2016/02/ (Accessed on January 4, 2018).

Hairsine, K. (2016), "Using social media for good during Ghana's elections", www.dw.com/en/using-social-media-for-good-during-ghanas-elections/a-36646065 (Accessed on September 19, 2018).

Kalyango, Y. Jr and Adu-Kumi, B. (2013), "Impact of social media on political mobilization in East and West Africa", *Global Media Journal*, spring, pp. 1–20 (Accessed on January 5, 2018).

Khasawneh, R.T. and Abu-Shanab, E.A. (2013), "E-Government and social media sites: The role and impact", *World Journal of Computer Application and Technology,* 1(1): 10–17, www.hrpub.org, DOI:10.13189/wjcat.2013.010103 (Accessed on December 20, 2017).

Media Foundation for West Africa (2017), "Media and good governance", www.mfwa.org/programmes/media-good-governance-and-development/ (Accessed on January 10, 2018).

Media "Media development's role in social, economic, and political progress", www.mdif.org/wp-content/uploads/2014/08/Media (Accessed on January 4, 2018).

Oxfam (2013), "Civil society engagement with political parties during elections, Lesson from Ghana and Sierra Leone", https://www.oxfam.org/.../rr-civil-society-engagement-political-parties-elections-1812 (Accessed on January 3, 2018).

Paul, S. (2012), How Ghana is using social media to promote voter registration, http://mashable.com/2012/03/27/ghana-voter-registration-social-media/#JlH6ecK7Daqx (Accessed on January 5, 2018).

Penplusbytes (2017), "Social media and political campaigning in Ghana", www. penplusbytes.org/site/ wp-content/uploads/2017/01/SOCIAL (Accessed on January 15, 2018).

Praveen, A. (2014), "Role of media in democracy and good governance", www.lawctopus.com/academike/role-media-democracy-good-governance/ (Accessed on December 28, 2017).

Riaz, S. (2010), "Effects of new media technologies on political communication", *Journal of Political Studies*, 17(2), 161–173.

"Role and impact of mass media", download.nos.org/srsec335new/ch3.pdf (Accessed on January 7, 2018).

MyJoyOnline.com (2016), "Social media tracking centre for Ghana elections 2016 ready to commence operations", www.myjoyonline.com/news/2016/November-23rd/social-media-tracking-centre-for-ghana-elections-2016-ready-to-commence-operations.php (Accessed on December 22, 2017).

Stapenhurst, R. (2000), "The media's role in curbing corruption", siteresources.worldbank.org/.../Resources/media.pdf (Accessed on 2nd January 2017).

Stremlau, N. and Price, M.E. (2009), "Media, elections and political violence in Eastern Africa: Towards a comparative framework", global.asc.upenn.edu/.../PDFs/PostelectionViolencereport.pdf (Accessed on December 18, 2017).

Today (2015), "Role of media in promoting good governance", July 27, 2015, www.todaygh.com/role-of-media-in-promoting-good-governance/ (Accessed on January 7, 2018).

Treisman, L. (2016), "Mistrust elections? There's an app for that", http://edition.cnn.com/2016/11/30/africa/ghana-elections-2016/index.html (Accessed on January 12, 2018).

UKEssays (2013), "Social media and new media in Ghana media essay", www. ukessays.com/essays/media/social-media-and-new-media-in-ghana-media-essay.php (Accessed on January 16, 2018).

Yazav, L. B. (2001), "Role of media in promoting good governance", www.nepaldemocracy.org/media/role_media.htm (Accessed on January 11, 2018).

3

The Role of e-Government in Nigeria: Legal Issues and Barriers against Complete Implementation

Ishaya Martins

CONTENTS

3.1 Introduction

It is interesting to note from the onset that, with the advent of the computer age, the worldwide adoption of e-government has immensely altered and enhanced human interaction and the way of life of people (Abdel-Fattah and Galal, 2008). Since the return of a democratically elected government in Nigeria, e-government has become popular. The administration of the former president, Olusegun Obanjo, who led the government at that time, introduced e-government in the country. Nigeria—indeed, the world—is gradually becoming a global village as a result of electronic government in the era of information and communication technology (ICT). e-Government immediately began in Nigeria once the country was returned to a civilian government in 1990, since then, the Internet and communication technology started becoming popular. It was initially received with a lackadaisical approach, coupled with ignorance of the potential benefits of ICT. Today, Nigeria is the fastest in the development of ICT in West Africa, and indeed, in Africa as a whole. It was in the years 1999 and 2000 that the federal government realized the importance of e-government; that is, information and telecommunication technology decided to revolutionize the civil service both at federal and state levels. This was due to the demands to improve civil service accountability, transparency, accessibility, the need to keep accurate data of civil servants (Ajayi, 2003), and so on. e-Government has become an important tool in revolutionizing business activities between government and private sectors, government and individuals, and between Nigeria and other nations of the world, through the use of the Internet and electronic messages. The Internet has added more value and quality life to citizens. The working of e-government in Nigeria has become an instrument in improving its own nationals and non-nationals resident in the country to engage effectively in assessing government infrastructure and the running of the government and its accountability to the people.

3.2 Definition of Electronic Government

In Nigeria, the word electronic is defined as a means relating to electrical, digital, magnetic, wireless, or optical technology, and references carrying out any act electronically. An electronic communication system refers to or means a system of creating, generating, sending, receiving, storing, displaying, or otherwise processing electronic documents and data. An electronic document means information that is created, generated, communicated, stored, displayed, or processed by electrical means, and it defines an electronic signature to mean information that is created in, or attached to, an electric document, and is used by a signatory to indicate his or her adoption of the content of the document. While information includes data, text, images, sounds, codes, computer programs, software, and databases, information technology requirements include software requirements (Electronic Transaction Act, 2007).

From the definition provided, the Act did not define electronic government but merely defined electronic, electronic communication, electronic documents, electronic signatures, and what information technology is. This is a deficiency of the Act, however, as government simply means the body with the power to make and enforce law to control a country, land area, people, or organization, or the relationship between a word and its dependents, or a group of people who hold a monopoly on the legitimate use of force in a given territory or the management, or control, of a system. So the use of the word e-government implies the management of electronic systems for better services and accessibility. A comprehensive definition of e-government is the one provided by the U.S. law known as the E-Government Act of 2002, which states that the purpose of e-government is to improve the management and promotion of electronic government services and processes by establishing a federal chief information office within the office of management and budget and by establishing a framework of measures that requires using the Internet base information technology to improve the access of government information for citizens (Justice, 2013).

3.3 Objectives of Nigeria's Electronic Transaction Act

The objectives of the E-Transaction Act are:

1. To facilitate electronic transaction by means of reliable electronic documents
2. To promote the development of legal and business infrastructure necessary to implement secure electronic commerce
3. To eliminate barriers to electronic commerce resulting from uncertainties of writing and signature requirements and establish uniformity of legal rules and standards

4. To promote public confidence in the integrity of electronic documents and electronic transactions
5. To facilitate electronic filing of information with government agencies and statutory bodies and to promote efficient delivery of government services by means of reliable electronic documents

The provision of the Act does not apply to certain transactions set out in the first schedule and to the extent specified in the first schedule. Moreover, the Act does not impose an obligation on any person to create, give, store, or receive information electronically but it applies between parties who agreed to conduct transaction electronically. The Act though did not impose obligations on the parties as regards to its provisions, yet it made a provision that any person who violates the Act is liable to a fine or imprisonment. From the provisions of the U.S. E-Government Act of 2002, and the provisions of Nigerian Electronic Transaction Act 2007, it is safe to say that e-government is to provide among other things, effective leadership, promote the use of the Internet, promote inter-agency collaboration, promote the use emerging technology, reduce the cost and burden of business, and transparency. This led to the question to be asked, what is governance? Governance can be used in different ways or contexts such as local governance, national governance, regional governance, for instance, the European use of the bill of lading otherwise known as BOLERO, international governance, and partnership and corporate governance. e-Governance can be applied on all these. Having defined governance, let us relate it to the Internet.

Internet governance refers to regulatory mechanisms put in place to ensure the equitable allocation of Internet resources such as domain names and Internet protocol (IP) addresses. Some notable regulatory mechanisms in this regard have evolved; these include the Internet Corporation for Assignment of Names and Numbers (ICANN) and the Nigerian Internet Registration Association (NIRA). Although there is presently no adequate or potent regulatory framework to guide conduct on the Internet, efforts have been made at intergovernmental level. However, e-government in the modern day of technology has many benefits attached to it. For instance, Olufemi (2012) said that developing states have slowly understood the various benefits of e-governance in administration and its application; developed and developing countries now adopt e-governance because it is faster, more convenient, and increases efficiency, revolutionary reforms, and transparency in all facets of human endeavor.

3.4 The Role of e-Government in Nigeria

1. One of the major roles of e-government in Nigeria is to facilitate the electronic payment of wages and salaries of civil servants in order to eliminate ghost workers and save money in the running of the government.
2. The use of electronic bill of ladings in international shipping.
3. The use of electronic transfers in banking business transactions.
4. The use by the Joint Admission and Matriculation Board in setting and administering examination questions and the marking of scripts. Results are released three working days after the examination.

5. The encoding of the particulars of every vehicle in Nigeria, especially in Abuja and state capitals in the country.

It is important to know the distinction between e-government and e-governance. The two concepts are sometimes used interchangeably but they are not same. Ayo (2014) is of the view that e-governance is described as the application of ICT to transform efficiency, effectiveness, transparency, and accountability of the exchange of information and transactions, while Grant and Chau (2005) define e-government as broadbased initiatives that leverage on the capabilities of the delivery of high-quality, seamless, and integrated public services. So e-governance in the public sector is broader while e-government is a subset of e-governance.

3.5 The Institutional and Legal Framework of e-Government in Nigeria

The institutional agency and legal framework of e-government includes the following:

The Nigeria Communication Commission (NCC) Act 2003; the National Broadcasting Corporation (NBC) LFN 2004; the National Information Technology Development Agency (NITDA) Act 2007; and the National Environmental Standards Regulation Agency and the Standard Organization of Nigeria (SON) all exist in Nigeria. The legal frameworks are the Constitution of the Federal Republic of Nigeria 1999 as amended; the Nigeria Communication Act; the Wireless and Telegraph Act; the National Film and Video Censors Board; and Cybercrimes (Prohibition, Prevention, etc.) Act 2015. The government of Nigeria has established various agencies to supervise and regulate e-government in Nigeria and has also enacted laws to regulate Internet services and punish violators or offenders, yet there are still legal problems, barriers, and hiccups in the full implementation of e-government in the country today.

3.6 Legal Issues and Barriers in Implementing e-Government

1. One of the major challenges of e-government in Nigeria is the issue of jurisdiction for trial and enforcement against violators, fraudsters, breaches of contract, and so on. To find an appropriate court of competent jurisdiction to bring a trial is a problem. For instance, after a click on the mouse of a computer in Nigeria, a message will pass through Niger, Libya, France, and other different countries before it reaches London. In the event of breach of a contract, which country's court has the jurisdiction to try the matter? International law has attempted to provide a solution to this issue through a forum state system and an integrated state system.
2. Another legal issue is the right of privacy of individuals. The collection of data from customer's information can be used as a key input or know your customer (KYC) constitutes a legal issue around the right of privacy. The gradual collection of customer's details shows an immediate window into a citizen's details, thus violating their right of privacy while online (Backus, 2003). In Nigeria, there is no

strict security procedure in place to protect citizens. However, the constitution provides the right of privacy of citizens, homes, correspondence, telephone conversations, and telegraphic communications, and all are guaranteed and protected by law [section 37 of the 1999 constitution as amended].

3. There is an inadequate legal and institutional framework at the local government level for coordination with e-government.
4. The problem of consumer protection is another major challenge of e-government today. Basically, ICT posed a serious challenge to the product, i.e., the Internet. However, the regulatory bodies in the country have created a good environment to protect customers. Despite the legal framework enacted by the government, the regulatory regime is still inadequate to protect the consumers in cases of inadequate Internet services provided by the service provider and compensation is poor in cases of failure on the part of the provider.
5. Lack of legal enforcement mechanisms, international policy, and delays in cases of disputes between residents or businesses in Nigeria and businesses in another continent. There is also the legal issue of competition law, which provides a level playground for Internet service providers. Competition law obligation requires institutions to secure appropriate service providers in the market. The regulatory agency requires efficient tools to create a conducive environment for competition, quality, and better services for Nigerian citizens, the government, and private organizations.
6. An inadequate power supply is another major challenge or barrier in the successful implementation of e-government.
7. Insufficient ICT infrastructure in government ministries, government parastatals, and educational institutions and universities.
8. Lack of zeal and willingness of the people to embrace change in new technology along with conservative attitudes and resistance to change.
9. Lack of qualified and trained personnel to handle digital systems in various ministries and parastatals.
10. Insufficient funds to acquire the latest digital system by the government for their own use. The cost and affordability of ICT is a big issue in Nigeria, but a bigger one is the lack of knowledge and understanding of the technology. Studies show that over 75 per cent of the Nigerian population do not have the opportunity to learn how to use a computer. If the educated populace do not know how to use a computer, then Internet proficiency is a challenging task. This is a difficult issue to address, as it implies changes in both education and mentality, as well as investments in e-services.
11. The Freedom of Information Act 2011 in Nigeria was a welcome addition for the Nigerian media and the objective was to enhance the role of e-government in Nigeria. The Act supersedes the official secrets act and provides under section 2[1] that anyone can request information and this information must be given within seven days. The Act urges public institutions to keep proper records and e-records, which will enhance e-government in Nigeria. But the Act fails to take into consideration the bureaucrats in the civil service, which states that no public servant should provide information to the media until permission is obtained from the chief executive officer, which may take one month before permission is obtained in order to disclose any information. Public servants who fail to give information may be liable to incur liabilities of 500,000 naira for their ministry.

3.7 Findings

Most local government councils are yet to embrace or connect to e-government for the ease of government business. In addition, data of streets and houses in their locality could be used for the purpose of security and for payment of revenue. Some state governments are yet to capture the number of houses for the purpose of collection of taxes or revenue for the government. Also, the transportation system is lacking e-government initiatives, especially as Nigeria is a major maritime state. The electronic bill of lading is yet to take effect and the bill for that purpose is still pending at the National Assembly. It was also discovered in the course of this study that there are inadequate trained police to detect, investigate, and prosecute cybercrimes in the country.

3.8 Recommendations

1. Government should declare a state of emergency in the power sector to put an end to inadequate and persistent power failures in the country, otherwise the development of e-government and governance will have a drastic setback.
2. The National Assembly should be proactive in enacting laws that are adequate in regulating e-government in the digital age and to deal with issues of detection, investigation, and prosecution of cybercrime in Nigeria. This will go in a long way to development customer's confidence in the sector.
3. The government should set up a high-power implementation committee consisting of professionals, technocrats, and men and women of integrity for the monitoring and evaluation of e-government in all government ministries, parastatals, and the private sector.
4. There is a need of iterative capacity building of individuals for their professional development so that they can understand the E-Government Act and ICT to upgrade their skills. The government should also collaborate and partner with other technologically advanced countries for training of Nigerians for better international exposure.
5. The government should release adequate or sufficient funds to procure the latest ICT infrastructure and to grant loans to public servants to acquire laptops. Public awareness and orientation on the benefits of e-government is very important and it will spur people's interest in this technological age.
6. International forums for the settlement of e-government disputes is advocated and for the establishment of the Alternative Disputes Resolution for West Africa with a branch office in Nigeria for West Africa.

3.9 Conclusion

Today, e-government is fundamental in all spheres of human activities that Nigeria, and indeed, other developing countries, cannot afford to be left behind in the wheel of progress and the economic development in technology. The development of e-government and governance is not solely one day's affairs; it requires synergy for the entire system to work. Every day, new innovations spring up in the area of ICT and Nigeria must enact adequate laws in tandem with this development. There are great prospects for the success and development of e-government and governance in Nigeria, provided the recommendations are implemented. There is a need to envisage the development of adequate and cost-effective service delivery, consolidation, and coordination of e-government in all sectors of government in Nigeria, and the need to coordinate policy and legal and institutional frameworks for e-government.

References

Abdel-Fattah, M. and Galal, E. (2008). Toward flexible evaluation for E-Government websites equality: A multi-perspective evaluation framework. *Proceedings of the 8th European Conference on e-Government*, Lausanne, Switzerland July 10–11.

Ajayi G.O. (2003). NITDA in Nigeria. Unpublished contribution delivered at the Round Table on developing countries, Italy, 2003.

Ayo, C.K. (2014). Information and communication technology as a lever for innovation in leadership. In T. Abioye, C. Awonuga, and A. Amuwo. *Leadership and Innovation in Africa's Development Paradigm* (pp. 71–90). Ota: Covenant University Press.

Backus, M. (2003). e-Governance and developing countries; introductions and examples. Research Report, no. 3, April, www.ftpiicd/org/research/reports/pdf.

Bamodu, G. (2004). Information communications technology and e-commerce: challenges and opportunities for the Nigerian legal system and the judiciary. *The Journal of Information, Law and Technology*, 2. Available at: http://www2.warwick.ac.uk/fac/soc/law/elj/jilt/2004_2/bamodu.

Cybercrime (Prohibition, Prevention, etc.) Act (2015). Nigeria Federal Act.

En wiktionary.org. https://en.wikipedia.org/wiki/ (Accessed on March 28, 2018).

Grant, G. and Chau, D. (2005). Developing a generic gramework for e-government. *Journal of Global Information Management (JGIM)*,13(1).

Olufemi, F.J. (2012). Electronic governance: Myth or opportunity for Nigerian public administration. *International Journal of Academic Research in Business and Social Sciences*, 2(9): 12–140.

The Constitution of the Federal Republic of Nigeria 1999 as amended.

The Freedom of Information Act (2011). Nigeria Federal Act.

The National Broadcasting Corporation LFN (2004). Nigeria Federal Act.

The National Information Technology Development Agency (NITDA) Act (2007).

The Nigeria Communication Commission Act (2003). Nigeria Federal Act.

United States E-Government Act of 2002. https://it.ojp.gov/PrivacyLiberty/authorities/statutes/1287 (Accessed on August 20, 2018).

4

ICT in Healthcare

Abid Sarwar, Jatinder Manhas, and Vinod Sharma

CONTENTS

4.1 Introduction

In the recent past, there has been revolutionizing advancements in mobile technology, social connectivity, broadband connectivity, personal digital assistants, and Internet coverage [1]. These advancements in one way or other are increasing awareness among the masses about the applicability of digital technology in healthcare and more and more people now accept healthcare solutions through the digital medium. This has the result that many governments dedicate significant budgets for e-health systems for ensuring even-handed and inexpensive access to healthcare.

Information and communication technology (ICT) is a way in which data is collected, classified, and processed to interpret the result in order to provide an integrated series of data for further communicating and analysis. In the recent past, the use of information technology has grown exponentially and today it has become an integral part of every branch of science. Governments across the globe have recognized the importance and benefits accrued by using information technology in governance leading to e-governance.

The health sector has apparently been considered as lagging behind as far as the use of ICT is concerned. However, in developed countries, information and communication technologies are heavily being used as the information exchange for various purposes of healthcare. Healthcare provision is characterized by complexity and uncertainty. In most circumstances, patients lack the ability to make an accurate diagnosis or to decide on an appropriate course of action on the basis of their symptoms. On the other hand, in low income countries, people are still largely dependent only on the diagnostic information provided by specialist doctors who they trust. The accomplishment of healthcare goals largely depends on how updated the medical professional is about the latest developments in medical science. However, this also depends on how the information is shared between the stakeholders. Any miscommunication can lead to serious consequences that can hamper the outcome of the course of treatment and thus the overall aims of healthcare.

The use of ICT in healthcare can be categorized into four major areas: education; application software; research; and data management.

4.2 Health and Education

When medical education is governed by ICT, it is possible to provide high-quality education across India seamlessly and to a majority of the people.

Application software for hospital management and expert systems for medical diagnosis: In rural areas, healthcare workplaces are not satisfactorily administered. With the help of application software, the management of such institutions of healthcare, such as hospitals and colleges, can be reinforced significantly and the diagnosis of diseases can be made on the basis of proper evidence and support.

Health research: ICT has the potential to change medical science in our country by making a major change in the way research in medicine is carried out. There is an immense opportunity in the application of information technology in traditional medical science to contemporary bioinformatics research. The availability of data through ICT for ongoing problems such as prevention, diagnosis, and the management of cancer, and many other diseases, can help in reducing the concerning mortality rates.

Management of data: Electronic medical records (EMR) are a fundamental requirement in using ICT seamlessly in healthcare. While EMR is available in several forms, size, shape, and format, the Indian medical community needs a specific mandate to standardize EMR and to create and establish ICT platforms for using EMR based systems for universal benefits.

The overall objective of this endeavor is to study and critically analyze present functioning of the health and education sectors using IT and related tools. In order to achieve this objective, the objectives of the study are to study the existing systems of healthcare and the education sector in India, to analyze present functioning, and the initiatives adopted.

4.3 Role of ICT in the Healthcare System

On March 20, 1876, Alexander Graham Bell made the world's first call over a telephone when he inadvertently spilled battery acid on himself [2]. Bell would have never realized that this was the world's first telephonic call for medical consultation. We have come a long way since then. Distance in healthcare had initially been overcome by a variety of "signaling systems," including bonfires, bells, flags, and mirrors. Telemedicine is a remote way by which patients can be examined, investigated, monitored, and treated, with the patient and doctor physically located in different places [3,4]. Most of the projects since the 1960s to early 1980 have failed to deliver any significant results because they suffered from a lack of funding. In the 1960s and 1970s, the concept of artificial intelligence was introduced in expert systems. An expert system is a knowledge-based system containing expert knowledge encoded in some form such as production rules, network of frames, and other representation schemes and loaded on a system to get accurate outputs. DENDRAL was the first expert system used by chemists [5]. This was followed by a number of expert systems, namely MYCIN, GUIDON, CASNET, HASPART, and so on. The main use of expert systems in the medical field is to get accurate diagnoses in medicine, infection, carrying out experiments in biology, and so on, for example, CASNET is used to detect and diagnose glaucoma, which causes blindness.

The cost of telecommunication was too high and technologies present at that time were too complicated. One pioneer telemedicine project (1972–1975) was STARPAHC, or space technology applied to Rural Papogo Advanced Health Care, which was developed by NASA to deliver healthcare to the Papogo Indian Reservation in Arizona. The main aim was providing the best healthcare facilities to the isolated Papogo Reservation. A van carried two medical healthcare workers and other healthcare instruments such as X-ray machines and ECG instruments [3]. The staff were linked via a microwave transmission to two expert medical doctors at public hospitals. The first project in reference to medicine by NASA was conducted in 1989, it was named Space Bridge to Armenia/Ufa. It was so named because it was started after a devastating earthquake in 1988 that shook the Soviet Republic of Armenia.

Neural networks were designed on the pattern of the human nervous system and the machines designed to behave like expert humans. One neural-based expert system developed by Stephen Gallant in 1988 was used to diagnose and treat acute sarcophagus disease. A major goal of ICT in health is to eliminate unnecessary traveling of patients and their escorts.

Healthcare is full of uncertainty and complexity of decision making. Human expertise is required because multiple diseases are characterized by overlapping symptoms. It is experience over many years that makes a budding doctor become a specialist. ICT can be used as an aid to healthcare doctors to reach precise diagnostic decision at an early stage. The data saved in hospital records can be used to train various artificial intelligence-based algorithms that can be used to work as expert systems in smaller domains. Table 4.1 lists some of the IT tools and software applications that are being used in healthcare. These tools are intended for aiding medical doctors for making expert medical decisions and also managing healthcare information.

4.4 Issues in e-Health

There are many issues pertaining to the application of information technology to the healthcare sector. Although a lot of work has been done in this sector in developed countries, in developed countries and countries having low resources and a booming population, there are issues of a lack of trust in technology, low awareness about IT, a lack of trained personnel, and so on. The availability of IT infrastructure is also a major challenge. Similar problems are being faced in India, which is currently witnessing a big change in the technological awareness of the masses (having the world's largest young population). There is another issue of interoperability, that is, in hospitals there are some systems that are sophisticated while others are old but are not easy to replace. Every system is supposed to perform well and a deliver good performance, especially when it comes to healthcare. The systems that are manageable behave like an old and docile dog. Configuring such a system means something as routine and unchallenging as this:

- Read the administrators' manual.
- Open the system and find the same screen as in the manual.

TABLE 4.1
Technology, Devices, and Applications

Technology	Devices and software	Applications
Diagnostics	Stethoscope	Consultations
	EKG	Telehomecare
	X-ray/CatScan, and medical image analysis software	
Videoconferencing	Cameras (e.g., videocams, webcams)	Consultations
	Computer-based desktops	Teledermatology
	Portable communications and data systems	Telementalhealth
Digital imaging	Instruments	Telepathology
	Media (e.g., film, magnetic tape)	Teleradiology
	Scanners/viewers	Teledentistry
	Digital cameras	Teledermatology
	Videocams with scopes	
IT	Data storage systems	Electronic medical
	Servers	records
	Software/informatics: DBMS/GIS	Data mining
	Middleware	Web portals
		Decision support systems
		Administration
Store-and-forward	Data/image/video/audio card capture/scanners	Electronic medical record
	Computer/camera/microphone and image management software	Report generator
Simulation and training	Multimedia graphics software	e-Learning
	Audio-visual	Curriculum
		Conferencing

- Change the setting.
- Sit back and see that the change is effective.
- Many times, the systems that are already set do not allow others to take over. In such a scenario, the administrator may need to do the following:
- Deliberate with someone senior in an organization.
- Open a data-repository.
- Create new files and modify or delete different files.
- And so on ...

4.5 Healthcare Systems

Discussion of the application of information technology in healthcare is quite vast owing to the continuous pace of change in technology, the volumes of application areas, and the lack of a precise definition. Speaking in general, IT facilitates healthcare providers to store, collect, transform, and use information electronically. New technologies have an important effect on healthcare systems and concerned higher education institutions. The students of medicine also need to be trained in such a way that they have a full understanding of the technological aspects of healthcare systems. They should be very comfortable in adopting new techniques and use intelligent tools for delivery in real time. Some new universities are introducing subjects that involve engineering to give some knowhow of technical medical equipment in such a way that future doctors can use the latest technological equipment in full confidence.

Computerized Provider Order Entry (CPOE) is a tool that can be used to reduce the errors that creep in due to the handwriting of physicians or other supplementary care providers who key in medical prescriptions into a computer system [6,7]. This system is not only applicable to the prescription of drugs but also includes tests and other reports ordered by medical doctors such as x-rays or other images. For other electronic medical records, multiple software tools exist, which depends on the consultation with the doctor. Such tools can be used as passive tools that can send a reminder and alert patients (Table 4.2).

In addition to the tools mentioned in Table 4.2, various other IT enabled technologies have healthcare facilities including:

1. *Electronic health records*: Earlier electronic health records were seen as digital files containing data of a patient obtained from various sources, which could include handwritten notes, x-rays, MRI images, and so on [8]. Now they are largely viewed as a subpart of a patient tracking system that provides an in-depth record of medical and treatment conditions of a patient
2. *Computerized provider order entry*: Computerized provider order entry is essentially a digital medication ordering system. The advanced version of such systems would also provide facilities of various pathological tests, lab diagnostic procedures, referrals, and so on.
3. *Clinical decision support system*: A clinical decision support system provides artificial intelligence and machine learning–based programs that supplements doctors and other healthcare workers with recommendations for reaching expert diagnosis [9].
4. *Picture archiving and communications system*: A picture archiving and communications system is a system that enables technology to keep a digital record and the integration of diagnostic and radiological images obtained from variety of sources such as a CT scan, x-ray, or an MRI. This technology enables a multidimensional view of a patient's medical condition and thus helps the medical doctor to reach a precise diagnostic decision.
5. *Radio frequency identification*: Radio frequency identification technology is used to track patients throughout the various sections of hospital like diagnostic labs, associated hospitals where patients may be referred to, the drug store, and so on.
6. *Automated medicine dispensing machines*: Automated medicine dispensing machines are used to automatically dispense medications to the patient as mentioned in the prescription [10].

4.6 Healthcare in India

India is having a boom in population numbers, but only about 33 per cent of the whole population has access to the modern medicines. The industrialization of pharmaceuticals was started in the 1980s, but even then, we were not able to make them available to the far

TABLE 4.2

Examples of IT Applications Being Used by Physicians and Hospitals

Type of Information Technology Used in Hospitals	Applications
Administrative and financial	Billing
	General ledger
	Cost accounting systems
	Patient registration
	Personnel payroll
	Electronic materials management
Clinical	Computerized provider order entry for drugs, lab tests, procedures
	Electronic health record
	Picture archiving and communication system for filmless imaging
	Results reporting of laboratory and other tests
	Clinical decision support systems
	Prescription drug fulfillment, error-alert, transcription, physician orders, and medical records
	Barcoding technology for drugs, medical devices, and inventory control
	Information security systems
Physicians	
Administrative and financial	Billing
	Accounting
	Scheduling
	Personnel and payroll
Clinical	Online references (drug compendia and clinical guidelines)
	Receiving lab results and other clinical information online
	Electronic prescribing
	Computerized provider order entry
	Clinical decision support systems
	Electronic health record (EHR)
	E-mail communication with patients
Infrastructure	Computers
	Handheld technology
	Servers and network

reaches of the country. It is estimated that nearly 80 per cent of the people leaving in India do not have access to the vital medicines they require. India lacks health infrastructure to a large extent; people living in rural areas are referred to hospitals in urban areas for medical care. A major reason for this is the absence of qualified medical doctors in rural areas. According to a survey published in a leading magazine, only 38 per cent of primary health centers have qualified medical experts and the remaining 62 per cent are only attended by pharmacists and other healthcare support staff. People in poor villages are especially left at the mercy of unqualified registered medical practitioners. It is indicated by a report of the planning commission that essential drugs for routine medical care are not supplied to most healthcare institutions in India. The report also states that there is a serious shortage of essential healthcare infrastructure in most states. To meet the requirements in rural areas, many pharmaceutical companies have come up with a proposal that they shall involve the post office network to sell drugs over the counter. Experts from industry and the medical field are of the opinion that although the proposed plan could mitigate the requirement to a certain extent, this has potential side-effects. In the latest five-year plan, the Government of India has dedicated a significant amount toward strengthening the healthcare infrastructure in rural India. With this development, the giants of pharmaceutical industries are also looking toward investing in rural markets in a bigger way. The government announcement of a five-year tax holiday for hospitals in rural areas will further help in facilitating basic healthcare amenities. In spite of all these developments, we need to keep in mind the limited purchasing power of a large number of people. It was a recommendation of the Bhore Committee that no one in this country should be denied medical care on account of an inability to bare the expenses of it.* A significant percentage of deaths that occur every year are attributed to an inability to purchase lifesaving drugs. In the current scenario where the inflation rate is increasing day by day, the three-tire plan of the government to provide comprehensive preventive and curative facilities to the entire population lies in shambles.

4.7 Health Sector Reforms in India

In order to bring healthcare facilities on par with that of developed countries, there is a need to bring about changes in the fundamental design of policies and institutional arrangements. Elementary transformations are required be done in the workforce, infrastructure, logistics, monitoring, and so on, with governments in power at the union level starting the reorganization of healthcare from the 1980s. These reforms are broadly covered in the following domains:

- Reorganization and restructuring of the existing government healthcare system
- Involving the community in health service delivery and provision
- Health management information system quality of care

1. *National Rural Health Mission (NRHM)*: The National Rural Health Mission was launched by the Government of India in 2005, further extended to 2020 in March 2018. This program is the main vehicle for providing the amenities of health facilities to the masses of rural India. This is an umbrella program that has multiple programs for health and family welfare within it [11,12]. The program has statistically identified 18 low performing states where the healthcare infrastructure is below average as compared with the other states in India (Figure 4.1).

   NRHM has the following vision:

   - To enhance the healthcare system throughout the length and breadth of the nation with a particular focus on prioritized states that lack basic infrastructure.

* Bhore Committee was set up by Government of India in 1943. It was a health survey taken by a development committee to assess health condition of India. The development committee worked under Sir Joseph William Bhore, who acted as the chairman of committee. The committee consisted of pioneers in the healthcare field who met frequently for two years and submitted their report in 1946.

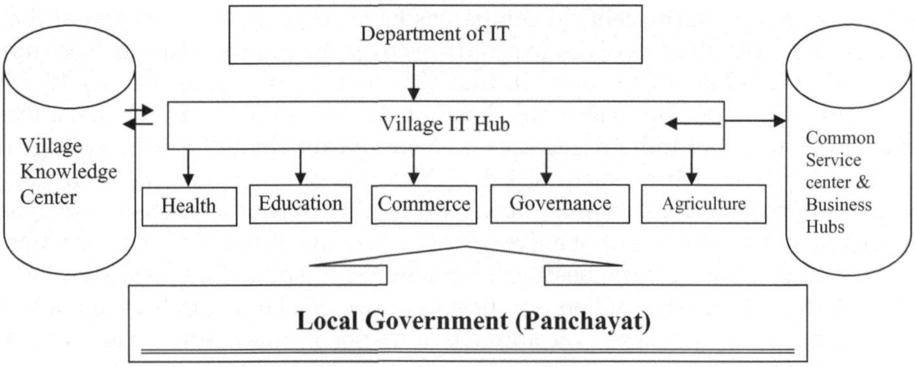

FIGURE 4.1
Overview of the NRHM program.

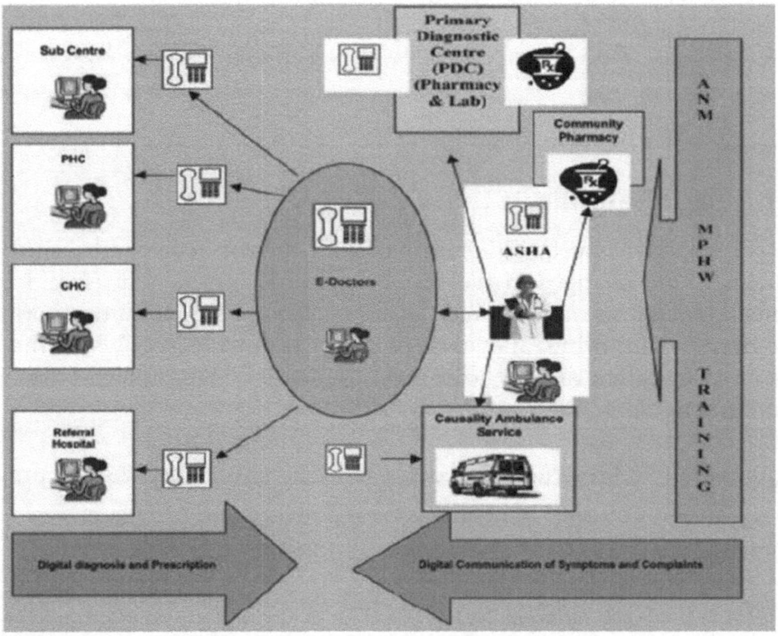

FIGURE 4.2
Modus operandi of the NRHM program.

- To enhance the ease-of-access and availability of excellent healthcare facilities, particularly in rural areas for financially backward and vulnerable sections of the population that cannot afford health-related facilities.
- To upgrade the health and determinants of good health like nutrition, sanitation, hygiene, safe drinking water, and much more.
- To implement the mainstream Indian Systems of Medicine in Public Health.
- To increase the absorptive capacity of the healthcare system to enable it to handle the growing population (Figure 4.2).

2. *Telemedicine*: Telemedicine refers to the use of information and communication technology centrally for patients with an aim to provide improved health services,

especially at remote locations. In many developed countries, the use of telemedicine has advanced to a great extent and is not just limited to maintaining patient information, rather it has advanced to tracking the medical status of an individual from birth to death. It is, however, paradoxical that despite India's strength in information technology, the use of telemedicine is still at a nascent stage, especially in the public health sector. With the growing cost of healthcare becoming a major headache for governments across the world, telemedicine could provide a solution to India and other countries grappling with the problem. Listing the advantages of telemedicine, Alice Lee, the chief of the UN program on space applications, said that developed countries were now relying on telemedicine as well [13,14] (Figure 4.3).

3. *National Health Portal (e-Health)*: To take up the Digital India initiative, the Ministry of Health and Family Welfare, Government of India, has set up the National Health Portal in pursuance to the decisions of the National Knowledge Commission, to provide healthcare related information to the citizens of India. e-Health is broadly defined as the use of information and communication technology in health. It will make a world of difference in India, where mobile technologies are growing at a speedy rate. As India has a strong presence in IT, the integrated health information system serves the needs of all stakeholders by contributing approximately 8 per cent to the gross domestic product.

   The eHealth initiatives have a vision to delivery better health outcomes in terms of:

   - Access to information
   - Quality of data provided
   - Affordability
   - Lowering of disease burden
   - Efficient monitoring of health entitlements to citizens

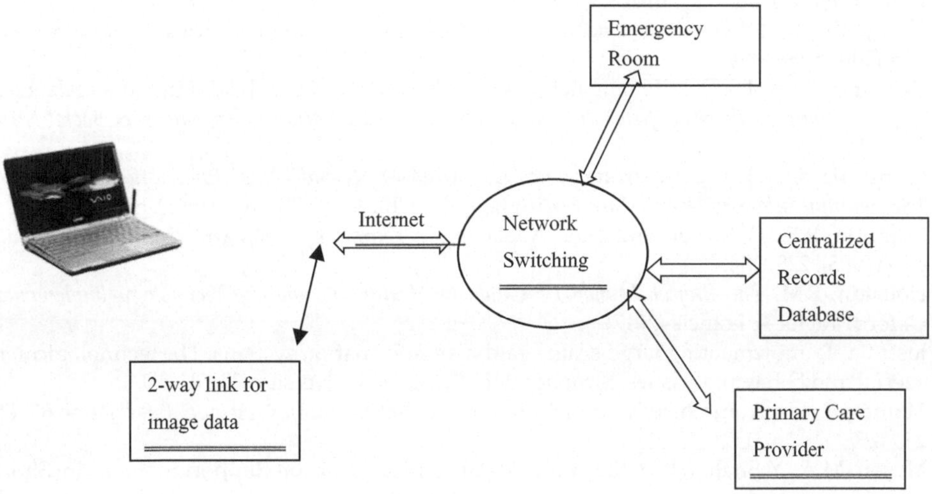

FIGURE 4.3
Telemedicine.

The main aim of this initiative was to make all medical facilities available at any time from any part of the world through web portals, mobile applications, SMS, or call center services. Broadly, the intent is to cover online medical consultations, online medical records, online medicine supply management, and exchange of patient information, but not limited to the said services.

The benefits of e-health can be described as follows:

- e-Health helped in avoiding duplicative or unnecessary diagnostic or therapeutic interventions, thereby decreasing the cost.
- By increasing efficiency, e-health not only reduced cost but also increased the quality of healthcare systems by allowing comparisons between different providers, giving consumers an additional power for quality assurance and directing patient streams to the best quality providers.
- Each intervention made using e-health is based on evidence not assumed.
- It enables patient involvement as evidence is clearly available.
- It enhances the relationship between the patient and the health professional and decisions are made in a shared manner.
- It has led to the possibility of educating medical professionals online.
- It has provisions for the exchange of data and communication between healthcare organizations in a standardized way.
- It has enabled people to seek treatment at global level by extending the boundaries of medical organizations worldwide.

References

1. Blaya, J.A., H.S.F. Fraser, and B. Holt. E-health technologies show promise in developing countries. *Health Affairs* 29.2 (2010): 244–251.
2. Ganapathy, K. Telemedicine and neurosciences in developing countries. *World Neurosurgery* 58.6 (2002): 388–394.
3. Dasgupta, A. and S. Deb. Telemedicine: A new horizon in public health in India. *Indian Journal of Community Medicine: Official Publication of Indian Association of Preventive & Social Medicine* 33.1 (2008): 3.
4. Bashshur, R.L., P.A. Armstrong, and Z.I. Youssef. *Telemedicine: Explorations in the use of Telecommunications in Health Care.* Springfield, IL: Charles C Thomas (1975).
5. Shannon, R.E., R. Mayer, and H.H. Adelsberger. Expert systems and simulation. *Simulation* 44.6 (1985): 275–284.
6. Houston, S.M. *The Project Manager's Guide to Health Information Technology Implementation.* Oxford: Taylor & Francis (2017).
7. Justinia, T. Implementing large-scale healthcare information systems: The technological, managerial and behavioral issues. Swansea, UK: Swansea University (2009).
8. Mantas, J. Electronic health record. *Studies in Health Technology and Informatics* 65 (2002): 250–257.
9. Musen, M.A., Y. Shahar, E.H. Shortliffe (2006) Clinical Decision-Support Systems. In: Shortliffe E.H., Cimino J.J. (eds) Biomedical Informatics. Health Informatics. New York, NY: Springer
10. Chudy, D.S., R.A. Jobus, and D.A. Schultz. Automated method for dispensing bulk medications with a machine-readable code. US Patent No. 6,370,841. 16 April (2002).

11. Dasgupta, R. and I. Qadeer. The National Rural Health Mission (NRHM): A critical overview. *Indian Journal of Public Health* 49.3 (2005): 138–140.
12. Singh, M.K., J.V. Singh, N. Ahmad, R. Kumari, and A. Khanna. Factors influencing utilization of ASHA services under NRHM in relation to maternal health in rural Lucknow. *Indian Journal of Community Medicine: Official Publication of Indian Association of Preventive & Social Medicine* 35.3 (2010): 414–419.
13. Buntin, M.B., S.H. Jain, and D. Blumenthal. Health information technology: Laying the infrastructure for national health reform. *Health Affairs* 29.6 (2010): 1214–1219.
14. Brewer, E., M. Demmer, B. Du, et al. The case for technology in developing regions. *Computer* 38.6 (2005): 25–38.

5

e-Governance in Education: A Comparative Analysis of Education Systems in Developed and Developing Nations

Satyajee Srivastava

CONTENTS

5.1 Introduction

e-Governance means quick and effective transmission of government policies and services to the public with the help of information technologies. It helps the government to reach the public at a fast pace to deliver services in an efficient manner without any bureaucratic delay.

e-Governance leads to a corruption free system and fixes accountability. Through e-governance, it is possible for the government to successfully implement policies in the healthcare sector by means of spreading awareness among the citizens regarding public hygiene and various preventive measures to combat fatal diseases and so on. Similarly, through e-governance, it is possible to spread and enhance the quality of the education system as well as reforming the education system to meet future challenges.

In the agriculture sector, it is possible to educate farmers regarding methods to be adopted to enhance agricultural growth, income, and so on. Through e-governance, government streamlines the basic services regarding taxation, licensing, and other related services in an effective manner.

e-Governance facilitates transparency, accountability, and increased efficiency in the system. It also reduces corruption, provides prompt communication between central, state, and local government agencies, and interdepartmental communication for taking quick administrative measures.

5.2 Concept of Education

As per the Oxford English dictionary, the word "Education" has its origin in the mid-16th century; it comes from the Latin verb "educare" [1]. The dictionary defines education as a "process of receiving or giving systematic instruction, especially at a school or university" [1]. The concept of education has been of great concern around the world for a long time. Many great philosophers and social reformers gave various definitions of this word. According to ancient Greek philosopher and scientist, Aristotle, "Education is the process of training a person to fulfill aim by exercising all the faculties to the fullest extent as a member of society" [2]. And philanthropist and ex-president of South Africa, Nelson Mandela, "Education is the most powerful weapon which you can use to change the world" [3]. American philosopher and educational reformer, John Dewey defined the word as follows: "Education is a process of living through, a continuous reconstruction of experiences" [4]. India's first Nobel laureate, philosopher and artist, Rabindranath Tagore's view was "Education means enabling the mind to find out that ultimate truth which emancipates us from the bondage of dust and gives us the wealth, not of things but of inner light; not of power but of love, making truth of its own and giving expression to it" [5]. An Islamic scholar and historiographer of the 18th century defined education as "the art of developing the sense of good and bad, so that a person can accept the good and reject the bad." Many people, many views, but the goal of all was same: "Education for All."

5.3 Importance of Education in the Development of a Country

Education plays a key role in the sustainable development of any country. It is defined as one of the basic human rights by the United Nations [6]. Quality education provides the capability to understand and develop skills to take up challenges faced by citizens of a country at both a national and global level. Educated citizens are well aware of the social, economic, and political situations of a country, thus helping a nation to flourish. For any country to utilize its workforce and reap the benefits, one needs to understand the potential of the human brain. This can be attained only when there is education. As stated by the former president of South Africa, Nelson Mandela, no country can really develop unless its citizens are educated. Educated minds always lead to innovations, which improves social, economic, and medical conditions of a nation, thus making it developed.

5.4 Developing and Developed Countries

A developing nation is a country with less developed industries and a low human resources development index with respect to other nations. Kofi Annan, former Secretary General of the United Nations [6], defined a developed country as "one that allows all its citizens to enjoy a free and healthy life in a safe environment." According to the United Nations Statistics Division, there is no criteria for the description of "developed" and "developing" countries or areas in the United Nations [6] system, the naming "developed" and "developing" are meant just for statistical analysis and does not judge on the stage attained by any country or area with respect to the development process.

On the contrary, a developed country is referred to as a nation whose economy has already progressed highly and has great technological and industrial advancements. Developed countries provide a healthy and secured environment for their citizens, whereas developing countries lack these.

In this chapter, we will first analyze the education systems in various developed countries. In most developed countries, it is believed that education is a must for the development and growth of the nation and thus education is a fundamental right, that is, education is compulsory for every child and is mainly controlled by the government. Funding for the education system mainly comes from government agencies at various stages. In these countries, stress is given not only on academic achievement but also on extracurricular activities like sports, music, dance, art, and so on, and the teaching staff are well compensated.

5.5 Comparative Study of Education Systems in Developed Countries

1. *The education system in the United States*: Developed countries like the United States attain a literacy rate of 97 per cent [7]. The standards of education are fixed by the department of education under the state government. The age criteria for students admitted to primary schools is 5 or 6 for kindergarten and they normally complete their secondary education by 18 years of age. In exceptional cases, for example, a child with a disability, parents may choose to educate their child at home. Parents may form groups to interact with each other and make common syllabus and teaching assignments, which resemble courses of the regular school going students. There is no national curriculum set in the United States. Instead, individual state boards set the curriculum.
2. *The education system in Japan*: In Japan, minimum standards for textbook content are fixed by the government education ministry. However, schools have the autonomy to set their own standard of content in the syllabus above the minimum standards set by the government education ministry. Free education is provided up to classes of the ninth standard and schools practice the trimester system. Students are supposed to wear a uniform during school hours. The screening tests are done for entry into various stages, for example, upper secondary, four-year university, two-year junior college, or other postgraduate institutions. Japan has a national curriculum that covers the entire country. Students are responsible for the cleaning of classrooms and grounds after their classes are finished.

5.6 Challenges for Providing Education in Developing Nations

Even though funds and policies are available for promoting education in developing countries, the literacy rate in these countries remains low. Below are the factors that lead to low literacy rates in developing countries [8]:

- In most of these countries, access to education is not free. The cost of books and other resources for providing quality education is borne by the parents of students enrolled in school.
- The quality of teaching is poor. In most rural areas of developing countries, there is a scarcity of teachers, either teachers are not available or they are untrained. This in turn leads to a poor quality of education for the next generation.
- There is a lack of good infrastructure and classrooms, which again leads to a lack of interest amongst pupils toward education. Children in many places are either squeezed in overcrowded classrooms or made to sit out in the open under the scorching sun. Children do not even get basic sanitation and drinking water facilities, which forces them to drop out of school.
- Another problem that is a hindrance in education for any developing country is gender discrimination. People in developing countries still consider females as weaker and believe that they should only be made to do household work. As a result, girls do not even get a chance to go to school.
- Distance of school from home is another hindrance. There are many places in which schools are situated a large distance away and students need to walk for as long as three to four hours to reach their schools. This leads to children getting fatigued, malnourished, and unable to concentrate on studies. Being malnourished even leads to poor development of the brain and thus the sole purpose of education is defeated.

5.7 Comparative Study of Education Systems in Developing Countries

1. *The education system in India* [9]: India is a nation that has a developing economy in the continent of Asia. It is politically divided into 28 states and 7 union territories. The right to education is a fundamental right of every citizen of India. Salient features are below:
   a. The education system is based on pattern of 10 + 2 + 3, where an initial 10 years represents high school, the next 2 is for higher secondary level, followed by 3 years of graduation.
   b. There are both private and public sectors associated with education. These are determined as per the funding received either by the government or borne by individuals.
   c. There are different boards or administrations associated with various institutions for designing and governing curriculum.

   The education system is divided into sections as described below [10]:
   - *Primary education*: Primary education is further divided as lower primary (nursery to standard fifth) and middle school (standard sixth to eighth). Education is mandatory and free for all children of the country until the age of 14 years.
   - *Secondary education*: Like primary education, secondary education is also divided into two categories, high school (classes 9th and 10th) and higher

secondary (classes 11th and 12th). Students get a chance to choose and learn the subjects of their interest. Based on the same, the various subjects offered are classified into three broad streams, namely science, commerce, and humanities.

- *Tertiary education or university education*: This level of education is highly regulated by the University Grants Commission (UGC), which grants funds and is the authority for the recognition of institutes and the quality of education provided. Depending on the course offered by the institutes, various councils are set up in India for the regulation of higher education. These councils include: AICTE for technical and engineering studies; BCI, for studies related to law and order; COA for studies related to architecture; and INC for nursing courses.
- *Vocational studies*: Students who fail to qualify or do not wish to pursue their education at university level can also enroll for various courses offered by privately owned vocational schools. These schools offer a variety of courses to choose from. Examinations are conducted at the end of courses by All India or state boards for vocational studies.

2. *The education system in Ghana* [11]: Ghana is a developing economy in the continent of Africa and is a unitary presidential constitutional democracy. A nation with cultural diversity, Ghana has a population of around 29 million, comprising a variety of religious, social, and ethnic groups. Some of the features of its education system are as follows [12]:

   a. The education system is based on a pattern of a 6-3-3-4 system, where the initial 6 years is for primary school, the next 3 years are for junior high school, followed by 3 years of senior high school, and then 4 years of university completing a bachelor's degree.

   b. At a basic level, emphasis is given to literacy, developing problem-solving skills, and creative thinking

   c. Metropolitan, municipal, and district assemblies are responsible for maintaining infrastructure and the quality of education until senior high school.

   d. Focus is given on improving information and communication technology (ICT) and science and technology.

   The education system is divided as below:

   - *Primary school*: At primary school, emphasis is given on the learning of languages, mathematics, social studies, and science. English is the official language of the country.
   - *Senior secondary school/senior high school*: This level of schooling is regulated by the Basic Education Certificate Examination (BECE) and offers seven to eight subjects. Admission to schools at this level is based on results in competitive exams. At the end of senior high school, students sit the West African Senior Secondary Certificate Examination (WASSC) for all selected subjects.
   - *University education*: Ghanaian universities [13] offer a wide range of subjects such as engineering, medicines, law, business, and pharmacy. It is highly competitive and universities are regulated by the National Accreditation Board. The quality of education at this level is considered to be very good and Ghana attracts people from overseas to pursue education in their country. All these universities work on the semester system.

3. *The education system in Argentina* [14]: Argentina is a federal republic, located in the southern half of South America. It is the second largest country in South America and was classified as upper-middle-income economy due to growing market size and stability. Salient features of the education system are [15]:
   a. Four levels of education. These levels are further classified into two different systems: initial level (kindergarten), primary level, secondary level, and tertiary level.
   b. The education system is taken care of by all levels of government, that is, the national government, the states, federal districts, and individual institutions.
   c. Public universities at university or tertiary level have free tuition and they are open to anyone.
   - *Primary education*: This level of education is mandatory and is governed by the Ministry of Education at national, state, and federal levels. This phase is divided into three phases of three years that represent junior primary, senior primary, and middle school.
   - *Secondary education*: At this level, the student is free to choose the subject of their choice. The subjects are broadly divided into three streams: *bachiller* (studies related to the field of humanities); commercial (focusing on commerce); and *escuelas técnicas* (related to science and technology).
   - *Vocational education*: This is an alternative to secondary education and it offers many options for studying. It is regulated by the National Technological University.
   - *Tertiary education:* Higher education is divided into various phases, that is, a three-year degree for teachers or technician training and a four to six-year degree course for engineering, medical, or graduates in legal fields, and graduate qualifications.

5.8 Analysis of Certain Factors that Developing Countries Are Focusing On

Here, we take the cases of three countries that are still developing, India, China, and Russia, and focus sharply on education. India and China are compared because of their population strengths. These two countries are also the leaders in the race of developing countries. Their analysis becomes important as it will show other developing nations their way to e-governance in education.

1. *Broadband penetration*: From Figure 5.1, we can see that Russia is the leader in introducing Internet [16] connectivity to its citizens. India has lacked in this aspect, while China, owing to its reforms, has quite successfully increased connectivity.
2. *Share of individuals using the Internet*: As shown in Figure 5.2, Russia has led the way, while China has followed quite successfully.
3. *Number of cellular subscriptions per 100 people*: Both India and China are quite successful in increasing the rate of cellular connections to its citizens.
4. *Government expenditure on education as per cent of gross domestic product (GDP)*: India and Russia have spent more as percentage of GDP on education than China. But despite this fact, China has made their way further in e-governance in education.

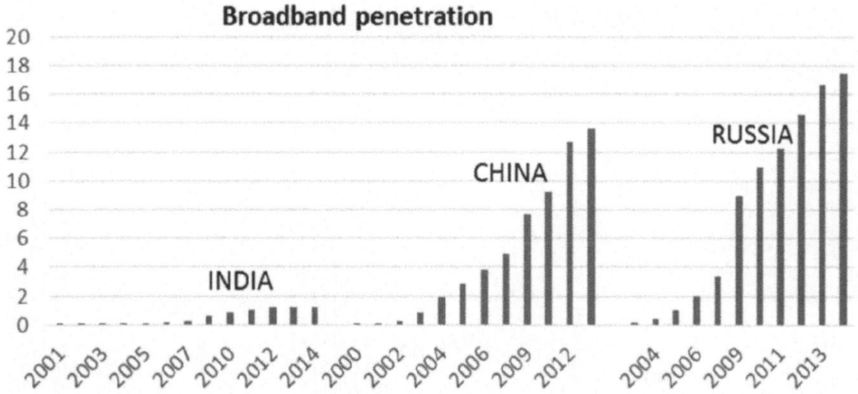

FIGURE 5.1
Broadband penetration. Source: https://ourworldindata.org/internet (Retrieved January 21, 2018) [17].

5.9 Results

Russia is somewhat less than a developed country, therefore, it is still a developing country. China and India are the largest populated countries, that is why their schemes and plans can work efficiently on other countries as well. Also, these countries are also the fastest growing economies [18] and they already have worked on malnutrition, disease control, and so on, and following their path can be beneficial for some countries (Figure 5.3).

5.10 Analysis of Apex Factors of Leading Developed Countries

Here, we take the cases of the developed countries of the United States, Japan, Australia, Singapore, and Finland; they are also the leaders in implementing e-governance in education.

1. *Broadband penetration*:

   Figure 5.1 shows that Finland is very successful in introducing broadband connectivity to its citizens.

2. *Share of individuals using the Internet*:

   Individuals who use the Internet are more likely to accept the e-system in education. As shown in Figure 5.2, Finland also takes the lead.

3. *Number of cellular subscription per 100 people*:

   The cellular subscription data of a country indicates that citizens are connected to the Internet everywhere using their phones. Figure 5.3 shows the connectivity of citizens.

4. *Government expenditure on education as per cent of GDP*:

   Figure 5.4 clearly shows that Finland is the country that spends most on e- governance in education.

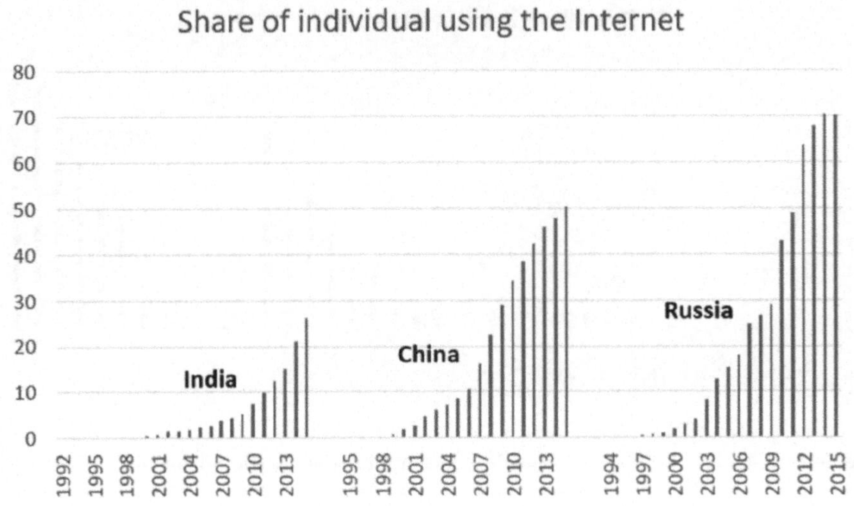

FIGURE 5.2
Share of individuals using the Internet. Source: https://ourworldindata.org/internet (Retrieved January 21, 2018) [17].

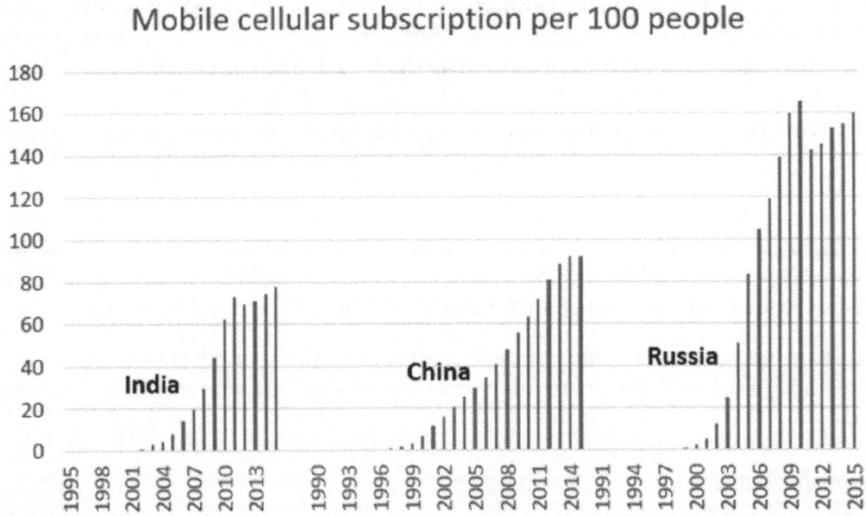

FIGURE 5.3
Number of cellular subscription per 100 people. Source: https://ourworldindata.org/internet (Retrieved January 21, 2018) [17].

5.11 Results

We can clearly see from the above study that network connectivity should be implemented while applying e-governance in education. A good share of GDP should be spent on education. Finland has the best school system in the world, why is this? We can clearly see from Figures 5.5 through 5.8.

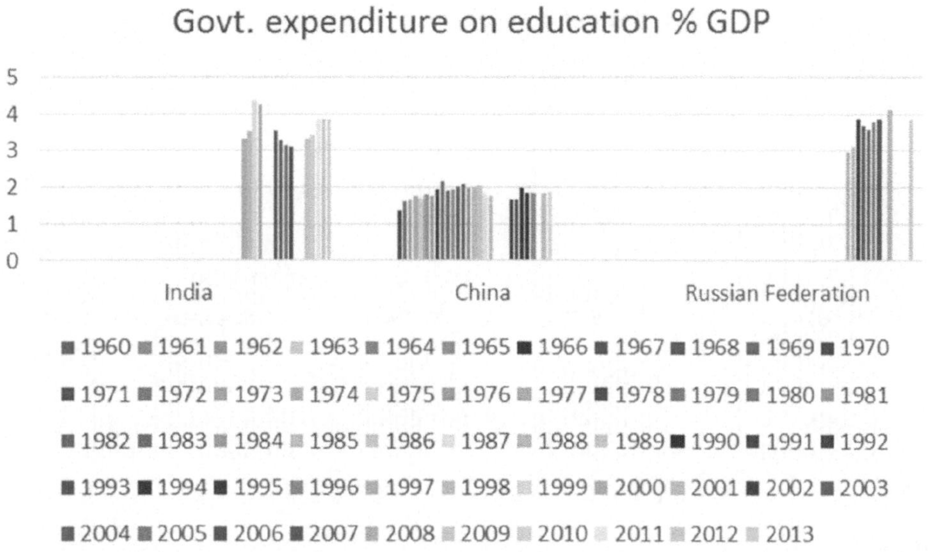

FIGURE 5.4
Government expenditure on education as per cent GDP. Source: https://ourworldindata.org/internet (Retrieved January 21, 2018) [17].

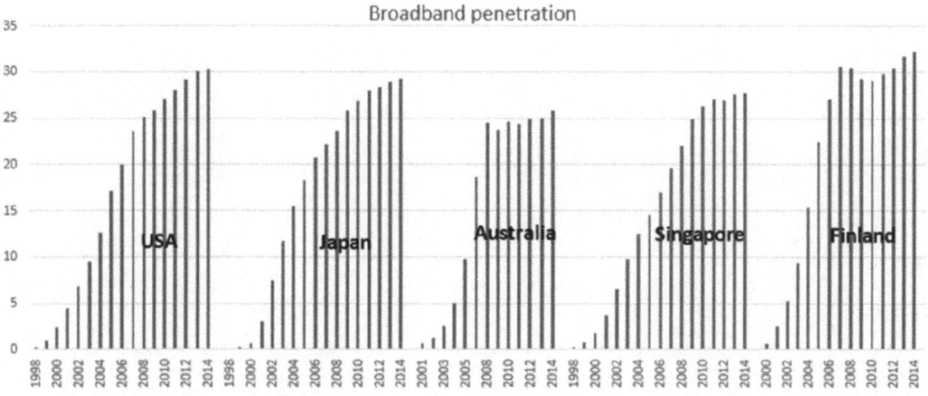

FIGURE 5.5
Broadband penetration. Source: https://ourworldindata.org/internet (Retrieved January 21, 2018) [17].

5.12 Conclusion

In this chapter, we studied various education systems in both developed and developing countries. We initially analyzed what impact education has in the development of a nation and saw that education is important socially, economically, and politically. Only through education can people understand how to face challenges and deal with them. Education also builds a sense of disciple in people and it also helps to improve communication skills, problem-solving skills, logical thinking, information gathering, and how to work together.

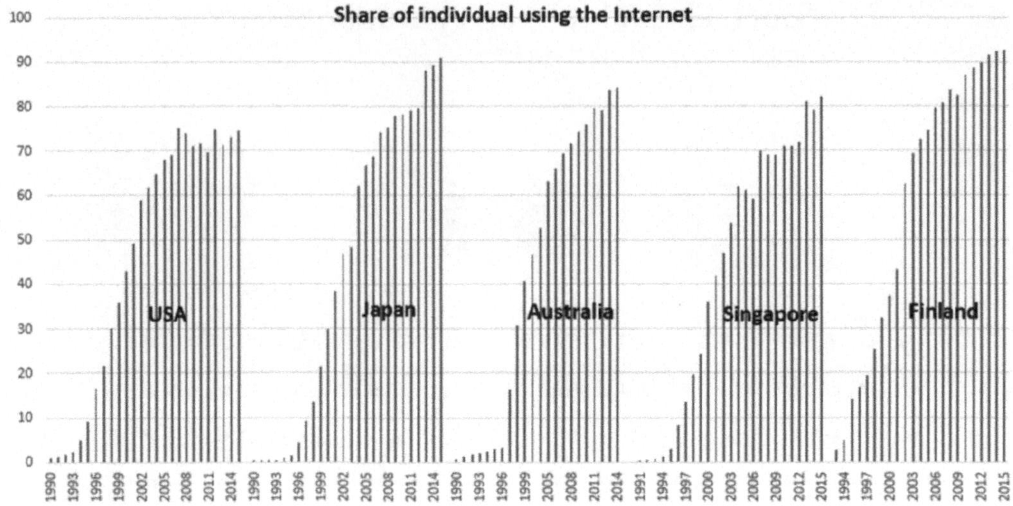

FIGURE 5.6
Share of individuals using the Internet. Source: https://ourworldindata.org/internet (Retrieved January 21, 2018) [17].

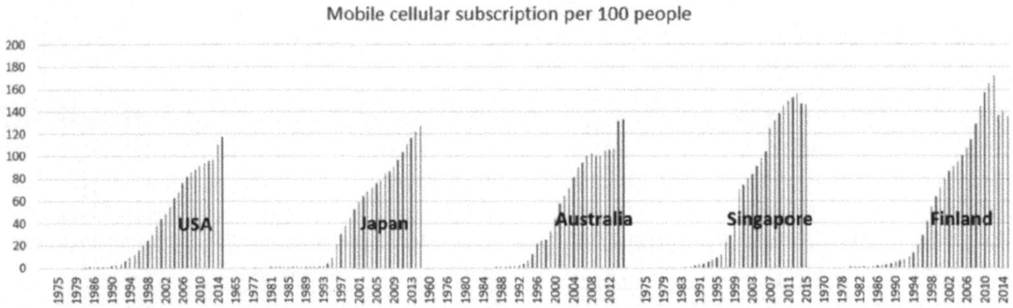

FIGURE 5.7
Number of cellular subscription per 100 people. Source: https://ourworldindata.org/internet (Retrieved January 21, 2018) [17].

We then discussed the education system in developed countries in which we took examples of three developed countries, that is, the United States, Japan, and China. We found that in these countries, education is compulsory. People do not have a choice of whether to pursue education or not, thus there are no illiterate citizens in these countries. Not only students, but parents are also motivated about studying.

After discussing developed countries, we looked at developing [19] countries. In comparison, we found that in developing countries, a huge percentage of people are left uneducated. This might be because of poverty, as the parents are unable to pay the school fees of their children, or because of the children are employed in some kind of labor during school hours, or maybe in rural areas, young girls are asked to get married at a young age, binding them to household work, leaving them no time to study. Therefore, not all citizens are able to acquire education in these developing countries.

If we compare India and China, we find that India attained independence in 1947 and China attained independence in 1949, that is, two years later than India. Although China

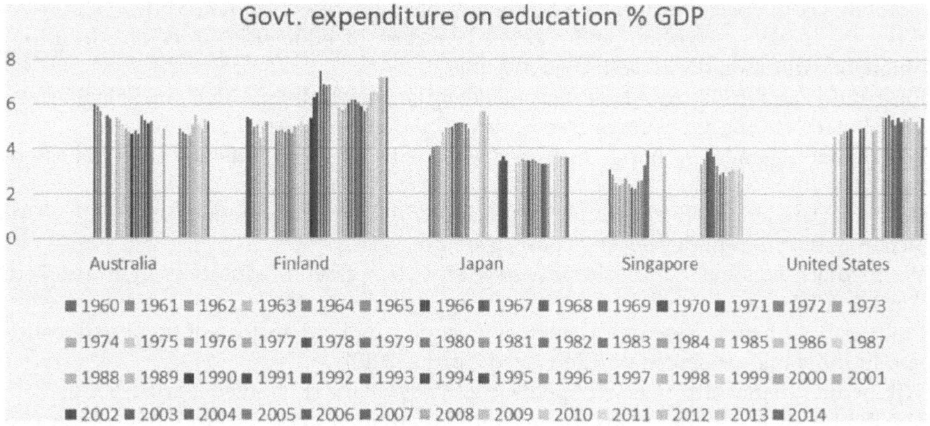

FIGURE 5.8
Government expenditure on education as per cent GDP. Source: https://ourworldindata.org/internet (Retrieved January 21, 2018) [17].

has the largest population in the world, it still managed to become a developed nation, while India is still struggling in its development. The lack of education is one of the major reasons that India is yet to be a developed country.

We noticed some similarities between developed and developing countries. In Japan, for example, students are supposed to wear school uniforms during working hours, which is similar to the fashion followed in India.

In Japan, students are supposed to clean their classrooms and grounds after their lectures. This not only makes the students independent but they also learn to respect every job. No such trend is followed in developing countries like India, therefore, there are differences between rich and poor people.

In developed countries, teaching professionals receive more compensation and have a better scope to excel in their jobs as compared with that in developing countries. People are more interested in adopting teaching as their profession in developed countries, and therefore, the quality of education delivery improves as they do their job not out of compulsion but as a choice.

Thus, after our comparison, we realize that education should be a must in every country and governments should take an active part in delivering education to all parts of their country. Also, well qualified teachers should be appointed and good compensation and opportunities must be given to them so that an increasing number of students are interested in the teaching profession—people should not hesitate in choosing this profession because they are scared that their income might not support their families. In addition, students must be taught how to respect all professions and not to look down upon poor people or people coming from rural areas.

References

1. Global Partnership for Education. www.globalpartnerhip.org (Retrieved April 2, 2018).
2. Maqbool Ahmad (2008). *Comprehensive Dictionary of Education*. London: Atlantic Publishers
3. Rod Ennis-Smith (2013). *The Last Call to Witness*. Plantation, FL: Llumina Press.

4. Academia.edu: Social Networking Site for Academics. www.academia.edu/25724141/definition_of_education_tradition_and_modern_concept_of_education_aims_of_education_definition_of_education (Retrieved April 2, 2018).
5. Bhagirathi Sahu (2002). *New Educational Philosophy*. New Delhi: SARUP and SONS.
6. The United Nations. www.un.org/en/index.html (Retrieved April 2, 2018).
7. Wikipedia: Literacy in India. https://en.wikipedia.org/wiki/Literacy_in_India (Retrieved April 2, 2018).
8. Academic Credentials Evaluation Institute, Inc. (2014). https://acei-global.blog/2014/03/06/15-facts-on-education-in-developing-countries/
9. Wikipedia: Education in India. https://en.wikipedia.org/wiki/Education_in_India (Retrieved April 2, 2018).
10. Pralhad P. Chhabria Research Center. www.ppcrc.in/blog/history-of-higher-education-system-in-india-and-present-state/(Retrieved April 2, 2018).
11. Wikipedia: Ghana. https://en.wikipedia.org/wiki/Ghana (Retrieved April 2, 2018).
12. U.S. Embassy in Ghana. https://gh.usembassy.gov/education-culture/educationusa-center/educational-system-ghana/ (Retrieved April 2, 2018).
13. Ghana Nursing and Health Centre. www.ghananursing.org/ (Retrieved April 2, 2018).
14. Willamette University (2015). https://blog.willamette.edu/worldnews/2015/04/29/the-educational-system-in-argentina-differences-similarities-and-the-challenges-ahead/ (Retrieved March 21, 2018).
15. Class Base. www.classbase.com/countries/argentina/education-system (Retrieved March 2, 2018).
16. Fortune (2015). http://fortune.com/2015/10/06/worst-internet-access/ (Retrieved April 2, 2018).
17. World Bank (2015). Broadband penetration by country, https://ourworldindata.org/internet (Retrieved January 21, 2018).
18. MoneyControl.com (2017). www.moneycontrol.com/news/business/economy/budget-2017-spendeducation-sector-seen-falling-short-1004364.html (Retrieved April 2, 2018).
19. Wikipedia: Developing country. https://en.wikipedia.org/wiki/Developing_country (Retrieved April 2, 2018).

6

Internet of Things (IoT) and e-Governance: The Arrival of a New Era

Rajeev Srivastava

CONTENTS

6.1 Introduction

The Internet of Things (IoT) is one of the leading emerging technologies. Presently, almost every device is connected to the Internet, or in other words, all devices communicate with each other with the help of the Internet [1–3]. IoT refers to the network of these connected devices using an IP address for communication. These connected devices, and the communication between them, generates a huge amount of data, which we can call "Big Data." e-Government can utilize the data generated by these devices to make the right decision at the right time. With the help of IoT technology, governments can establish better communication between citizens and e-governance [4]. By combining IoT with e-governance and analyzing data, governments can form better policies and increased economic development [5]. This chapter focuses on the benefits to the citizen of combining IoT with e-governance.

The benefit of IoT is that with the help of sensors, we can connect with surrounding objects and perform analysis [6]. For example, we can analyze the flow of traffic and find traffic jams and even the length of those jams using network sensors and digital cameras.

With the help of IoT, integrated sensors within embedded systems can take corrective action to any potentially dangerous situations. For example, by using sensors to indicate the water level of a river or the sea, a system can automatically send an alarm related to flooding and corrective measures can be taken in advance to save lives and infrastructure.

Based on the available literature, the benefits of IoT and e-governance will be presented in section two. IoT and e-governance for the purpose of road management in smart cities will be discussed in section three. Finally, conclusions will be drawn in section four. The results show that IoT can benefit e-government in different ways, such as at the tactical, operational, and strategic levels to make the services of government more effective and transparent.

6.2 Benefits of IoT for e-Governance

The main advantage of IoT is that it is a mix of several technologies and provides communication solutions such as sensors (wired or wireless), tracking technologies, distributed intelligence for numerous small objects, RFID (radio frequency identification) technology, and ZigBee technology [1,7].

IoT includes not only devices connected to the Internet but also devices connected to each other, generating signals based on sensors. The best thing is that by just installing applications on the device, it will work like a sensor in the network. For example, while driving or cycling, potential potholes can be detected by using accelerometers. In riots or robberies, microphones and cameras can be used to identify the culprits by just measuring the concentration of fine particles [1,7–10]. Many organizations today look at IoT as a new source of data, which can be used to monitor various things in different situations, for example, in determining a cutoff temperature.

With the help of IoT, huge amount of data can be gathered, which is known as Big Data, and Big Data can be very beneficial for e-governance [12]. For example, by sharing data with citizens, governments can improve transparency, or by extracting information from Big Data, governments can make better decisions for good governance [1,2,7–9,11,12]. IoT can also help in giving useful advice to users, such as help in intelligent car driving, smart highways, and traffic management [6,11].

There are many value drivers of IoT that results in better governance [2], these drivers and their benefits are given in Table 6.1.

With the help of sensors, companies can easily know what is going on in the real world [13]. Automated data collection and identification technologies like RFID can help companies to optimize processes in terms of increased accuracy and competitive advantage [14]. In summary, we can say that IoT is beneficial for citizens as well as for the government for better governance by analyzing the sensor data to know historical trends over time. The list of possible benefits of IoT in terms of strategic/political, tactical, and operational divisions [15,16] suitable for e-governance research is given in Table 6.2.

TABLE 6.1
Drivers of IoT for Better Governance

Driver	Benefits
Manual closeness	Improvement in job satisfaction, empowerment of consumers, reduction in labor cost and better data quality
Automatic closeness	Reduction in the cost of labor and process failures, provide quality data for better process management
Automatic sensors	Improvement in quality of service, enhanced efficiency of process management, and providing quality data for further improvements in process management
Feedback of user	Improvement in quality of service and its effectiveness by making process management more flexible, quick, and accurate
Broad user feedback	Improvement in trust by making new customer contacts, creating new opportunities of advertisement, and generating additional revenues

TABLE 6.2

IoT Benefits for e-Governance

Title	Benefits
Political and strategic	Improvement in trend analysis and forecasting, more transparent government, and improved citizen and government relationship
Tactical	Improvement in maintenance and planning, efficient enforcement of regulations, and reduction in cost and improvement in safety and health measures
Operational	Improvement in efficiency and effectiveness of various services

6.3 Road Management in Smart Cities

For the management and maintenance of national highways there is a requirement for accurate data. Over the years, many methods have been adopted to gather data, and on the basis of that, teams are working for better traffic and road management. Now with the help of IoT, accurate data can be easily captured by using sensors at different locations on the road. The Big Data collected from the sensors can be analyzed and used in the planning and projection of safety measures, as well as service efficiency regarding traffic and road management. One of the major problems in road management is the overloading of heavy vehicles because these vehicles lead to damage of the road and reduce the service life of the road [17,18]. With the help of IoT, governments can effectively reduce the overloading of vehicles and avoid damage to the road as well as reducing the frequency of maintenance. By reducing the frequency of road maintenance, traffic disruption can be reduced and there can be a large cost saving.

Another major problem of smart cities is traffic congestion. The two possible ways to handle this problem are managing the existing capacity and building more roads [11]. For managing the existing capacity, there is a requirement for more integrated tools. With the help of IoT, the driver of the car can be provided with all the necessary information, such as which routes have less traffic or which routes have ongoing repair work. So by collecting data from various sources, and analyzing that data better, traffic management can be accomplished.

All the important information like maximum speed limits, parking places, nearest petrol filling station, and so on, can be provided to the motorist during driving in the form of text, pictures, or sound.

Even safety information can be provided, such as sharp turns or damage to the road to avoid accidents or traffic jams [19].

By using the above techniques of road safety, traffic congestion can be managed effectively and the efficiency of the road network can be improved. With the help of IoT, the driving pattern of the motorist can also be observed and, depending upon behavior such as whether the driver is following all the traffic rules and regulations, he or she can be punished or rewarded, even the grading can be done depending upon the driving pattern.

6.4 Conclusion

With the help of IoT, the physical world can be monitored and controlled from distance by accessing remote sensor data. By integrating and analyzing the captured data from sensors, the government can develop and improve services. It has also been observed in the literature that limited research was done in the field of IoT and e-governance. This chapter provides a systematic insight toward the benefits of IoT for e-governance and the benefits range from the political to the operational level. Through IoT, e-governance can be improved in terms of effectiveness, efficiency, and the flexibility of various services to reduce cost, empower citizens, and improve transparency between governments and citizens. Finally, we can say that IoT may have a major impact on the services offered by governments in the future and it will beneficial for governments at all levels. However, IoT may have a negative influence for e-governance, which is the future scope of this study.

References

1. Atzori, L., Iera, A., Morabito, G.: The Internet of things: A survey. *Comput. Netw.* 54, 2787–2805 (2010).
2. Fleisch, E.: What is the Internet of things? An economic perspective. *Econ. Manag. Financ. Mark.* 5, 125–157 (2010).
3. Kopetz, H.: *Internet of Things. Real-Time Systems*. pp. 307–323. Springer, New York (2011).
4. Marche, S., McNiven, J.D.: e-Government and e-Governance: The future isn't what it used to be. *Can. J. Adm. Sci. Rev. Can. Sci. Adm.* 20, 74–86 (2003).
5. United Nations, Department of Economic and Social Affairs: United Nations e-government Survey 2014: e-Government for the future we want. United Nations, New York (2014).
6. Ramos, C., Augusto, J.C., Shapiro, D.: Ambient intelligence-the next step for artificial intelligence. *IEEE Intell. Syst.* 23, 15–18 (2008).
7. Chen, X.-Y., Jin, Z.-G.: Research on key technology and applications for Internet of Things. *Phys. Procedia.* 33, 561–566 (2012).
8. Gubbi, J., Buyya, R., Marusic, S., Palaniswami, M.: Internet of Things (IoT): A vision, architectural elements, and future directions. *Future Gener. Comput. Syst.* 29, 1645–1660 (2013).
9. Boulos, M.N.K., Al-Shorbaji, N.M.: On the Internet of Things, smart cities and the WHO Healthy Cities. *Int. J. Health Geogr.* 13, 10 (2014).
10. Chui, M., Löffler, M., Roberts, R.: The Internet of Things. *McKinsey Q.* 2, 1–9 (2010).
11. Hounsell, N.B., Shrestha, B.P., Piao, J., McDonald, M.: Review of urban traffic management and the impacts of new vehicle technologies. *IET Intell. Transp. Syst.* 3, 419–428 (2009).
12. Coetzee, L., Eksteen, J.: The Internet of Things—promise for the future? An introduction. *IST-Africa Conference Proceedings*(2011), Gaborone, Botswana. pp. 1–9 (2011).
13. Haller, S., Karnouskos, S., Schroth, C.: *The Internet of Things in an Enterprise Context*. Springer Berlin, Heidelberg (2009).
14. Spiess, P., Karnouskos, S.: Maximizing the Business Value of Networked Embedded Systems through Process-Level Integration into Enterprise Software. Presented at the *Second International Conference on Pervasive Computing and Applications* (2007), Birmingham, UK.
15. Ivanov, D.: An adaptive framework for aligning (re)planning decisions on supply chain strategy, design, tactics, and operations. *Int. J. Prod. Res.* 48, 3999–4017 (2010).
16. Ackoff, R.L.: Towards a system of systems concepts. *Manag. Sci.* 17, 661–671 (1971).

17. Mulyun, A., Parikesit, D., Antameng, M., Rahim, R.: Analysis of loss cost of road pavement distress due to overloading freight transportation. *J. East. Asia Soc. Transp. Stud.* 8, 1020–1035 (2010).
18. Bagui, S., Das, A., Bapanapalli, C.: Controlling vehicle overloading in BOT projects. *Procedia-Soc. Behav. Sci.* 104, 962–971 (2013).
19. Rijkswaterstaat: Feiten en cijfers, www.rws.nl/wegen/feiten_en_cijfers/statistische_verkeersgegevens/index.aspx.

7

Managing Community University Engagement with Information Technology

Minali Banerjee, Manju Singh, and Bhaskar Arora

CONTENTS

7.1 Introduction

Higher education refers to the tertiary or final level of formal learning that is provided by colleges, universities, and other similar establishments. The Indian higher education system is characterized by a continuous increase in enrollment and decreasing sources of quality education. This is primarily because the Indian higher education system is at an initial stage of establishment, although it has been decades that India has provided education. Although from the gurukul system to e-learning, a lot of economical, technological, and social changes have been witnessed, still, India is far behind in providing quality education to its increasing population and fails in attracting foreign students.

One reason is the lack of coverage and access. Until now, not all of the rural population have access to colleges and universities. This is because government educational policies are not that accessible. The policies are prepared on obsolete data that does not portray the current needs of the population. The reason behind this is because they are not in constant contact with those for whom the policies are to be framed. Periodical surveys and research are required to formulate policies, especially for those who are incapable of accessing the government for their problems.

Universities can play an important role here. Universities can bridge the gap between policymakers (government) and policy seekers. They can become an agent of the government by engaging and educating rural communities through Community University Engagement (CUE). CUE will give an ethical platform to these universities to work for the health and well-being of society (Weiss, 2016).

7.2 Community University Engagement

Higher education is crucial to the development of human resources in any country (Banerjee and Singh, 2018). Therefore, it is considered as an essential component for development. Any university has three main functions: teaching, research, and community connect or outreach. As education is a social good, higher education institutions (HEIs) become the providers of the social good and therefore are liable to work for society by taking its third function as the heart of its functioning. These days, the functioning of universities is driven more by profit (Blake, 2013). The profit driven approach deviates these universities from being a not-for-profit organization and tends to divert their resources toward earning rather than providing learning. With this approach the provider of social good cannot sustain for long.

In order to do justice with their existence, it is necessary for universities to work in accordance with the needs and demand of its stakeholders. Stakeholders here refer to the group of people, global or local, who are affected by the work of these universities. University stakeholders comprise of the staff (both teaching and administrative), students, government, societies (one residing nearby preferably rural communities), and industries (The UNIBILITY Consortium, 2017) (Figure 7.1).

Universities are liable to these stakeholders as they are responsible for funding them in numerous ways. In order to do so, they need to work for these stakeholders through partnering with them and by considering their needs and suggestions in their policymaking and administration. This partnership is formally known as CUE.

The life of villagers is difficult and a lot can be done by university stakeholders toward training and educating them (Hall et al., 2015). CUE works by providing sustainable

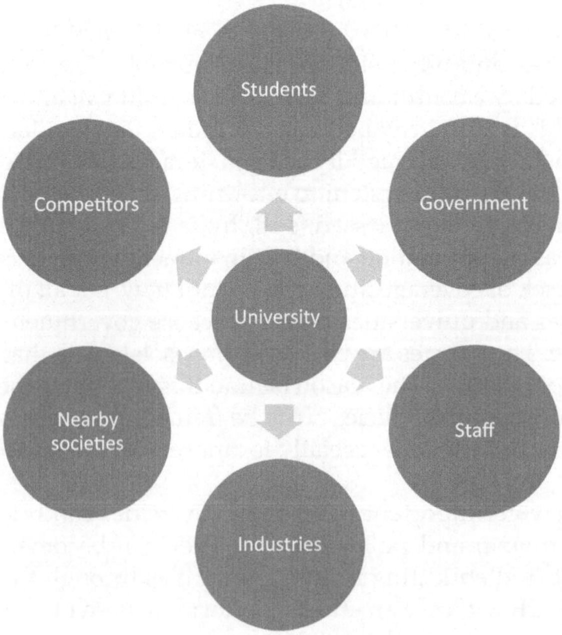

FIGURE 7.1
University stakeholders.

services to society in the form of joint workshops and projects with communities. These projects could involve planting trees, medical camps, educating the rural population about current technology, engaged research, where researchers can involve the people from the population they are targeting, the creation of local self-help groups, conducting surveys, and gathering traditional knowledge and practices from villagers. As the Indian education system is at its developing phase, universities are not in constant contact with their respective stakeholders, which weakens the partnership. This weak string can be strengthened through information technology.

Bhagat Phool Singh Mahila Vishwavidyalaya (BPSMV), Sonepat, Haryana, has taken the initiative of promoting CUE by creating a structure known as "the Centre for Society University Interface and Research (CSUIR)." The center has come up with a course on folk medicines by combining their academic expertise with the indigenous knowledge of communities. The rural women have immense knowledge of herbs and indigenous medicines and therefore the students are sent to rural communities to learn and document these medicines and treatments and convert them into academic literature.

7.3 e-Governance

India needs to globalize its higher education sector in order to meet the ever-rising competition and to fulfill the urge to become a world power. The increasing demands for education needs qualitative and quantitative improvement in universities. The biggest challenge for Indian universities is to meet the global pace of educational development; therefore, to become world class, information technology, or more specifically, e-governance, stands out as the best tool (Shrivastava et al., 2014).

e-Governance refers to an exchange of information electronically. It is basically confined to involving information and computer technology (ICT) or simply computers in the administration. The formal concept has four basic models: government to government; government to citizen; government to employees; and government to business (Garson, 2006). But e-governance is not only limited to government undertaking but can be used by any institution or undertaking in order to have transparent and real-time governance. This cost-effective technology helps in increasing productivity as administrators can access and control a wide range of activities simultaneously.

In universities, ICT can play a crucial role in administration, teaching, and training by involving a large group of people. The technology can be used from student teaching and learning to general administration including the library system, inventory management, and finance (Maki, 2008). It can also be used in the evaluation of the students through online exams. This will make the exam system more transparent and flexible and will help provide quality education (Akbar and Qureshi, 2015).

7.3.1 e-Governance for Community University Engagement

CUE for responsible education is a tool for practicing social responsibility in the education system. e-Governance can help in bringing together local and global stakeholders of universities in order to carry out a unanimous approach toward responsible implementation of CUE.

CUE is started by knowing the needs of the university stakeholders. As CUE involves knowledge sharing and a participatory approach of learning and interest, the exchange of information plays a key role here. e-Governance can help to provide information to the masses in a short timespan; an online portal can be created for this. It will work as an educational grid where all sorts of information regarding training, projects, and related work can be provided to the stakeholders simultaneously. This portal will make an "educational quality circle" that will bring together all the stakeholders and each stakeholder will have to provide an input to carry out the working of CUE.

As per the accessibility of the stakeholders, the educational quality circle will be divided into two types: "global educational quality circle (GEQC)" and "local educational quality circle (LEQC)."

7.3.2 Local Educational Quality Circle

The word "local" here signifies the stakeholders who reside in the country of the respective university. There could be further subdivision of LEQC, as shown in Figure 7.2.

The university can start by making a portal and connecting all its internal stakeholders to it. Students and staff, both teaching and administration, are required to provide suggestions on how the university could work on engaging with communities. With the suggestions received, the university arranges workshops and projects and asks its internal stakeholders to take these projects to the nearby communities. This will help in collecting data from nearby rural communities.

For instance, the university through the online portal informs its students and staff members about a medical campaign being organized by the university in a nearby village. The university can ask for suggestions about the campaign. After taking suggestions, the students, along with the teachers, could be sent to the nearby village to carry out the medical campaign. The results can then be uploaded to the LEQC with a request for further suggestions.

This information then can be shared on a government created LEQC where it will reach other universities, government departments, and industry members. The external stakeholder will also give suggestions after going through the information on the portal. The policymakers can then act accordingly. This will help the government to know the grounded realities of the unreached areas that are otherwise left unnoticed by government surveys. This will also help in making the policies region oriented, which are far more effective.

A similar practice is being conducted by the Government of India. An online portal, "MyGov" serves as a platform for citizen engagement in good governance. Here, the Indian Government invited suggestions from the public under the Rurbanization scheme.

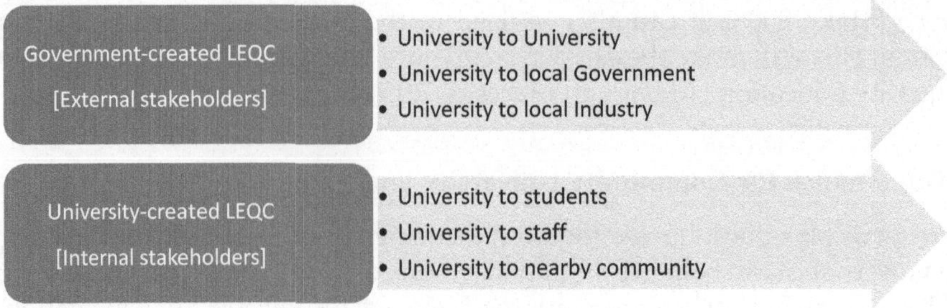

FIGURE 7.2
The LEQC model.

The suggestions were invited between March 24 and April 13, 2018 on how to deal with the key areas of Rurbanization, namely: treating solid waste, village sewage, accessibility of road transport, a cost-effective approach to street lightning, improvement in healthcare services, digital literacy at village level, facilitating infrastructure for women in villages, and creating employment opportunities for village women. A large number of suggestions were received from students, teachers, and the general public.

The Samarth Bharat Abhiyaan Programme launched by the University of Pune was a classic example of CUE. Under it, each college adopted one village for its overall development. The development program was started by taking 12 key aspects, including environment awareness, health and drug addiction, soil and water health, and so on (Tandon, 2014). The initiative was carried out using the methodology explained above, as the university gathered suggestions from its staff and students on how to create awareness among the people of the targeted society. The staff members can also be trained by field experts through videos and online discussions on how to carry out these campaigns.

M.M. College, Haryana, stands out as another example of CUE. The college, with the help of NSS students, conducted a survey on the status of birth and death registrations in Haryana. The findings were shared with local municipal officials. This could be recaptured using the online tool where the survey results were computerized and shared with the government directly through the online portal. This will help the state and the local government implement the region-related policy on birth and death registration.

7.3.3 Global Educational Quality Circle

Global here refers to university stakeholders residing in foreign countries. It includes foreign governments, foreign universities, teachers, and students. No country can globalize its education sector by operating only within its boundaries. Universities need to come up with partnerships in order to increase learning and innovation. Similarly, the CUE approach can not be limited to a region or a single country, it needs to be globalized as well. Therefore, universities, along with their stakeholders, should come up with a common means of communicating and mobilizing knowledge and ideas concerning CUE.

GEQC provides the required means of communication among global stakeholders without being physically present. The global portal asks different universities to contribute their valuable knowledge and experience on CUE with other universities and governments. The data collected at a local level can be shared on this global platform where all the agents involved can analyze the data and take the required action.

The University of Victoria is offering a course on Community Based Participatory Research (CBPR) for effective CUE globally. This UNESCO certified course is being delivered on the Moodle platform, which has three components: online, face to face, and field work. The programme is led by Dr. Budd Hall and Dr. Rajesh Tandon, UNESCO co-chair in Community Based Research and Social Responsibility in Higher Education. The target is to enhance capacities among academia and practitioners regarding CBPR so that CUE can be completed in a more responsible manner.

Participatory Research in Asia (PRIA) is a center for developing participatory research in Asia, particularly in India. It was also involved in the formulation of the UNESCO chair in Community Based Research and Social Responsibility in Higher Education, launched in 2012 (Hall et al., 2015). The chair is working for producing partnerships and engagements between universities and communities in an efficient manner. The chair carries out its projects and trains its subordinates through online teaching methodology.

7.4 Conclusion

Information technology or e-governance serves as a remedy to rising problems in developing and developed countries (Mittal et al., 2004). e-Governance in CUE practices help universities to participate in policy making. The educational quality circle helps in providing an open access and transparent database for universities to learn and innovate their CUE practices.

The circle enables multiregional mobilization of knowledge using online discussions, videos, live chat, and so on, and brings trainers and learners together. Similarly, the concept of CUE helps achieve the aim of providing responsible education by each university.

Periodical updating of these portals is required. There is a strong need of organizations like PRIA, who work with different universities, to encourage CUE. UNESCO are working on achieving Sustainable Development Goals (SDGs) and they have identified the concept of CUE as an effective measure of achieving SDGs globally by integrating internationally received ideas. These organizations will provide a framework for such kinds of models. Therefore, organizations like UNESCO should also be made part of this quality circle.

PRIA partners with various universities to prepare courses on CUE. PRIA combines their field expertise, along with the theoretical knowledge of university teachers, for the preparation of a wide variety of certificate courses. One of these courses is "International perspective in participatory research and evaluation." This is an online course where through videos, case studies, and online learning, the learner is provided with the knowledge of participatory research (PR). The course prepares the learner for the conduct of effective PR projects in their own university with the help of their surrounding communities.

References

Akbar, S. & Qureshi, A. Q. (2015). Role of information and communication technology (ICT) in a good examination system. *American Journal of Educational Research*, 3(11), 1438–1443.

Banerjee, M. & Singh, S. (2018). Is higher education a potential means of promoting labour mobility? *International Journal of Emerging Multidisciplinary Research*, 2(1), 27–31.

Barta, B.-Z. et al. (1995). *Information Technology in Educational Management*. Chapman and Hall, London.

Blake, P. (2013, January 06). The profit motive is threatening higher education. *University World News*. www.universityworldnews.com/article.php?story=2013010422115451 (Retrieved on April 12, 2018).

Garson, D. G. (2006). *Public Information Technology and* e-Governance. Jones and Bartlett Publishers, Sudbury, MA.

Hall, B., Tandon, R., & Tremblay, C. (2015). Strengthening Community University Research Partnerships: Global Perspectives. British Columbia, University of Victoria. http://dspace.library.uvic.ca/bitstream/handle/1828/6509/Hall_Budd_StrengtheningCommUniversityPartnerships_2017rev.pdf?sequence=6&isAllowed=y (Retrieved on March 25, 2018).

Maki, C. (2008). Information and communication technology for administration and management for secondary schools in Cyprus. *Journal of Online Learning and Teaching*, 4 (3), 18–20.

Mittal, A. et al. (2004). A framework for e-Governance solution. *IBM Journal of Research and Development*, 48(5/6), 717–733.

Shrivastava, R. K., Raizada, A. K., & Saxena, N. (2014). Role of e-Governance to strengthen higher education system in India. *IOSR Journal of Research and Method in Education (IOSR-JRME)*, 4(1), 57–62. www.iosrjournals.org/iosr-jrme/papers/Vol-4%20Issue-2/Version-1/J04215762.pdf (Retrieved on April 4, 2018).

Tandon, R. (2014). Fostering social responsibility in higher education in India. http://unescochair-cbrsr.org/unesco/pdf/Fostering_Social_Responsibility.pdf (Retrieved on March 18, 2018).

The UNIBILITY Consortium (2017). Universities meet social responsibility (UNIBILITY) - 2015–2017. www.iauhesd.net/sites/default/files/documents/io8_guidelines_final_version_2017-09-12_print.pdf (Retrieved on March 11, 2018).

Weiss, B. (2016). The rise of social responsibility in higher education. *University World News*, 423. www.universityworldnews.com/article.php?story=20160811095808959 (Retrieved on May 2, 2018).

8

Appraising the Societal Approach of India through the Social Cost Benefit Matrix

Deepa and Prateek Gupta

CONTENTS

8.1 Introduction

Capacity building is required within government and the creation of general awareness about e-governance among citizens. The consequent benefits can be a reduction in corruption, enhanced transparency, better convenience, growth in revenue, and/or cost reduction. Hence, e-governance has gained more popularity in the complex business world. e-Governance allows citizens to communicate with the government, participate in the government's policy making, and to communicate with each other. e-Governance creates opportunities for the government to revolutionize the procedure of the creation and execution of a sustainable approach from a system-focused to an actor-driven one.

Identifying the increasing use of electronics, the Government of India established the Department of Electronics in 1970. By the 1980s, a large number of government officers had computers but they were typically used for "word processing." The escalation of e-governance first stared with the National Informatics Centre (NIC) being established in 1977, and it was a first important footstep on the road to e-governance in India. The establishment of NICNET in 1987 was the major pushing force for e-governance. The National e-Governance Plan (NeGP) commenced in 2006, which showed a striking agenda for embryonic e-government services. "eKranti" or NeGP 2.0 was also gestated with a spotlight on electronically driven services. Later, Digital India, which commenced on July 1, 2015, became an initiative to make certain that government services are provided to citizens electronically by recuperating online infrastructure and by increasing Internet connectivity.

Gradually, several states started measures to introduce e-governance to improve their governance process such as the e-Seva and e-Procurement Project in Andhra Pradesh, Project e-Sampark in Chandigarh, e-procurement in Gujrat, Project Bhoomi and Khajane in Karnataka, project FRIENDS (Fast, Reliable, Instant, Efficient Network for the Disbursement of Services) in Thiruvananthapuram (Kerala), project Gyandoot in Dhar district (Madhya Pradesh), projects Lok Mitra and Jan Mitra under project e-Mitra in Rajasthan, the Lokvani project at Sitapur District in Uttar Pradesh, and so on. As per the United Nations E-Government Survey 2016, e-government in support of sustainable development was launched in July 2016.

As per Ministry of Information and Technology, Government of India has collaborated with many countries toward the effective implementation of e-governance in the world. These countries are Armenia, Australia, Azerbaijan, Bangladesh, Taiwan, Belarus, Bhutan, Russia, Canada, China, South Africa, Egypt, Estonia, Serbia, France, Finland, Georgia, Germany, Ghana, Indonesia, Israel, Japan, Kazakhstan, Kyrgyzstan, Latvia, Sweden, Singapore, Lesotho, Malaysia, Mongolia, Myanmar, Poland, Saudi Arabia, South Korea, Tanzania, Tajikistan, Tunisia, Turkmenistan, the United States, Uzbekistan, and Vietnam, as well as BRICS and the European Union.

8.2 Review of the Literature

To make conducive research, the following literature was reviewed and analyzed.

Rizvi A.H. (2016) discussed Vidya-Vahini, an educational project and promotion scheme by the Indian government to improve quality services for their people, which means there is enormous scope for the development and growth of e-governance in different areas. Agangiba W.A. and Agangiba M.A. (2013) take an impressive e-governance study as the most demanding applications of information and communication technology for public services. Al-Khouri Ali M. (2011) aimed to help in bridging the gap between policy makers and implementers by providing greater clarity and reducing misalignment on key elements of e-government transformation. Antonio Cordella and Jakob Hesse (2010) indicated that the negotiation that occurs among different involved performers constantly shaped the nature of the services delivered and the socio-economic expansion supported by the project and the resultant changes the project itself experienced. Asaduzzaman M. (2011) suggested that the major impediments in implementing e-governance initiatives in Bangladesh are the lack of awareness of e-governance, a strong tactical plan, centralization of e-governances, a dearth of an e-based official community culture, and an incoherent political culture. Ching-Heng Pan (2010) discussed the development of "e" as a starting point for the practical use of cost benefit analysis on e-government in Taiwan. Chowdhury M.H. and Zaidi Satter A. (2012) identified and scrutinized the part of e-governance that generated "Digital Bangladesh." The study foresees that the actual implementation of e-governance is a complex and lengthy task that may proceed well beyond the government's target of 2021. Dhamuniya S. (2015) conducted a pragmatic overview of the state of higher education in Rajasthan, one of the major Indian states. Dhindsa B. et al.

(2013) focused on use of an e-governance portal that provides users with easy access to all government information and services, while downplaying the structure of government or which ministry provides the service. It is directed toward the development of recent services and strategies. Dwivedi S.K. and Bharti A.K. (2010) discussed the basic problems and acceptability of e-governance in India. Effectual promotion schemes by the Indian Government were also shown, which enhanced the availability of quality services to citizens, and implies that there is vast prospective for the growth and development of e-governance in various sectors. Dwivedi S.S. (2015) focused on the challenging issues lying ahead for e-governance, that is, security, and the government needs to make significant investments in areas such as IT training, assessment, and awareness. Gupta M.P. (2010) considered the evolution of e-governance in India. The study showed the initiatives and projects engaged in by the Government of India in the span of five years and the missions and objectives in the creation of a "Transparent and Efficient Governability" from the grassroot level. Sharma M and Gupta P (2017) discussed that in the era of e-governance and digitalization, public sector accounting and auditing should be transparent and public funds should be used to provide more convenient access to government accounting information for citizens in India like private sector accounting information. The use of e-governance facilities for greater transparency in India should address the efficiency and effectiveness of the public sector with new public financial management systems, which is possible through the effective use of e-governance services. Khan I. et al. (2015) focused on how government and public sector units around the world are altering their public administration units and providing more well-organized and cost-effective services, as well as improved information and openness to their stakeholders. Malik P. et al. (2014) put more emphasis on building a bridge between the government and people to make helpful and competent services available, to augment productivity, and for other benefits to citizens, in addition, many other important e-governance applications are introduced by governments of different countries. There are differences between a citizen's intention to get government information and a citizen's intention to conduct government transactions on an e-government website. Gupta P., Choudhary D., and Deepa (2016), highlighted the effective use of e-governance in the area of agriculture development through Kisan Seva Kendra (KSK). The only issue identified was a lack of awareness of KSK among farmers in India. Jalal A. and Mistry J.J. (2012) focused on the relationship between e-government and corruption in developed and developing countries. The outcomes suggested that there is an increment in usage of e-government related to ICT that results in the decrement of corruption. The study also revealed that the impact of e-government is advanced in developing countries in comparison with developed countries between 2003 and 2010. Gupta P. and Bhanti P. (2013) discussed various issues and challenges regarding the sustainable management of education and identified the use of e-governance in management education through ICT. Governance through ICT was identified as a major tool for the effective use of management education in the present era. Panda B.P. and Swain D.K. (2009) showed that the system may become more transparent by developing information kiosks at the rural and urban level as part of e-government initiatives for creating transparency in different systems and procedures so that people can get information by the means of online services and can give their feedback on various issues. Patel A. et al. (2013) concentrated on generating a high level of awareness about e-capacity related to governance provided by the Government of Gujarat. The author highlighted the service challenge provided by the

Gujarat Government toward e-governance. Kumar P. and Bhanti P. (2012) focused on the existing eminence of e-governance in India and several areas where e-governance can perform an important role in society. Singh A. (2014) highlighted the triumph of an e-governance proposal in how it increased and improved people's involvement in the functioning of the government through extensive ICT access, promoted accountability, transparency, and responsiveness, and ensured that government works better at a minimal cost. Singla S.K. and Aggarwal H. (2011) focused on the impact of e-governance to control corruption based on an analysis of various projects implemented in India, especially in the state of Punjab. The paper provides submissions for setting effectual e-governance projects and concludes with an argument about the advantages of such projects. Yadav K. and Tiwari S. (2014) explored the latest technology to be adopted by governments to make the workings of government more efficient and transparent.

8.3 Problem Identified

To receive the optimum benefits of ICT, there is an urgent need to setup adequate infrastructure along with investing sufficient capital. The innovative e-governance approach helps in improving service delivery of information with its involvement in decision making. Implementing e-governance provides consistent, opportune, and convincing information for broadcasting to the population and other related organizations. The "Virtual Interaction" is counted as a disadvantage for rural people who lack access to technology, on the other hand, the public usually face corruption and harassment issues while using technical services. The initiatives regarding e-governance may boost the access to information, which leads to decreased corruption. In addition, there is always a need of an appropriate strategy to measure the tangible and intangible benefits of e-government. It should be understood that e-governance has increased transparency and efficiency toward dissemination of information but there is still a way to go to achieve social and economic growth in the lives of people. Keeping these problems in view, this study aims to identify and analyze the social cost, benefits, threats, and opportunities for e-governance in India.

8.4 Objectives of the Study

There is an urgent need for adopting and encouraging advanced ICT in public administration. The present study is an attempt toward identifying the need, scope, and strategies of e-governance in India, the identification and analysis of shortcomings, and to provide an appropriate solution, which may lead to e-government capacity building in India. This study is has the following objectives:

- To identify the need and scope of e-governance in India.
- To analyze and correlate the cost and benefits generated by e-governance in India.

- To re-look at the policies framed and strategies adopted by the Indian Government in the context of societal development through e-governance in India.
- To compare the policies framed and strategies adopted with the philosophy of the Indian Government in the context of e-governance in India.
- To analyze the role of government, semi-government, and other various agencies in promoting e-governance facilities with high societal benefits in India.

8.5 Hypothesis

To have a constructive conclusion, analysis was done on the basis of the following hypotheses:

H_{0a}: The implication of e-governance will adversely affect socio development in India as it carries a high cost.

H_{1a}: The implication of e-governance in India will be effective and may provide a large benefit to society.

H_{0b}: The availability of e-governance facilities to every citizen of India is not effective for social factors, that is, education and living standards of the citizens of India.

H_{1b}: e-Governance facilities can reach every citizen of India effectively for improved social factors.

8.6 Research Design

The following research methodology took place in the present study:
Sampling: The sampling in the research was as following

- *Sample size*: 1000 respondents (members of the public) were selected (from different area of Delhi and West Uttar Pradesh of India).
- *Sampling method*: Judgmental sampling is followed.
- *Research instrument*: To attain the designed objectives of the present study, a structured survey was conducted containing 20 questions, excluding personal information. The survey questions targeted individuals' approach toward e-governance services and so on.
- *Mode of survey*: The survey was conducted through personal interviews and interactions.
- *Place of survey*: The identified areas were New and Old Delhi, Noida, Ghaziabad, Sahibababd, Modinagar, Meerut, Hapur, Bulandshar, Mujjafarnagar, and so on. The research was concentrated on citizens of India in Delhi and West Uttar

Pradesh. It was not possible to analyze all citizens available in the said area in one go, ten major cities of this area were selected for the survey purpose.

- *Research method*: The collected data was justified and analyzed with the help of SCBA matrix and SCBA formula, which includes the following:

$$\textbf{Social Cost}\,(\mathbf{SC}_x) = \text{Adverse to society} = -1$$

$$\textbf{Social Benefit}\,(\mathbf{SB}_x) = \text{Favorable to society} = +1$$

$$\textbf{Neutral}\,(\mathbf{N}_x) = \text{No impact to society} = 0$$

$$\mathbf{NSCB}_x = \Sigma\,\mathbf{SB}_x + \Sigma\,\mathbf{SC}_x + \Sigma\,\mathbf{N}_x$$

$$\mathbf{SB}_x = \{\text{No. of Factors} \times (+1)\}$$

$$\mathbf{SC}_x = \{\text{No. of Factors} \times (-1)\}$$

$$\mathbf{N}_x = \{\text{No. of Factors} \times (0)\}$$

If $\mathbf{NSCB}_x$ = Positive value…net social benefit

If $\mathbf{NSCB}_x$ = Negative value…net social cost

If $\mathbf{NSCB}_x$ = Zero value…no benefit, no cost

If $\mathbf{NSCB}_x \geq 5$, it is represented as "effective social benefits"

If $\mathbf{NSCB}_x \geq 1 < 5$, it is represented as "favorable social benefits"

If $\mathbf{NSCB}_x = 0$, it is represented as "zero effect i.e., no benefit no cost"

If $\mathbf{NSCB}_x < 0$, i.e., $(-\text{ve})$, it is represented as "affecting social cost"

where:

$\mathbf{SB}_x$ = Social benefit

$\mathbf{SC}_x$ = Social cost

$\mathbf{N}_x$ = Neutral

$\mathbf{NSCB}_x$ = Net social cost benefit of factor X

8.7 SWOT Analysis of e-Governance in India

The present study helps in segmenting the status of e-governance in India according to SWOT analysis (Singh & Chander, 2012) (Table 8.1).

TABLE 8.1
SWOT Analysis of e-Governance in India

SWOT	Urban society	Rural society	Government/society
Strengths	• Literacy rate is consistently increasing • Increasing IT infrastructure • People eager to learn e-governance services • Transparency in government services • Increasing IT education at school level	• Removal of unwanted intermediaries between farmers and the government • Transparency in government services • Increasing access of e-services • Increasing IT education at school level	• Higher per capita income • IT literacy rate is consistently increasing • Increasing IT infrastructure • People eager to learn IT skills • Transparency for government services
Weakness	• Low IT literacy • Language barrier • Inefficient cyber laws • High ongoing cost of the Internet • Fear factor towards the use of e-services • Short term approach of IT companies • Weak connectivity	• Very low IT literacy • Language barrier • Reach to all rural areas • Very low awareness about e-governance • Inefficient IT infrastructure • Lack of IT standards • Fewer number of Customer Service Centers (CSCs) • Weak awareness	• Low IT literacy • Low investment in IT sectors • Language barrier • High cost of Internet • Cost of IT infrastructure • Inefficient cyber laws • Lack of IT standards • Short-term approach of IT companies
Opportunities	• Increase in employment • Open market for IT companies • Improvement in the education system • PPP mode for technology outsourcing • Government services at finger tips	• Increase in employment • Increment in literacy level • Improved agriculture • Support in transportation • Linking of Government schemes	• Increase in employment • Emergent market for IT companies • Improvement in the education system • Liaising of all schemes with the Internet • Higher cost efficiency in the long run
Threats	• High information technology illiteracy levels • Security and privacy • Dependence over technology • Brain drain of skilled IT individuals	• Inadequate power supply in rural areas • Lack of awareness about e-governance initiatives • Improper use of ICT • Improper use of the Internet	• Non-availability of user-friendly interfaces • Lack of awareness about e-governance initiatives • Security and privacy • High IT illiteracy levels

This SWOT matrix is prepared on the basis of feedback collected from rural and urban citizens, government officials, and the literature.

8.8 Social Cost Benefit Analysis (SCBA) of e-Governance in India

See Table 8.2.

8.9 Analysis of SCBA Matrix

The data collected is analyzed in Table 8.2 as social costs and benefits for urban and rural societies in form of Yes (Y) and No (N). To analyze and present better conclusions, these benefits and costs are structured in SCBA matrix as in Table 8.3.

Using Net Social Cost Benefit Formula:

(Factor X is "U" for urban, "R" for rural, "G" for government)

For Urban Society:

$$\begin{aligned}\mathbf{NSBC_U} &= \mathbf{\Sigma SB_U + \Sigma SC_U + \Sigma N_U}\\ &=\{7\times(+1)\}+\{2\times(-1)\}+\{1\times(0)\}\\ &=+7-2+0\\ &=+5\end{aligned}$$

For Rural Society:

$$\begin{aligned}\mathbf{NSBC_R} &= \mathbf{\Sigma SB_R + \Sigma SC_R + \Sigma N_R}\\ &=\{7\times(+1)\}+\{2\times(-1)\}+\{1\times(0)\}\\ &=+7-2+0\\ &=+5\end{aligned}$$

For the Government of India:

$$\begin{aligned}\mathbf{NSBC_U} &= \mathbf{\Sigma SB_G + \Sigma SC_G + \Sigma N_G}\\ &=\{5\times(+1)\}+\{5\times(-1)\}+\{0\times(0)\}\\ &=+5-5+0\\ &=+0\end{aligned}$$

This impact may also be observed with the help of a graphical presentation (Figure 8.1).

Interpretation: The analysis of the SCBA matrix of e-governance in India is as follows: out of *10 points SCBA* for Urban Society shows *7 positive points* against *2 negative points* and *1 point with no impact*. Net impact is +5 which shows that there are *effective social benefits* for urban society. For Rural Society, there is no change and remains the same with *7 positive points* against *2 negative points*, and *1 point with no impact*. Net impact is +5 which shows that there are *effective social benefits* for rural society too. Where the Government of India is concerned, the scenario is slightly changed as SCBA shows *5 positive points* against

TABLE 8.2

Matrix Representing Social Cost Benefit Analysis (SCBA) of e-Governance in India

		For urban society			For rural society			For the Government of India		
S.N.	**Factors**	**Cost**	**Benefit**	**Remark**	**Cost**	**Benefit**	**Remark**	**Cost**	**Benefit**	**Remark**
1.	Access of government services	N	Y	Need of society	N	Y	Need of society	N	Y	Duty of government
2.	IT literacy	Y	N	Involves cost t- have IT skills	Y	N	Involves cost to have IT skills	Y	N	Involves cost to provide IT skills
3.	Access to the Internet	Y	N	Involves regular cost to use the Internet	Y	N	Involves regular cost to use the Internet	Y	N	Involves high cost as the use of Internet is regular
4.	Access of e-government services	N	Y	Eliminating the cost of travelling to government offices and other irrelevant costs	N	Y	Eliminating the cost of travelling to government of-ices and other irrelevant costs	Y	N	Government requires spending more money
5.	Awareness about e-government services	N	Y	Increases knowledge about various government services	N	Y	Increases knowledge about various government services	N	Y	Provides knowledge about various government services
6.	Campaigning about e-government services	N	Y	No cost is involved but benefits in the long run	N	Y	No cost is involved but benefits in the long run	Y	N	Cost is involved for awareness campaigning
7.	Impact of e-government services	N	Y	Provides awareness, knowledge, access about various subsidies, schemes, features of government	N	Y	Provides awareness, knowledge, access about various subsidies, schemes, features of government	N	Y	Provides awareness, knowledge, access about various subsidies, schemes and features of government

(Continued)

TABLE 8.2 (CONTINUED)

Matrix Representing Social Cost Benefit Analysis (SCBA) of e-Governance in India

		For urban society			For rural society			For the Government of India		
S.N.	**Factors**	**Cost**	**Benefit**	**Remark**	**Cost**	**Benefit**	**Remark**	**Cost**	**Benefit**	**Remark**
8.	Investment toward e-governance infrastructure	N	N	No impact	N	N	No impact	Y	N	Heavy cost is involved
9.	Availability of CSCs	N	Y	Easy access of transfer of e-service has become possible	N	Y	Easy access of transfer of e-service has become possible	N	Y	Easy access of transfer of e-service has become possible
10.	Effectiveness of CSCs toward execution of e-government services	N	Y	To execute all services on behalf of the government	N	Y	To execute all services on behalf of the government	N	Y	To execute all services on behalf of the government

This matrix is the result of discussions made with the people of urban areas and rural areas.

TABLE 8.3

Analysis of SCBA Matrix of e-Governance in India

			Cost/benefit*		
S.N.	**Factors**	**Analysis**	**For Urban society**	**For Rural society**	**For Government of India**
1.	Access of government services	Access to government services are always being treated as benefits for all as it is required for society as well as the government	+ 1	+1	+1
2.	IT literacy	IT literacy is important, but it involves a cost to have IT skills for both urban and rural people as well as for the government	−1	−1	−1
3.	Access to the Internet	Access to the Internet involves a high and regular cost as the use of the Internet is increasing day by day for all	−1	−1	−1
4.	Access of e-government services	Accesses of e-government services are treated benefits for all as it helps in eliminating the cost of travelling to government offices and other irrelevant costs. Whereas the government currently requires money to spent on this	+1	+1	−1
5.	Awareness about e-government services	Awareness about e-government services increases knowledge about various government services and schemes, hence treated as benefits for all.	+1	+1	+1
6.	Awareness about campaigning for e-government services	People from urban and rural areas do not bother about awareness campaigning and do not pay anything, hence it is treated as no cost/benefit for them. Whereas for the government, a cost is involved for awareness campaigning	+1	+1	−1
7.	Impact of e-government services	e-Government service provides awareness, knowledge, access to various subsidies, schemes, features of the government, hence it is treated as benefits for all	+1	+1	+1
8.	Investment towards e-governance infrastructure	There is no impact of investment toward e-governance infrastructure for the general public but a heavy cost is involved for the government	0	0	−1

(Continued)

TABLE 8.3 (CONTINUED)
Analysis of SCBA Matrix of e-Governance in India

			Cost/benefit*		
S.N.	**Factors**	**Analysis**	**For Urban society**	**For Rural society**	**For Government of India**
9.	Availability of CSCs	CSCs play the role of intermediators between the government and the public, by which easy access of transfer of e-services becomes possible	+1	+1	+1
10.	Effectiveness of CSCs toward execution of e-government services	CSCs are able to execute all services on behalf of the government, hence they are treated as benefits for all	+1	+1	+1
Total benefits			**+7**	**+7**	**+5**
Total costs			**−2**	**−2**	**−5**
No impact			**1**	**1**	**0**

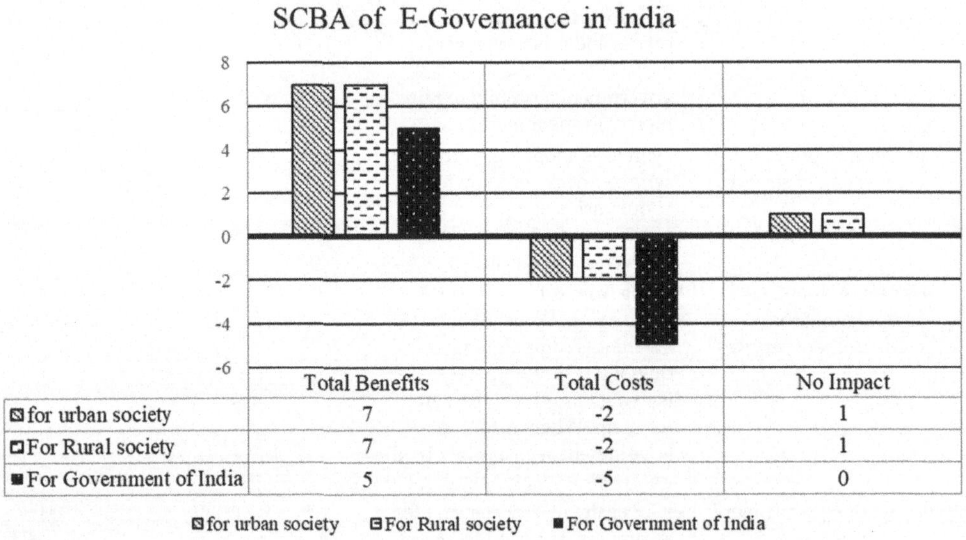

FIGURE 8.1
Social cost benefit analysis (SCBA) of e-governance in India.

5 negative points and *0 points with no impact.* Net Impact is "0" which shows that there is no impact for the Government of India. This shows that urban and rural society benefits from the availability of e-governance in India. Whereas it seems that the government requires an increased effort to run e-governance activity effectively and to invest funds for infrastructure; however, in the long run, there will be a win-win situation for all. It also reveals that there is an urgent need of high level e-governance facilities with sound infrastructure.

8.10 Testing of Hypothesis on the Basis of Analysis

The data analyzed so far has assisted in accepting or rejecting the hypothesis set earlier. The result is discussed in Tables 8.4–8.6.

8.11 Conclusion and Suggestions

Illiterate people (specifically non-technical) and the inadequate technical infrastructure are the most challenging issues in India toward the effective implementation of e-governance. The present study highlights the following challenges faced in India toward the effective implementation of e-governance:

- It was found with the help of the survey that there is a huge lack of awareness about the availability of various e-governance facilities in the different areas.

TABLE 8.4

Hypothesis Testing: "a"

Hypothesis set	Result
H_{0a}: The null hypothesis was set by assuming that the *implication of* e-governance will affect socio development in India adversely as carrying a high cost H_{1a}: The alternative hypothesis was set by assuming that the *implication of* e-governance *in India* will be effective good enough and may a large benefit to society	It may be analyzed with the help of data studied that this null hypothesis is **rejected** and the alternative hypothesis is **accepted** as e-governance is increasing in India daily and it is influencing people positively

TABLE 8.5

Hypothesis Testing: "b"

Hypothesis set	Result
H_{0b}: The null hypothesis was set by assuming that the means of making available e-governance facilities to every citizen of India is not effective toward social factors, that is, education and living standards of the citizens of India H_{1b}: The alternative hypothesis was set by assuming that the e-governance facilities can reach every citizen of India effectively for improved social factors	The null hypothesis is **accepted** as the means of making available e-governance facilities to every citizen of India are not focused toward social factors, that is, education and living standards of the citizens of India rather than only providing government services to the public

TABLE 8.6

Socio-Economic Costs and Benefits of e-Governance in India

Costs	
• High investment for technical infrastructure • Cost of building the e-governance portal • Cost of e-governance portal administration and maintenance • Cost of training (CSCs/public/administrators) • Cost of awareness campaigning • Cost of making e-governance facilities available • Cost of security of online data	
Benefits	
Benefits to the governmental agency	• Easy flow of e-governance operations • Saving in direct workplace costs • Reduction in delivery time of e-services
Benefits to CSCs/agencies	• Improved work efficiency and effectiveness of e-services. • Automation of governance process • Reduction in errors/frauds and complaints
Benefits to the citizen	• Panacea for all government services • Easy and quick communication • Cost saving • Single window interface as no need to visit various governmental offices • Time saving, increased control over operations
Benefits to society	• Transparency • Increasing reach to society • Bridging the gap between citizens and the government

- Many citizens do not use e-governance services as they felt that there was high ratio of technical illiteracy.
- The respondents felt that accessing the Internet was still expensive.

It may be observed that the major issues against the effective implementation of e-governance are "technical literacy," "lack of awareness," "Internet connectivity," and "easy flow of services." The possible suggestions identified through this project required for society are discussed as follows (Kumar, 2016):

1. It is urgently required to deliver all types of public services electronically, which will make the service process transparent, citizen centric, easily accessible, and effective in favor of the public and government.
2. This major issue of spreading awareness can be solved by involving technical education institutions. At their teaching faculty, students can create awareness to make it possible for nearby areas to learn about e-governance quickly and at a very low cost. This is expressed with the help of the model in Figure 8.2.

The major issue identified by the study, which is the inappropriate flow of e-governance service due to a lack of awareness, was the government somehow unable to reach each citizen or to spread awareness. The above model suggests that this issue may be

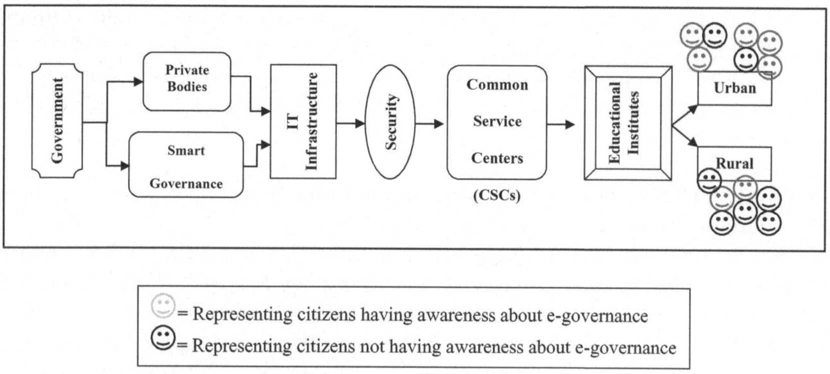

FIGURE 8.2
Suggested model for effective flow of e-governance to end users.

solved if educational/technical institutes are involved. The technical students under the guidance of their mentors/teachers may spread such awareness quickly as well as in a cost-effective manner.

References

Agangiba W., Agangiba M. (2013), e-Governance justified, *(IJACSA) International Journal of Advanced Computer Science and Applications*, Vol. 4, No. 2, pp. 223–225.

Al-Khouri Ali M. (2011), An innovative approach for e-government transformation, *International Journal of Managing Value and Supply Chains (IJMVSC)*, Vol. 2, No. 1, Doi: 10.5121/Ijmvsc.2011.2102.

Asaduzzaman, M. (2011), e-Governance initiatives in Bangladesh: Some observation, *Nepalese Journal of Public Policy and Governance*, Vol. XXVIII, No. 2, July-December, pp. 42–54.

Ching-Heng P. (2010), Methods for Costs-Benefits Analysis on E-Government Projects, 09640d002503 (Commissioned Research Reports), Client: Taiwan e-Governance Research Center, R.O.C. (Taiwan).

Chowdhury M.H, Satter A. (2012), The role of e-Governance in creating digital Bangladesh, *International Journal of Advances in Science and Technology*, Vol. 4, No. 6, pp. 24–32.

Cordella A., Hesse J. (2010), E-government in the making: Socio-economic development in the Akshaya project. In: *European Conference on Information Systems 2010*, 6–9 June, Pretoria, South Africa. The London School of Economics and Political Science.

Dhamuniya S. (2015), e-Governance in Rajasthan State Universities: Impacts and impediments, *International Journal of Social Sciences and Management*, Vol. 2, No. 1, pp. 31–35.

Dhindsa B., Narang M., Choudhary K. (2013), Benefits and challenges of e-Governance portal, *International Journal of Soft Computing and Engineering (IJSCE)*, Vol. 3, No. 5, pp. 121–123.

Dwivedi S.K. (2015), Enabling good governance through e-Governance in India: Moments for retrospection. *XVI Annual Conference Proceedings*, DSPSR, Delhi.

Dwivedi S.K, Bharti A.K (2010), e-Governance in India – Problems and acceptability, *Journal of Theoretical and Applied Information Technology*, Vol. 17, pp. 37–43.

Gupta M.P. (2010), Tracking the evolution of e-Governance in India, *International Journal of Electronic Government Research*, Vol. 6, No 1, pp. 46–58.

Gupta P., Choudhary D., Deepa (2016), "An e-Governance step through Kisan Seva Kendra (KSK) towards Indian rural development: A study of need and role of KSKs in Ghaziabad. In e-Governance *in India: Problems, Prototypes and Prospects*. Eds. Puneet Kumar, Rajesh Sharma, Urmani Kaushal. Nova Science Publishers Inc, Hauppauge, NY, pp. 173–184.

Jalal A., Mistry J.J. (2012), An empirical analysis of the relationship between e-government and corruption, *The International Journal of Digital Accounting Research,* Vol. 12, pp. 145–176.

Khan N., Nazia K.I (2015), e-Governance reforms in India: Issues, challenges and strategies - an overview, *IJCSI International Journal of Computer Science,* Vol. 12, Issue 1, No. 2, pp. 42–53.

Kumar S. (2016), e-Governance in India, *Imperial Journal of Interdisciplinary Research (IJIR),* Vol. 2, No. 2, p. 482.

Kumar P., Bhanti P. (2012), Prospects of e-Governance in India, *International Journal of Engineering and Innovative Technology,* Vol. 2, No. 3, pp. 335–339.

Malik P., Dhillon P., Verma P. (2014), Challenges and future prospects for e-Governance in India, *International Journal of Science, Engineering and Technology Research (IJSETR),* Vol. 3, No. 7, pp. 1964–1972.

Panda, B.P. and Swain, D.K., (2009). Effective Communications through e-Governance and e-Lerning. *Chinese Librar-Anship: An International Electronic Journal,* (27), pp. 1–9.

Patel A., Patel M., Biju S. (2013), A survey on e-Governance facility provided by Gujarat Government, *International Journal of Scientific and Research Publications,* Vol. 3, No. 8, pp. 407–409.

Rizvi, A.H. (2016), A study of e-Governance educational projects in India. *Global Journal for Research Analysis,* Vol. 5, No. 1, pp. 37–38.

Sharma M., Gupta P. (2017), Public-sector accounting and e-Governance in developing countries: Case of India, *International Journal of Science Technology and Management,* Vol. 6, No. 2, pp. 17–626.

Singh A. (2014), An impact study on e-Governance in India (applications and issues), *Asian Journal of Technology & Management Research,* Vol. 4, No 1, pp. 6–12.

Singh V., Chander S. (2012), e-Governance in Punjab – A SWOT analysis. *International Journal of Management, IT and Engineering,* Vol. 2, No. 6, pp. 99–110. www.researchgate.net/publication/280738116_e-Governance_in_Punjab-A_SWOT_Analysis.

Singla S.K., Aggarwal H. (2011), Combating corruption through e-Governance in public service delivery system, *Journal of Global Research in Computer Science,* Vol. 2, No. 7, pp. 96–100.

Yadav K., Tiwari S. (2014), e-Governance in India: Opportunities and challenges. *Advance in Electronic and Electric Engineering,* Vol. 4, No 6, pp. 675–680.

9

Econometric Estimation of the Relationship between Unemployment Rate, Economic Growth, and Information and Communication Technology in BRICS Countries

Sushil Kumar Rai and Bhartendu Kumar Chaturvedi

CONTENTS

9.1 Introduction

Today, the development of information and communication technology (ICT) plays a significant role in carrying out the process of development in a nation. The rapid development of ICT has made the world a global village where all economic activities related to humans and material resources are used for optimum results. In the process of economic development, the optimal use of available resources plays a vital role to increase the rate of effective employment in the country. The advent of ICT works as a bridge between available resources and its efficient use through dissemination and exchange of information. The development of information and communication technology in a developing economy has become a source of job creation among youths. The spillover effects of ICT are substantial. Various studies show that digital jobs are generated up to two to four times in comparison with employment in other sector of the economy (Oliner and Sichel, 2000). Although some economists argue that technology offers only technical benefits to economies, there is evidence that ICT has a social benefit as well as job creation in the economy (Gurumurthy, 2006).

The relationship between ICT, economic growth, and employment rate could be explained from the demand as well as the supply side. From the demand side, the growth of ICT and its equipment leads to more demand for producing new relevant commodities and services, thus accelerate the process of growth in the economy. From the supply side, development of ICT increases the quantity of products by enhancing the productivity of existing factors as well as employing additional factors in production activity. After recognizing the significant role of ICT in economic activity of a country, an important question raised among economists, analysts, researchers, and policy makers: Does the development of "ICT" cause "economic growth" through addressing the problem of unemployment, or alternatively, does "economic growth" cause development of "ICT" via addressing the problem of unemployment? Therefore, the purpose of the present study is to empirically examine the causal relationship between ICT, economic growth, and the unemployment rate in BRICS (Brazil, Russia, India, China, and South Africa) countries.

The subsequent sections of the chapter include a brief discussion of available literature, limitations of existing literature, the objective and hypotheses, and the significance of the present study. Methodology that contains the source of the data, definition of variables, and the proposed empirical model has also been presented. Finally, the last section deals with data analysis, interpretation of results, and conclusions along with policy implications.

9.2 Review of Literature

Recently, a number of studies have been conducted on this issue that reveals the relationship between ICT and economic growth for different countries. Most of the findings of the available results are verifying the presence of a relationship between economic growth and ICT. Some of the studies are mentioned here and arranged in chronological order.

Niebel (2018) analyzed the impact of ICT on economic growth on a sample of 59 developing, emerging, and developed countries over the period 1995 to 2010. The study reported a positive relationship between ICT and gross domestic product (GDP) growth. Further, the study found that developing and emerging countries did not gain more from investment in ICT than developed countries.

Latif et al. (2018) investigated the dynamic relationship between ICT, foreign direct investment (FDI), economic growth, trade, and globalization for BRICS economies over the period 2000 to 2014. The study suggested the following findings: (a) ICT positively contributes to economic growth; (b) a bidirectional causality exists between economic growth and FDI, between globalization and economic growth, and between trade and economic growth; (c) unidirectional causality is running from globalization to trade; and (d) bidirectional causality existing between globalization and ICT.

Qureshi and Naijar (2017) in their study examined the relationship between ICT usage and growth in per capita GDP of 32 very small island states. The study found a positive impact of the use of ICTs on GDP.

Alderete (2017) analyzed the relationship between ICT access, ICT use, and socioeconomic development on a sample of 163 countries for the year 2013. The result indicated that ICT usage and ICT skills enhance the effect of ICT access on socioeconomic development.

Khan et al. (2017) examined the relationship between ICT, patent applications, research and development expenditure, and growth factors in the context of group of G7 countries over the period of 1995 to 2013. The study suggested the following findings: (a) a significant and positive relationship between high-technology exports and growth factors; (b) a negative relationship between residential patent applicants and per capita GDP; (c) a negative relationship between research and development expenditure and GDP per capita.

Samoilenko (2016) examined the framework of the neoclassical growth model for investigating the process by which various macroeconomic outcomes of the investment in ICT are associated with re-investment in ICT. The study supported the notion of the cyclical relationship between investment in ICT and economic outcomes as growth in GDP.

Ishida (2015) in his study applied an autoregressive distributed lag (ARDL) model to estimate the long-run relationship between ICT, energy consumption, and economic growth in Japan over the period 1980 to 2010. The study revealed a long-run stable relationship between ICT, energy consumption, and economic growth.

Jin and Cho (2015) examined the theoretical assumption that ICT factors affect national economic development. The study found a positive impact of ICT factors on national economic development.

The study of Mohammed and Sadiq (2015) revealed that ICT has contributed positively to human capacity building and job creation in developing economies.

The study of Mefteh and Benhassen (2015) investigated the relationship between ICT and economic growth for a sample of 43 countries over the period 1995 to 2011. The study found a positive and significant relationship between ICT and economic growth.

Yang (2015) examined the causal relationship between ICT trade and GDP over the period 1990 to 2010 for the United States, Japan, Korea, and China. The study found: (a) a strong impact of income on GDP and ICT trade for the United States; (b) a significant impact of GDP on ICT trade for China; (c) both ICT export and income have a significant impact on GDP for Korea; and (d) absence of a causal relationship between ICT trade and GDP for Japan.

Pradhan et al. (2014) found a bidirectional causality between the development of ICT infrastructure and economic growth in the G20 developed countries group as well as the G20 developing country groups.

The study of Nyeko et al. (2013) examined the impact of ICT enabled small and medium enterprises (SMEs) on generating employment in Kampala, Uganda. The result indicates that ICT enabled SMEs are creating employment, but mostly in the lower level of management hierarchy.

Sepehrdoust and Khodaee (2013) investigated the effects of ICT on the employment level of selected countries of the Organization of Islamic Conference (OIC) for the period 2000 to 2009. The result shows a positive and significant effect of the ICTs on the employment rate and the effects were diversified among oil and non-oil economies.

Iscan (2012) studied the relationship between ICT and economic growth over the period 1980 to 2011 for Turkey. He found clear evidence of a significant relationship between ICT and economic growth for the economy of Turkey.

Veeramacheneni (2011) examined the causal relationship between ICT and economic growth for ten Latin American countries using time series data for the period 1975 to 2003. The study found a bidirectional causal relationship between ICT and economic growth for seven Latin American countries.

Kim (2007) in his study found a bidirectional causality between ICT and economic growth, however, the causality was absent between employment and ICT.

Dutta (2001) examined the causal relationship between ICT infrastructure and economic activity in 15 developing and 15 industrialized countries. The study found the evidence of strong causality from ICT infrastructure to economic growth and the presence of weak causality in the opposite direction.

9.3 Limitations of Existing Literature

Most of these studies are based on individual countries and use time series data; however, results are different for different countries. One of the reasons for conflicting empirical findings lies in the size of samples. A short data span lowers the power of the unit root and cointegration tests (Johansen, 1988) and the estimation of causality could result in a misleading relationship between the variables. To overcome this problem in our study, we pooled data together that differed across individual countries. In the present study, we also include unemployment rate as a variable to understand whether ICT driven economic growth is employment friendly or not.

9.4 Objective and Hypotheses

The objective of the present study is to examine the causal relationship between unemployment rate, economic growth, and ICT. Based on the review of literature, the following hypotheses are constructed to achieve the objective of the study:

H1: There exists a long-run relationship between unemployment rate, economic growth, and ICT.

H2: There is a unidirectional causality between the considered variables.

H3: There is a bidirectional causality between the considered variables.

9.5 Significance of the Study

In any developing economy, it is important to know the relationship between the development of ICT and various economic activities, especially when the world economy is moving rapidly towards global integration. The relationship between the variables under study can help policy makers to develop a better insight of economic growth and to formulate effective policy to solve the problem of unemployment through the development of ICT. Therefore, the outcomes of this study will help to design a policy that addresses the problem of unemployment through the causal cyclical relationship between ICT and economic growth.

9.6 Methodology

9.6.1 Source of the Data

A secondary source has been used to collect the relevant information. The annual data on BRICS countries for the variables under study has been obtained from World Development

Indicators (WDI) 2017, published by the World Bank. The data used in the study is from 1998 to 2016. The present study is based on the panel data that comprises 95 observations.

9.6.2 Definition of Variables

In the present study, the variables, namely, unemployment rate (UEM), economic growth (EG), and ICT have been considered. The variables used in the study are taken in natural logarithms to minimize the variance in the data set. The definitions of the variables are as follows:

UEM: Refers to the share of the total labor force that is without work but available for, and in search of, employment.

EG: Refers to the annual percentage change in the gross domestic product in constant 2010 US$.

ICT: Refers to the summation of fixed broadband subscriptions, fixed telephone subscriptions, and mobile cellular subscriptions per 100 people.

9.7 Empirical Model

In order to find out an appropriate relationship between the considered variables; analytical tools like panel unit root test, panel cointegration test, panel vector error correction model (VECM), and Wald coefficient restrictions test have been used. As a first step of our analysis, four types of unit root tests, Levin, Lin, and Chu (LLC), Im, Pesaran, and Shin (IPS), augmented Dickey-Fuller (ADF), and Phillips-Perron (PP) are employed. The model is developed as follows:

$$\Delta y_{it} = \alpha_i + \gamma_i y_{it-1} + \sum_{j=1}^{k} \alpha_j \Delta y_{it-j} + e_{it} \tag{9.1}$$

where:

Δ = first difference

$t = 1,\ldots,T$ refers to the time periods

$i = 1,\ldots,N$ refers to members of the panel

The null hypothesis of the test is $\gamma_i = \gamma = 0$ for all i indicating that the panel data are non-stationary, while the alternative hypothesis is $\gamma_i = \gamma < 0$ for all i showing that the panel data are stationary.

In the second step, when all series are integrated of the same order, the Johansen Fisher, Kao, and Pedroni methods are applied to examine the panel cointegration relationship. The Pedroni and Kao tests are based on the Engle-Granger two-step cointegration tests. The Johansen Fisher cointegration test is highly influenced by appropriate lag length (Johansen and Juselius, 1990). To get the optimal lag length for the cointegration test, VAR lag order selection criteria are used. The hypotheses of the Johansen Fisher cointegration test are as follows:

$$H_0 : r = 0; H_1 : r \leq 1.$$

The null hypothesis of no cointegration is rejected, if there exists, at least, one cointegration vector. Cointegration indicates the existence of causality, although it does not point out the direction of causal relationships. Therefore, we applied the vector error correction model to know the direction of causality. The following vector error correction model is estimated:

$$\Delta LICT_{it} = \theta_{1j} + \lambda_{1i}\varepsilon_{it-1} + \sum_{k=1}^{q}\theta_{11ik}\Delta LICT_{it-k} + \sum_{k=1}^{q}\theta_{12ik}\Delta LEG_{it-k} + \sum_{k=1}^{q}\theta_{13ik}\Delta LUEM_{it-k} + \mu_{1it} \quad (9.2)$$

$$\Delta LEG_{it} = \theta_{2j} + \lambda_{2i}\varepsilon_{it-1} + \sum_{k=1}^{q}\theta_{22ik}\Delta LEG_{it-k} + \sum_{k=1}^{q}\theta_{21ik}\Delta LICT_{it-k} + \sum_{k=1}^{q}\theta_{23ik}\Delta LUEM_{it-k} + \mu_{2it} \quad (9.3)$$

$$\Delta LUEM_{it} = \theta_{3j} + \lambda_{3i}\varepsilon_{it-1} + \sum_{k=1}^{q}\theta_{33ik}\Delta LUEM_{it-k} + \sum_{k=1}^{q}\theta_{31ik}\Delta LICT_{it-k} + \sum_{k=1}^{q}\theta_{32ik}\Delta LEG_{it-k} + \mu_{3it} \quad (9.4)$$

where:

Δ = first difference
k = lag length
$t = 1,\ldots,T$ refers to the time period
$i = 1,\ldots,N$ refers to members of the panel
θ_{12ik}, θ_{21ik}, θ_{31ik}, θ_{13ik}, θ_{23ik} and θ_{32ik} = estimated parameter to examine short-run causality
λ = coefficient of error—correction term ε_{it-1} is used to evaluate long-run causality and speed of adjustment towards equilibrium.

Finally, the Wald coefficient restrictions test is applied to examine the short-run causality. The Wald test computes a test statistics based on the unrestricted regression. The Wald statistic measures how close the unrestricted estimates come to satisfying the restrictions under the null hypothesis. If the restrictions are true, then the unrestricted estimates should come close to satisfying the restrictions. The hypotheses of the Wald test:

$$H_0 : \beta_2 = 0; H_1 : \beta_2 \neq 0.$$

9.8 Analysis of Data

9.8.1 Interpretation of Results

A critical assumption of the regression model is that the series under consideration must be stationary because a non-stationary series leads to spurious and nonsense regression. The panel unit root test is applied to check the stationarity of the considered variables. The result of the test is shown in Table 9.1.

Table 9.1 shows the result of stationariness, which suggests the rejection of the unit root null hypothesis of non-stationary for the considered variables at 1 per cent level of significance. On the basis of unit root test, it is observed that the variables are integrated

TABLE 9.1

Panel Unit Root Test Results

	Levin, Lin, and Chu		Im, Pesaran, and Shin		ADF Fisher		PP Fisher	
Variables	**Level**	**First Diff.**	**Level**	**First Diff.**	**Level**	**First Diff.**	**Level**	**First Diff.**
LICT	1.13 (0.87)	−3.18 (0.00)[a]	1.43 (0.92)	−2.61 (0.00)[a]	3.01 (0.98)	22.64 (0.01)[a]	0.12 (1.00)	28.92 (0.00)[a]
LEG	−2.49 (0.00)[a]	−2.75 (0.00)[a]	−0.73 (0.22)	−1.99 (0.02)[b]	15.35 (0.11)	19.18 (0.03)[b]	11.51 (0.31)	19.17 (0.03)[b]
LUEM	−1.04 (0.14)	−5.87 (0.00)[a]	0.09 (0.53)	−5.75 (0.00)[a]	8.72 (0.55)	49.21 (0.00)[a]	11.66 (0.30)	64.70 (0.00)[a]

Source: Authors' analysis.
Note: *P*-value is given in parentheses.
[a] Significant at 1 per cent.
[b] Significant at 5 per cent.

at first order I (1). Having established that each of the three variables is I(1), the panel cointegration between the considered variable is checked using Pedroni, Kao, and Fisher Tests, and the results have been presented in Table 9.2. Prior to conducting the cointegration test, VAR lag order selection criteria are applied to get the optimal lag length (see Appendix 1).

Table 9.2 shows the series are cointegrated, thus proposing the rejection of the null hypothesis of no cointegration which means that the variables display a long-term relationship. The existence of a panel long-run cointegration relationship indicates the presence of causality between unemployment rate, economic growth, and ICT; therefore, the vector error correction model (VECM) is applied to find out the direction of causal relationships. The result of the vector error correction model is to find out the causality between unemployment rate, economic growth, and ICT, which is given in Table 9.3.

The result shows that coefficient {C(1)} of the error correction term is statistically significant at the 1 per cent level with a negative sign (−0.04) and reveals a long-run causality run from unemployment rate and economic growth to ICT. The coefficient of the error correction term of about −0.04 suggests that the speed of adjustment towards long-run equilibrium is slow. The coefficient {C(5)} of the error correction term indicates that the long-run causality run from ICT and an unemployment rate to economic growth is statistically significant, which suggests that economic growth is responsive to ICT and the unemployment rate in long-run and the system is progressing at a speed of 0.01 per cent per annum towards long-run equilibrium. The statistically insignificant value of coefficient {C(9)} of the error correction term shows that the unemployment rate is not responsive to economic growth and ICT in the long-run. To find out the short-run causality between the studied variables, the Wald test is applied and the result is shown in Table 9.4. It is evident from Table 9.4 that there is no short-run causality run from unemployment rate and

TABLE 9.2

Panel Cointegration Tests Results

Pedroni test		
Test statistics	Statistics	
Panel v-statistic	1.370127 (0.1514)	
Panel rho-statistic	1.091517 (0.2523)	
Panel PP-statistic	−5.348923 (0.0036)[a]	
Panel ADF-statistic	−2.340747 (0.0096)[a]	
Group rho-statistic	1.567172 (0.1571)	
Group PP-statistic	−8.932833 (0.0055)[a]	
Group ADF-statistic	−2.448924 (0.0072)[a]	
Kao test		
ADF	−1.982863 (0.0199)[a]	
Johansen Fisher test		
Null hypothesis	Maximum eigenvalue test	Trace test
$r = 0$	51.07 (0.0000)[a]	65.11 (0.0000)[a]
$r \leq 1$	13.67 (0.1886)	13.99 (0.1886)
$r \leq 2$	24.46 (0.0065)[a]	26.67 (0.0026)[a]

Source: Authors' analysis

Note: r denotes the number of cointegration equation, P-value is given in parentheses.

[a] Significant at 1 per cent.

TABLE 9.3

Panel Vector Error Correction Model Results

Estimated equation: D(LICT) = C(1) × (LICT(−1) − 0.172199962204 × LEG(−1) − 0.190490576844 × LUEM(−1)) + C(2) × D(LICT(−1)) + C(3) × D(LEG(−1)) + C(4) × D(LUEM(−1))

	Coefficient	Std. error	t-Statistic	Prob.
C(1)	−0.043913	0.010213	−4.299844	0.0000[a]
C(2)	0.564619	0.078086	7.230746	0.0000
C(3)	0.091246	0.220288	0.414210	0.6798
C(4)	−0.004904	0.108098	−0.045363	0.9639
Adj. R-squared	*0.641717*		*Prob.(F-statistic)*	*0.0000*

Estimated equation: D(LEG) = C(5) × (LICT(−1) − 0.172199962204 × LEG(−1) − 0.190490576844 × LUEM(−1)) + C(6) × D(LICT(−1)) + C(7) × D(LEG(−1)) + C(8) × D(LUEM(−1))

	Coefficient	Std. error	t-Statistic	Prob.
C(5)	−0.018866	0.007096	−2.658787	0.0100[a]
C(6)	0.046033	0.028335	1.624597	0.1081
C(7)	0.748339	0.079935	9.361824	0.0000
C(8)	0.112328	0.039225	2.863670	0.0053
Adj. R-squared	*0.488007*		*Prob.(F-statistic)*	*0.0191*

Estimated equation: D(LUEM) = C(9) × (LICT(−1) − 0.172199962204 × LEG(−1) − 0.190490576844 × LUEM(−1)) + C(10) × D(LICT(−1)) + (11) × D(LEG(−1)) + C(12) × D(LUEM(−1))

	Coefficient	Std. error	t-Statistic	Prob.
C(9)	0.004744	0.012016	0.394799	0.6940[b]
C(10)	−0.081648	0.091873	−0.888696	0.3768
C(11)	0.084123	0.259184	0.324568	0.7463
C(12)	0.154101	0.127185	1.211632	0.2292
Adj. R-squared	*0.008937*		*Prob.(F-statistic)*	*0.0891*

Source: Authors' analysis.
[a] Significant at 1 per cent.
[b] Insignificant.

economic growth to ICT in BRICS countries. The short-run causality is also missing from ICT and economic growth to the unemployment rate. Only in cases of economic growth, unemployment rate and ICT, does the short-run causality run from unemployment rate and ICT to economic growth.

To validate the result of the developed model, White's test of heteroscedasticity and Breusch-Godfrey serial correlation LM test is applied. The result of the diagnostic test has been depicted in Table 9.5. The insignificant p-value suggests absence of heteroscedasticity and serial correlation in the estimated model and the estimators of the developed model are efficient and reliable.

The causality tests are effective only within the sample period, therefore variance decompositions (VDCs) of the vector error correction model are applied to assess the validity of causality beyond the sample period. The variance of the forecast error in the independent variable can be ascribed to innovations in dependent variable as well as to its own innovations (see Appendix 2). In this way, the VDCs can be detected as out of the sample causality tests. The VDCs result is steady with our findings in the VDC model analysis. In the case

TABLE 9.4

Wald Test Results

Null hypothesis: C(3) = C(4) = 0				Null hypothesis: C(6) = C(8) = 0				Null hypothesis: C(10) = C(11) = 0			
Test statistic	**Value**	**Df**	**Prob.**	**Test statistic**	**Value**	**Df**	**Prob.**	**Test statistic**	**Value**	**Df**	**Prob.**
F-statistic	0.109	(2,81)	0.89[a]	F-statistic	5.33	(2,81)	0.00[b]	F-statistic	0.394	(2,81)	0.67[b]
Chi-square	0.218	2	0.89[a]	Chi-square	10.6	2	0.00[b]	Chi-square	0.789	2	0.67[b]

Source: Authors' analysis.

[a] Insignificant.

[b] Significant at 1 per cent.

TABLE 9.5
Diagnostic Test Results

Null hypothesis: $E(\mu_{it}^2)$=Constant			Null hypothesis: $E(\mu_{it}\,\mu_{is})=0,\ s \neq t$				
	Exclude cross terms	**Include cross terms**					
Chi-sq	59.60	104.35	Lags	1	2	3	4
Df	48	84	LM-Stat	15.62	8.90	11.58	13.38
Prob.	0.12[a]	0.06[a]	Prob.	0.07[a]	0.44[a]	0.23[a]	0.14[a]

Source: Authors' analysis.
[a] Insignificant at 5 per cent.

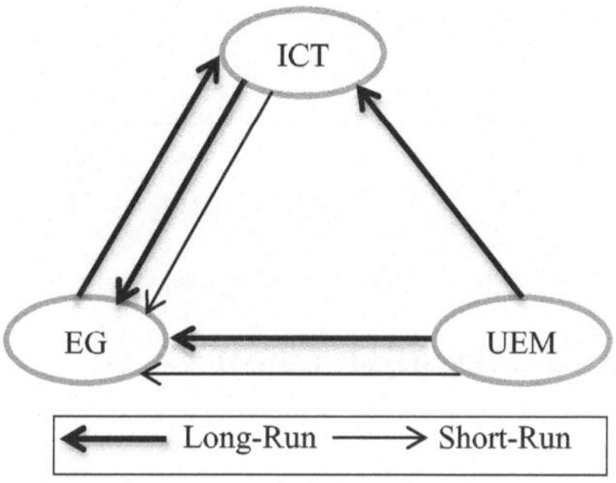

FIGURE 9.1
Panel causality relations for BRICS countries.

of BRICS countries, 97 per cent of innovation in ICT is explained by economic growth and the unemployment rate after 15 years, thus, approving that causality is running from economic growth and unemployment rate to ICT. On the other hand, 80 per cent of innovation in economic growth is explicated by ICT and the unemployment rate after 15 years and this confirms our findings of causality between these variables.

Based on the causality results, evidence shows that a higher economic growth can expand the usage of ICT as well as reduce the unemployment rate in BRICS countries. Additionally, evidence shows that the expansion of ICT can accelerate the economic growth in these economies through reduction OF the unemployment rate (Figure 9.1).

9.9 Conclusions and Policy Implications

The purpose of this study is to examine the causal relationship between unemployment rate, economic growth, and ICT in BRICS countries. The relationship will be beneficial to understand the importance of information and communication technology and its impact on economic growth through a reduction in the unemployment rate in these countries. The panel cointegration and panel vector error correction models are conducted to get the relationship between the considered variables. The results of the present study indicate the following: (1) all series are non-stationary at levels but stationary at the first difference, and there exists a long-run equilibrium relationship between unemployment rate, economic growth, and ICT; (2) a bidirectional long-run causal relationship exists between economic growth and ICT; and (3) there exists a unidirectional causal relationship running from unemployment rate and ICT to economic growth in the long-run as well as in the short-run.

The result of a bidirectional long-run causal relationship between ICT and economic growth exhibit their interdependency in BRICS nations. Therefore, the development policy of ICT in BRICS countries will accelerate the process of economic growth, while on the other hand, the higher economic growth will enhance the usage of ICT in these nations. Further, the present study also reveals that a unidirectional long-run as well as short-run causality is running from unemployment rate and ICT to economic growth. Hence, the increment in economic growth through increase in the practice of ICT in BRICS countries will reduce the rate of unemployment in these countries.

Appendices

Appendix 1

Endogenous variables: D(LICT) D(LRGDP) D(LUEM)
Exogenous variables: C
Date: 03/30/18 Time: 15:15
Sample: 1998 2016
Included observations: 65

Lag	LogL	LR	FPE	AIC	SC	HQ
0	240.3958	NA	1.35e-07	−7.304485	−7.204129	−7.264888
1	296.9308	106.1119[a]	3.13e-08[a]	−8.767102[a]	−8.365676[a]	−8.608714[a]
2	305.0691	14.52367	3.22e-08	−8.740587	−8.038092	−8.463408
3	308.4802	5.772752	3.84e-08	−8.568623	−7.565059	−8.172653
4	314.1263	9.033659	4.30e-08	−8.465424	−7.160792	−7.950663
5	318.5350	6.647029	5.02e-08	−8.324154	−6.718453	−7.690602

LR: Sequential modified LR test statistic (each test at 5 per cent level); FPE: final prediction error; AIC: Akaike information criterion; SC: Schwarz information criterion; HQ: Hannan-Quinn information criterion.
[a] Indicates lag order selected by the criterion.

Appendix 2

Variance decomposition of LICT				
Period	SE	LICT	LRGDP	LUEM
1	0.073637	100.0000	0.000000	0.000000
2	0.134297	99.96629	0.033371	0.000341
3	0.186674	99.90311	0.087257	0.009630
4	0.229891	99.81118	0.150518	0.038306
5	0.264684	99.68920	0.218976	0.091827
6	0.292293	99.53724	0.290108	0.172653
7	0.314009	99.35644	0.362023	0.281534

(Continued)

8	0.330994	99.14860	0.433237	0.418165
9	0.344237	98.91587	0.502595	0.581540
10	0.354548	98.66059	0.569243	0.770165
11	0.362579	98.38520	0.632585	0.982214
12	0.368848	98.09211	0.692249	1.215643
13	0.373762	97.78367	0.748044	1.468285
14	0.377639	97.46214	0.799924	1.737931
15	0.380726	97.12965	0.847955	2.022396

Variance decomposition of LRGDP

Period	SE	LICT	LRGDP	LUEM
1	0.026720	1.579427	98.42057	0.000000
2	0.050191	2.959376	94.43315	2.607469
3	0.074352	3.922498	90.55117	5.526327
4	0.098468	4.485898	87.63546	7.878646
5	0.122001	4.730906	85.55889	9.710205
6	0.144642	4.741319	84.09658	11.16210
7	0.166247	4.989536	83.06598	12.34449
8	0.186775	5.334119	82.33432	13.33156
9	0.206249	5.620471	81.80742	14.17211
10	0.224728	5.682470	81.41886	14.89867
11	0.242285	6.344353	81.12205	15.53359
12	0.259001	7.022572	80.88465	16.09278
13	0.274953	7.727485	80.68447	16.58805
14	0.290214	8.464831	80.50665	17.02852
15	0.304853	9.236975	80.34153	17.42150

Variance decomposition of LUEM

Period	SE	LICT	LRGDP	LUEM
1	0.086639	1.025725	30.61963	68.35465
2	0.131861	1.824944	29.42185	68.75320
3	0.166536	2.414023	28.50826	69.07772
4	0.195375	2.773182	27.82361	69.40321
5	0.220429	2.949136	27.30886	69.74200
6	0.242783	2.997208	26.91621	70.08658
7	0.263099	2.962838	26.61062	70.42654
8	0.281816	2.878891	26.36740	70.75371
9	0.299244	2.767668	26.16937	71.06296
10	0.315611	2.643679	26.00464	71.35168
11	0.331088	2.516041	25.86488	71.61908
12	0.345806	2.390263	25.74424	71.86549
13	0.359869	2.269497	25.63857	72.09193
14	0.373360	2.155397	25.54487	72.29974
15	0.386345	2.048672	25.46091	72.49042

Cholesky ordering: LICT LRGDP LUEM.

References

Alderete, M. V. (2017). Examining the ICT access effect on socioeconomic development: The moderating role of ICT use and skills. *Information Technology for Development*, 23(1), 42–58.

Dutta, A. (2001). Telecommunication and economic activity: An analysis of granger causality. *Journal of Management and Information System*, 17(4), 71–95.

Gurumurthy, A. (2006). Promoting gender equality? Some development related uses of ICTs by women. *Development in Practice*, 16(6), 611–616.

Iscan, E. (2012). The impact of information and communication technology on economic growth: Turkish case. *International Journal of eBusiness and eGovernment Studies*, 4(1), 17–26.

Ishida, H. (2015). The effect of ICT development on economic growth and energy consumption in Japan. *Telematics and Informatics*, 32(1), 79–88.

Jin, S. & Cho, C. M. (2015). Is ICT a new essential for national economic growth in an information society? *Government Information Quarterly*, 32(2), 253–260.

Johansen, S. (1998). Statistical analysis of cointegration vectors. *Journal of Economic Dynamics and Control*, 12 (23), 231–254.

Johansen, S. & Juselius, K. (1990). Maximum likelihood estimation and inference on cointegration with application to the demand for money. *Oxford Bulletin of Economics and Statistics*, 52(2), 169–210.

Khan, H., Zaman, K., Khan, A., & Islam, T. (2017). Quadrilateral relationship between information and communications technology, patent applications, research and development expenditures, and growth factors: Evidence from the group of G-7 countries. *Social Indicators Research*, 133(3), 1165–1191.

Kim, D.-K. (2007). Information technology, economic growth, and employment: Evidence from time-series analyses. *Journal of Applied Business Research*, 23(1), 71–78.

Latif, Z., Mengke, Y., Danish, N., Latif, S., Ximei, L., Pathan, Z. H., ... Jainqui, Z. (2018). The dynamics of ICT, foreign direct investment, globalization and economic growth: Panel estimation robust to heterogeneity and cross-sectional dependence. *Telematics and Informatics*, 35(2), 318–328.

Mefteh, H. & Benhassen, L. (2015). Impact of information technology and communication on economic growth. *International Journal of Economics, Finance and Management*, 4(2), 90–98.

Mohammed, M. & Sadiq, A. M. (2015). The role of information and communication technology in providing job opportunities for youth in the developing world. *Journal of Emerging Trends in Engineering and Applied Science*, 6(7), 174–179.

Nibel, T. (2018). ICT and economic growth-comparing developing, emerging and developed countries. *World Development*, 104, 197–211.

Nyeko, S., Kabaale, E., Moya, M., Amulen, C., & Kituyi, G. M. (2013). The role of information and communication technology small and medium enterprises in job creation in Kampala, Uganda. *Journal of Business Management and Administration*, 1(5), 75–82.

Oliver, S. D. & Sichel, D. E. (2000). The resurgence of growth in the late 1990s: Is information technology the story. *Journal of Economic Perspective*, 14(4), 3–22.

Pradhan, R., Arvin, M., Norman, N., & Bele, S. (2014). Economic growth and the development of telecommunication infrastructure in the G-20 countries: A Panel-Var approach. *Telecommunication Policy*, 38(7), 634–649.

Qureshi, S. & Naijar, L. (2017). Information and communication technology use and income growth: evidence of the multiplier effect in very small Island states. *Information Technology for Development*, 23(2), 212–234.

Samoilenko, S. V. (2016). Where do investments in telecom come from? Developing and testing a framework of sustained economic impact of investment in information and communication technologies. *Information Technology for Development*, 44(4), 584–605.

Sepehrdoust, H. & Khodaee, H. (2013). The impact of information and communication technology on employment of selected OIC countries. *African Journal of Business Management*, 37(39), 4149–4154.

Veeramacheneni, B., Ekanayake, E. M., & Vogel, R. (2011). Information technology and economic growth: A causal analysis. *Southwestern Economic Review*, 34, 75–88.

Yang, C.-G. (2015). A study on the relevance of ICT trade and GDP. *Advanced Science and Technology Letters*, 84, 35–39.

10

Role and Challenges of IoT in e-Government

Meena Thangaraj and Ravi Sankar Sangam

CONTENTS

10.1 Introduction

"e-Government" is the online administration by the concerned government, using information and communication technology (ICT), for boosting open administration conveyance to reinforce correspondence channels for the engagement and strengthening of the general population, and additionally, using these advantages for the better well-being of individuals. e-Governance in India started in 1970 with the appearance of the Department of Electronics set up by the Government of India. To help India in moving toward Digital India, numerous activities were embraced by the government, which incorporates the National Informatics Centre Network (India) (NICNET), the District Information Systems of the National Informatics Center (DISNIC), commencement of Union Ministry of Information and Technology, advancement of the National e-Governance Plan, and Smart Cities. The three primary target partners of e-government in India are the government, citizens, and business in three noteworthy segments: G2G (Government to Government), G2C (Government to Citizen), and G2B (Government to Business) [1]. G2C administrations incorporate different measurements, which includes e-education, e-medicine, air contamination control, e-transport, e-citizen, e-registration, and horticulture. Out of the different measurements expressed, air contamination control is among the most vital administrations given by the Government of India. Several Indian urban communities have additionally been recorded as the "dirtiest urban areas" by the World Health Organization (WHO). These insights demonstrate the significance of contamination control in India. The government has used different plans with moderate air contamination. Be that as it may, with a specific end goal to help moderate levels of air contamination, it is important to generate instructions for the Indian populace. Social networks are where individuals are associated through web-based social networking projects to post information, make online groups, have a live collaboration with each other, and offer insights [2]. There has been a sharp surge in the use of interpersonal organizations like Facebook, Second Life, Twitter, and WhatsApp. To create government as a learning society known worldwide includes increasing the personal satisfaction of its residents through instruction and human services, expanded efficiency in horticulture and partnered exercises, generating business potential by using devices and IT ventures, and good administration. Indeed, there is ample scope to harness the potential of social media because of the growth in numbers of social media users. The total number of social media users across the world in 2010 was 0.97 billion whereas it is expected to reach up to 3.02 billion by 2021 [3].

10.2 e-Governance Services for Public Awareness

The following will help in effective e-governance through e-learning:

- Social systems
- Internet of Things (IoT) based contamination sensor
- Machine learning calculations
- Smart ecological instruction courses modules

a. *Social systems*: To accomplish better conditions through e-governance, interest is vital [4]. To accomplish increased involvement, the Indian populace should be taught about their social conditions, air contamination, air quality in their area, essential drivers of air contamination, repercussions of air contamination both in the future and presently, the simple changes that occupants could accomplish to lessen air contamination, how these simple changes can have a huge impact on air contamination control, and how to accomplish change for their area. Person to person communication will happen as a successful e-learning stage to educate inhabitants because of the following reasons:

- Extensive utilization of informal communities both in urban and rural regions of India.
- Online networking of clients with new analyses.
- Active investment in discussions among clients.
- Bringing individuals together even though they are isolated by living in separate areas.
- Fostering collective intelligence among the general population. Due to the above reasons, informal communication was used to inform individuals.

b. *IoT-based contamination sensor*: Air contamination information is gathered intermittently utilizing air contamination IoT sensors set in urban areas across India. We have proposed the use of IoT based air contamination sensors instead of conventional air quality observational tools because the tremendous size and high cost of conventional tools make it unacceptable for utilizing it across India, which traverses an extensive geographical region [5]. These sensors can likewise be utilized to recognize the significant contamination in the city from vehicles or other industries that expel apparently large amounts of carbon dioxide, sulfur oxides, and other gases. The gathered information is used for investigations, such as foreseeing the amount of air contamination in the future, examining the data to discover the dirtiest regions, or similar investigations of air contamination in each city.

c. *Machine learning calculations*: To increase enthusiasm for discovering contamination control methods in the general population, it is important to pass on air quality measurements to individuals in an insightful way. However, individuals are more concerned about their local city/town or current place of living. To engage individuals on their conditions, air quality insights of their local city and area must be communicated to them, which will help in disseminating awareness among individuals about air contamination. This approach would be more compelling to achieve an individual's interest. To add this knowledge to our model, we use machine learning calculations [6]. There are three general classes of machine learning calculations: directed, unsupervised, and fortification learning; unsupervised learning was the best decision for our model as our model requires Big Data to be sorted and does not require forecasts, characterization, or activity picking. Amongst different unsupervised learning approaches, bunching calculation helps in sorting out unlabeled interpersonal organizations' client information into bunches regarding the local city/town or current place of living. Out of the different bunching systems, the best decision for our structure is various leveled grouping. Various leveled bunching calculations use the similarities of informal organization information to gather information, such as on occasions they are especially like each other and not like different occurrences in unique gatherings [6][7]. Our subjective model utilizes Ward's agglomerative various leveled bunching to help in gathering the general population into groups as per their present living area/local city or town. This is superior to any other agglomerative bunching strategies as Ward's technique uses the least fluctuation metric to group unlabeled information, rather than using the separation between the examples. This element of Ward's strategy is viable in limiting the intra group fluctuation. The information of every city or town gathered from the sensors, alongside small ecological training course modules, which are particularly intended for every city, are presented on the individual coordinating groups.

d. *Smart ecological instruction courses modules*: The course modules are exclusively created deliberately for every city after comprehensive research about the city's condition, history, socioeconomics, topology, air contamination status through years, any cases or episodes that had occurred because of air contamination, activities taken to diminish air contamination, and any air toxins in the city. The findings of the investigation from the IoT sensor are incorporated into the e-learning module. These city course modules are offered after intensive research and they are made considerably less difficult with key focuses that are comprehensible. This is the one of the critical areas of our intellectual system, as it is fundamental to meet our prime goal of instructing a larger number of Indian people about air contamination for e-administration benefit in India. The course modules show the client's local area in its current state and focuses on how nature was in the preceding decades, what the components are that prompted air contamination today, and undertaking the anticipated future if a similar situation happens again. It also incorporates graphical portrayals of the client's local or present living city/town and any air contamination related measurements, which are understandable to all clients [8]. e-Learning modules additionally incorporate reenacted sound and video modules that will grant ecological instruction in an intriguing and provocative way. The e-learning modules can give a platform to increase awareness amongst individuals about the climate, which may lead to an enormous decrease in air contamination.

10.3 Challenges of IoT in e-Governance

Currently, one of the foremost difficulties experienced by IT experts is to predict the negative and/or positive effects that everyday activities can cause in an association [9]. Administration and security are the most difficult issues in IoT [10]. Subsequently, there are numerous strategic issues associated with IoT by society. The ideas for IoT based governance are likewise not completely formulated and different definitions have been proposed by various industry and research associations.

According to the EU, administration alludes to "the tenets, procedures and conduct that influence the manner by which powers are worked out, especially as respects transparency, cooperation, responsibility, viability and intelligibility." Recently, the fusion of distributed computing and IoT, along with cloud computing, can create profits to various stakeholders through its boundless capacities [11]. The cloud can offer a powerful answer for IoT driven administrations. The cloud can profit IoT by stretching out its extension to manage genuine things in a more disseminated and dynamic way, and for conveying new administrations in a substantial number of situations. Incorporating IoT with distributed computing will create new difficulties as well, particularly in administration and security perspectives that identify with information changes and information in distributed storage. The primary parts that influence the administration of IoT are association size and heterogeneity [12]. The absence of trust in information security, protection, and loss of information administration by a client are some of the regular difficulties that are noted with IoT and distributed computing situations. In view of the this, leaders must be acquainted of such difficulties before embracing IoT. In addition, because of the trouble of finding a typical definition for IoT or a potential cloud administration, it would appear to be untimely to organize strategy improvements when there is no concession to exceptional tenets for IoT administration issues, which are isolated from other general guidelines. In any case, as there are no lawful systems for IoT administration, regardless of whether the contrasts amongst IoT and the distributed computing have been overestimated, an examination of the major IoT administration issues is by all accounts advantageous. In the IoT and cloud setting, it is hard to isolate the ideas of governance, security, and privacy, because protection and security perspectives in IoT would most likely need administration components. Specifically, information security has the goal to protect the privacy, trustworthiness, and accessibility of information.

10.4 IoT Security Challenges

The joining of distributed computing and IoT should improve authoritative execution considering the potential this association makes in creating novel answers for an extensive variety of businesses. Regardless, this association likewise has some conspicuous security challenges, from the association of sensors to clients, programming, and systems, up to the building and coordination of IoT applications with the cloud and their arrangement as administrations. Security, as far as the elements of systems, figures out what information needs assurance or which information should be controlled. This is surely testing because of layering and reflection in IoT, notwithstanding obscure dangers because of the variety in advances and the dynamic nature of the earth, as capacities and objectives powerfully change to suit an association.

10.5 Pivotal Role of e-Governance

Giving great governance, a corruption free organization, generating jobs, pulling in ventures, production of a good foundation and social frameworks, building up knowledgeable urban communities, and the development of a capital city of universal appeal, are among the highest points of the motivation for a new government. Obviously, a large portion of these activities call for improved budgetary and administrative assets throughout the following three to five years. In any case, repeating themes go through these activities. These are the viable utilization of the standards of e-government and e-governance, overwhelming advancement of the electronics and IT industry, and arrangement of developing SMAC innovations, which can provide the framework of the new state and can prompt a new start. e-Government has demonstrated, over and over, its ability to change the nature of the conveyance of open administrations as far as upgraded effectiveness and straightforwardness are concerned. Today, and from as far as 15 years ago, there are many e-government ventures from different administrations for a huge number of subjects on the web in India. Mee Seva (once in the past eSeva), Passport Seva, e-Procurement, FAST, CARD, and Mobile Seva are such cases. Some legislature has spearheaded work in the region of e-government. eSeva, launched in 1999, was the first stage for e-services, offering numerous G2C services. In the course of 15 years, further improvements have occurred in government. Presently, Mee Seva is appraised as the best e-administration activity in the country, as far as the qualities of its structure, its scope over the state, and the arrangement of its administration. There is a critical extension for the development of e-benefit conveyance as far as enhancing the nature of the administration by radical change and concentrating on the process of rebuilding the back-end divisions. The government ought to center incorporated administrations by combining the work procedures of all the government offices engaged with managing a specific administration. Another arrangement of flagship projects must be embraced in a genuine mission-mode. The arrangement of e-government should, this time round, incorporate all real government divisions and make a huge effect on the population. There should be a limited number of events for residents and business people to visit government workplaces to profit from any data or administrations. In this sense, we should move toward a "less-contact" government e-governance, which has "more contact" amongst government and residents. We are seeing the incredible ascent of social media as a powerful tool, not just for person to person communication between individuals, but as a constant channel for communicating feelings on any matters of significance, venting disdain against treachery or an absence of honesty in public life, and running protests that need contact with the general population. Similarly, as social media has become a capable instrument in the hands of the population for such purposes, governments too can exploit this media in an assortment of courses for setting up a participative governance or e-governance, which was, just ten years ago, a hypothetical idea. e-Governance is a capable thought whose time has now come. While the Government of India (GoI) had, in 2012, created an arrangement on the utilization of social media by government divisions, we have seen almost no utilization of it up until now. We have to build a system and a stage rapidly, ideally in an open private organization mode for understanding the fantasy of e-governance or a participatory governance.

10.6 The Advantages of e-Governance

A definitive objective of e-government is to have the capacity to offer an expanded arrangement of open administrations to subjects in a proficient and practical way. It considers government straightforwardness as it enables society to be educated about what the legislature is dealing with and in addition the approaches they are attempting to actualize. The principle advantage while executing e-government will be to enhance the productivity of the present framework. That would consequently save money and time. The presentation would likewise encourage better interchanges amongst governments and organizations. For instance, e-acquirement encourages G2G and B2B correspondence; this will allow smaller businesses to seek government contracts and more business, thus, the making an open market and more grounded economy. Business and residents can get data quicker whatever time of the day. Society is moving toward portable associations and the capacity of an e-taxpayer supported organization to be opened throughout the nation brings the possibility of a great advantages for an e-taxpayer driven organization, as we live in what is currently named as the knowledge era. The expected advantages of e-government incorporate proficiency, enhanced administration, more openness in administrations, and more openness and responsibility.

10.7 The Disadvantages of e-Governance

The fundamental burden concerning e-government is the absence of fairness in the community over access to the web, unwavering quality of data on the web, and the concealed plans of the government that could impact popular assessments. Potential ramifications of imposing e-government include miscommunication between the administration and residents, impacts on monetary, social, and political components, powerlessness to digital assaults, and aggravation to the norm in these territories. Hyper-reconnaissance happens once the administration has begun and it turns out to be more complex than initially thought, the residents will be compelled to collaborate electronically with the legislature on a bigger scale.

10.8 IoT Technologies for e-Governance

IoT is a broadband system that utilizes standard correspondence conventions though the Internet. The significant thought of IoT is the across the board presence of articles that can be estimated and deduced, and additionally can change depending on the circumstance. Appropriately, IoT is enabled by the extension of a few things and the corresponding hardware. IoT can include hardware, for example, cell phones, and different offices including food, apparatus, and points of interest that can team up to accomplish a joint goal. The principle for IoT is its impact on shoppers' lives [13]. For IoT, the cabling cost for multiple sensors is expensive, therefore, the correspondence between sensors ought to be remote. Low-control standard correspondence is reasonable for interconnection among numerous gadgets. As indicated by area and separation scope, a few systems are presented.

1. Home Area Networks (HAN) that utilize short-run models like ZigBee and Wi-Fi. All checking and control segments in a house are associated by HAN.
2. Wide Area Networks (WAN) give correspondence amongst clients and dispersion utilities that requires a substantially more extensive scope than HAN. The execution requires a fiber link or remote broadband like 3G and LTE.
3. Field Area Networks, which are utilized for association amongst clients and substations [14].

In IoT, two assignments, including detecting and preparing information, are performed, yet they are not bound together from a wireless sensor network (WSN) perspective. The attached arrangements are ThinkSpeak and iOBridge. ThinkSpeak is an investigation IoT stage for a social network of things, imagining and breaking down the live information in the cloud, analyze the information by MATLAB® coding. Interestingly, iOBridge has its own particular equipment modules that are associated with the cloud that can be gathered by web interfaces and the information can be amassed for other web administrations [15].

10.9 IoT Applications for e-Governance

IoT utilizes the Internet to blend different heterogeneous things and give a simple entry for these things, where every current thing must be connected to the Internet. The IoT based sensor systems can be used in the monitoring of excessive power usage, that is, light and ventilation system administration. To get to this point, sensors can be placed at different areas to gather and disseminate information for usage change [16]. It is also has vast advantages in the area of healthcare. The status of patients in a center or clinic is observed with a specific end goal to give better and quicker results for the doctor. Emergency vehicles, blood items, and organs for transplantation are observed to check their availability online. With a database, patients are shown to diminish the danger of a mix-up for getting incorrect medications, measurements, and techniques. Staff validation expects to enhance the worker's conduct toward patients. As to information gathering and detecting, it saves time for information handling and anticipating human mistakes. Through sensor information, for example, diagnosing conditions and giving ongoing data on tolerant well-being markers, the solution for the patient is executed by utilizing bio-flag checking, the patient condition is examined through heterogeneous remote access-based techniques to give the patient information at any time.

1. *Water and weather systems*: Climate frameworks utilize differing sensors to supply appropriate information, for example, temperature, rain, sun-oriented illumination and wind speed, and additionally to help improve the effectiveness of a city [17]. Water dissemination frameworks are fundamental parts of each city. Traditional techniques for water appropriation from the water source to the client's premises are not reasonable and effective, particularly in diagnosing any spillage in the pipeline or different parts of the framework. Along these lines, by placing sensors at proper areas of the appropriation framework, it recognizes any sort of deficiencies or different applications. Recognition of flaws like spillage, the content of the water, and the level of supply, can be actualized through setting sensors in an IoT based condition. In a similar manner, inside a capacity tank, the level of water is estimated by putting an ultrasonic sensor on the highest point of the tank and two weight transducers at the base. The nature of water can be estimated both before and after the capacity tank at key areas by a glass anode for estimating water pH. Besides that, when a city encounters excessive or too little rain, a significant number of them confront serious issues with water. As per the necessities of a district, neighborhood utilities can create inventive techniques to design and oversee the water system, understand faulty water utilization, monitor changes in water preservation, and allotting their rare assets adequately, mostly to flooding and wastewater administration amid a tempest through IoT. Dumping crude sewage into the nearby conduits will happen unavoidably in an area with no administration and planning. IoT helps in showing nearby specialists for administration and planning everything related to water, for example, controlling a colossal measure of crude sewage and readiness for storms. Urban areas through frameworks that screen the climate and those that control the water stockpile can assemble information for assurance of the water supply status. With a reasonable technique, urban areas will diminish the flooding of sewers and limit water sullying. Besides, utilizing an arrangement of sensors for information on the water level of groundwater sources and streams, it is conceivable to foresee surge occurrences. These framework sensors depend on ultrasonic range discoverers and they are set above neighborhood conduits to gauge the change in water level and anticipate any surge dangers.
2. *Transportation and vehicular traffic*: Vehicular movement data is a generous wellspring of information in semi-urban areas, where using the information and utilizing an appropriate investigation, occupants and the administration can benefit together [17]. Inhabitants can use the vehicular movement data to characterize the arrival time at their destination. Checking vehicular movement in the city by

urban IoT ought to be actualized. Nevertheless, camera-based activity observation is now accessible in numerous urban areas, however, they require a capable correspondence foundation to give more data. Activity checking is directed by detecting capacities, GPS on vehicles, and a blend of air quality sensors and acoustic sensors along the given street. This data is fundamental for experts and subjects to train and to send officers to any potential problem, as well as designing the best approaches.

10.10 Conclusion

The achievement of IoT substructures can empower urban communities, as the most vital research inspiration is communicated, and a short time later, primary and accommodating applications can be clarified. It shows how day-by-day exercises can be expanded and enhanced through utilizing them. Moreover, the difficulties emerging from actualizing the IoT framework were shown. Regarding this matter, the consolidation of the IoT stage into other autonomous and available frameworks to give clear and far reaching usage is amongst the most fascinating future proposals. In addition, furnishing a system to adapt to some critical difficulties, for example, the protection privileges of the clients/inhabitants, is a territory for research. A portion of the advancement in the real usage of enthusiastic urban areas over the world can be considered as tests or pilot ventures for future urban communities. IoT through its usefulness should, in fact, utilize suitable frameworks and sensors to guarantee the rights of occupants.

References

1. M. Pathak and G.D. Kaur, "Impact of e-Governance on public sector services", *International Journal of Emerging Research in Management & Technology*, vol. 3, no. 4, pp. 10–103, 2014.
2. M.A.M. Ganim and M. Kamruzzaman, "e-Governance using social network: A model for strong democratic environment in Bangladesh", *IEEE International Conference Computer and Information Technology*, 8–10 March 2014.
3. R. Nagarathna and R. Manoranjani, "An Intelligent Step to Effective e-Governance in India through E-Learning via Social Networks," 2016 IEEE 4th International Conference on MOOCs, Innovation and Technology in Education (MITE), Madurai, 2016, pp. 29–35.
4. S. Madakam and R. Ramaswamy, "100 new smart cities (India's smart vision)", *IEEE Information Technology: Towards New Smart World (NSITNSW), 2015 5th National Symposium*, pp. 1–6, 17–19 February 2015.
5. C. Xiaojun, L. Xianpeng and X. Peng, "IoT- based air pollution monitoring and forecasting system", *IEEE International Conference on Computer and Computational Sciences*, pp. 257–260, 27–29 January 2015.
6. E. Alpaydin and B. Francis, *Introduction to Machine Learning*, 3rd ed, MIT Press, Massachusetts, United States.
7. S. Cummins, A. Beresford and A. Rice, "Investigating engagement with in-video quiz questions in a programming course", *IEEE Transactions on Learning Technologies*, vol. 9, no. 1, pp. 57–66, 2016.

8. European Research Cluster on The Internet of Things, "Internet of things: IoT Governance, privacy and security issues", *European Research Cluster on the Internet of Things*, Click here to enter text. 2015.
9. R. Weber, "Governance of the Internet of things—From infancy to first attempts of implementation?" *Laws*, vol. 5, no. 3, p. 28, 2016.
10. M. Khaled and A. L. Hassan, "Governance, Risk and Compliance 'GRC' for Internet of Things 'IOT' Governance, Risk and Compliance 'GRC' for Internet of Things IOT," April, pp. 148–152, 2016.
11. R. Bhadauria, R. Chaki, N. Chaki, and S. Sanyal, "A survey on security issues in cloud computing", *International Journal of Innovations in Engineering and Technology*, vol. 5, no. 6, pp. 83–87, 2011.
12. Strategic Opportunity Analysis of the Global Smart City Market. Available online: www.egr.msu.edu/~aesc310web/resources/SmartCities (accessed on 24 February 2017).
13. G. Hancke, B. Silva, and G. Hancke, Jr., The role of advanced sensing in smart cities, *Sensors*, vol. 13, no. 1, pp. 393–425, 2012.
14. A. Botta W. de Donato V. Persico, A. Pescapé Integration of cloud computing and Internet of Things: A survey, *Future Generation Computing Systems*, vol. 56, pp. 684–700, 2016.
15. S. Talari, M. Shafie-khah, P. Siano, V. Loia, A. Tommasetti and J. P. S. Catalão, "A Review of Smart Cities Based on the Internet of Things Concept," Energies, vol. 10, no. 421, pp. 1–23, 2017.
16. N. Neyestani M.Y. Damavandi M. Shafie-khah and J.P.S. Catalão, Modeling the PEV traffic pattern in an urban environment with parking lots and charging stations. In *Proceedings of the 2015 IEEE Eindhoven PowerTech, Eindhoven, The Netherlands*, pp. 1–6, 29 June–2 July 2015.
17. M. Shafie-Khah E. Heydarian-Forushani, M.E.H. Golshan P. Siano M.P. Moghaddam M.K. Sheikh-El-Eslami and J.P.S., Catalão, Optimal trading of plug-in electric vehicle aggregation agents in a market environment for sustainability, *Applied Energy*, vol. 162, no. 1, pp. 601–612, 2016.

11

An Era of Smart Vehicle Ad Hoc Network for Intelligent Traffic Network Management

Monika Jain and Rahul Saxena

CONTENTS

11.1 Introduction

e-Governance is the application of information and communication technology (ICT) for delivering government services to the public. Wireless networks are a renowned trend today; there is not a single person who is not affected by the applications of wireless networks. A wireless ad hoc network is a special type of network in which each node acts as a router, which can also be called intelligent nodes, that is, it takes the decision itself where to send the information in the network.

A vehicular ad hoc network (VANET) is one of these types of network, in which the road infrastructure acts as the network and vehicles act as an intelligent node called the router. By this VANET-enabled feature, vehicles will collect all the information regarding running the network and they then have the capability to take decisions based on network traffic. VANET is the latest trend today, which keeps vehicles more aware about the network; Figure 11.1 shows the overall description of VANET. There are two types of communication in VANET: vehicle to vehicle communication and vehicle to infrastructure communication. When information is exchanged between vehicles, that communication is known as vehicle to vehicle, and when communication is exchanged between the vehicle and the infrastructure, then it is called vehicle to infrastructure communication (Jain and Saxena, 2017).

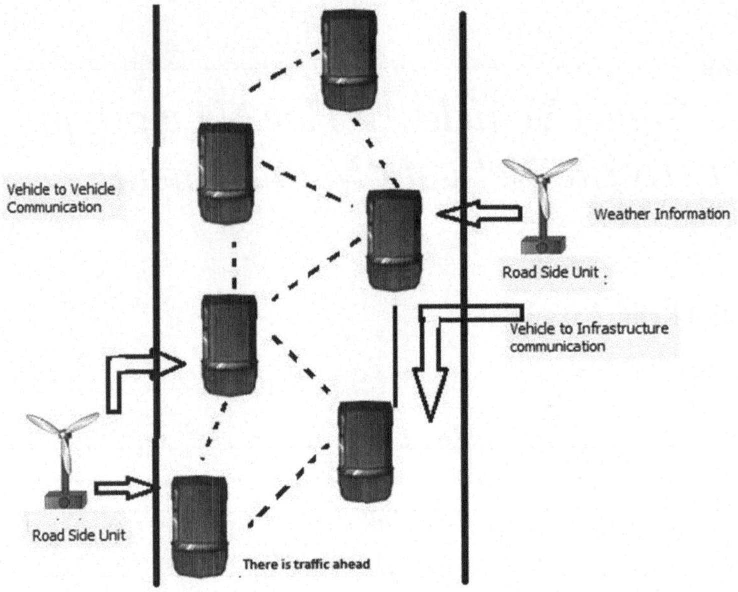

FIGURE 11.1
Overview of the VANET scenario.

11.2 Requirement of VANET in India

Road accidents are a major concern, especially in India, where the statistics of deaths are shocking. According to data collected by the World Health Organization, from 180 countries, the total number of road traffic deaths has plateaued at 1.2 million (World Health Organization, 2015).

11.3 Road Accidents in India

According to reports from the Ministry of Road Transport and Highways, we have plotted the number of deaths due to road accidents from 2003 to 2015; the graph shows the increase in the number of deaths from 2003 to 2015. According to other reports, Indian roads are found to be the most dangerous in the world. The main reason of these deaths is speeding by drivers, this reflects the challenge that we are facing today. Some safety measures need to be taken care of to decrease these numbers (Figure 11.2).

11.4 VANET: A Probable Solution

Vehicles are increasing every minute in the world, leading to traffic jams and collisions, especially in India and other developing nations, where the roads are not properly

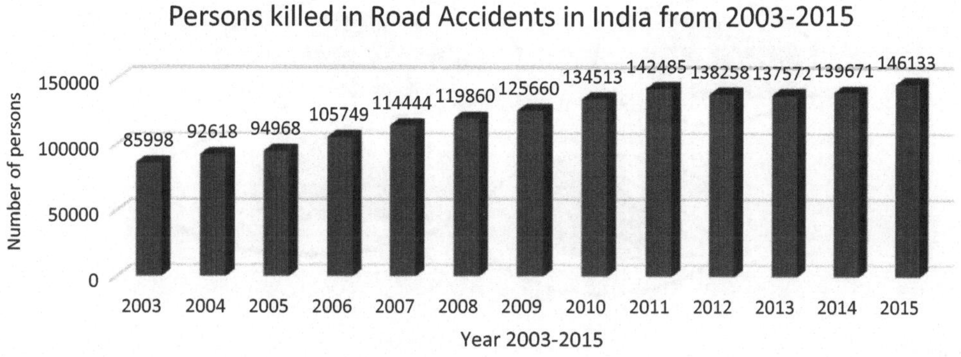

FIGURE 11.2
Total number of people killed in road accidents in India from 2003 to 2015.

structured and are poorly maintained, and where road accidents are frequent. VANET is a plausible solution for these problems. According to a study, if driver get a warning five seconds before an accident, subsequent deaths and injuries can be prevented.

Figure 11.3 describes how accidents occur without VANET, whereas Figure 11.4 describes the prevention of accidents with VANET, showing how vehicles within a network can share information about incidents to other vehicles. With the implementation of VANET, accidents can be prevented.

11.4.1 VANET Communication and Simulation of VANET

VANET has some special specifications that make VANET unique. As vehicles move around the road with different speeds, the topology of the network is not static; the nodes have a very high dynamic topology. It can be seen, due to the higher dynamic topology, that network disconnection takes place at a higher rate. VANET has an enormous application, which mainly includes safety, security and comfort to the driver (Qutayri, 2010). VANET provides intelligent transportation to the user, which significantly decreases the probability of a collision. A driver gets the notification about traffic and other conditions a

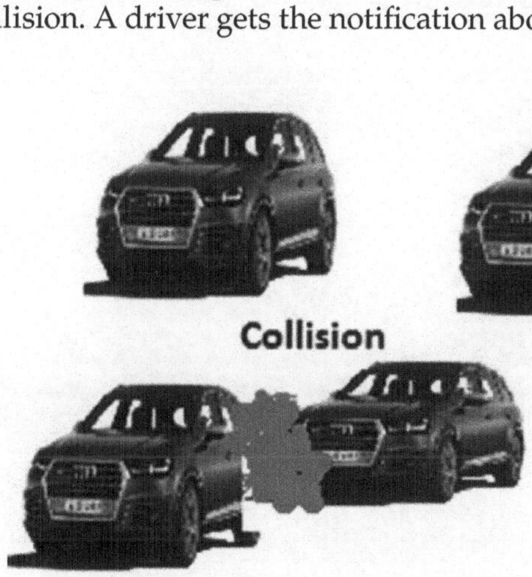

FIGURE 11.3
Collisions without VANET.

FIGURE 11.4
Collision prevention with VANET.

mile before, which gives sufficient time to be alerted. Not only does VANET provide collision prevention, it also provides other information such as weather conditions, poor road conditions, traffic information and so on to other nodes. Parking management and toll collection is also done automatically.

Vehicle to vehicle technology follows the mesh network topology, which means every vehicle can send the information to other vehicle nodes. The communication between vehicles is used by dedicated short-range communication (DSRC) (Howard, 2014). One of the possible frequencies used for communication is 5.9 GHz.

We have implemented VANET simulation through Network Simulator Version 2 (NS2); the network simulator is created and their properties are set according to the configuration of four nodes that are created along with their network, and the position of nodes is specified in the network. The nodes can communicate with other node in the same network (Figure 11.5).

VANET parameters in NS2 (Table 11.1).

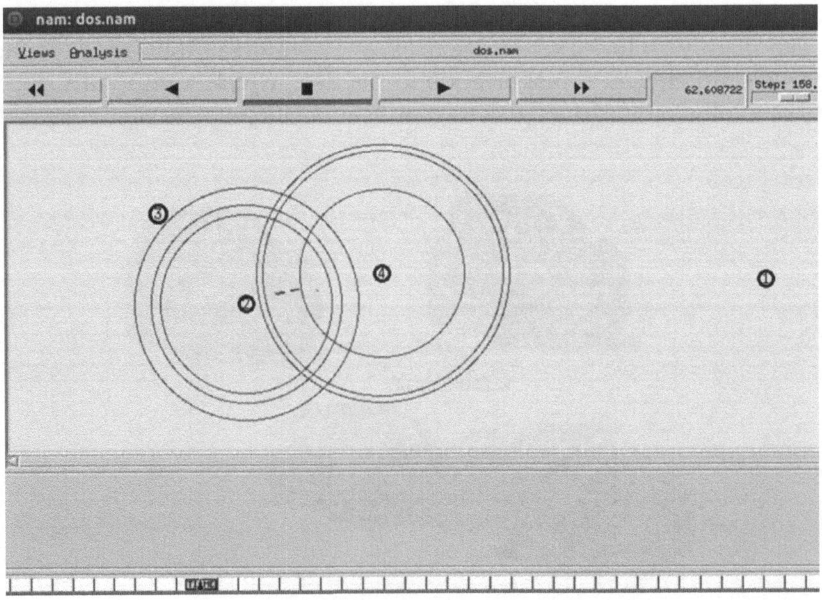

FIGURE 11.5
Simulation of VANET by NS2.

TABLE 11.1

Network Parameters Used in the Simulation

Network Parameters	Values Used
Visualisation	NAM
MAC	802_11
Number of nodes	4
Routing protocol	AODV

11.5 Conclusion

VANET is an emerging trend today, which can help us to build towards a smart future. The idea of having communication like mobile technology on a vehicle is remarkable. In this chapter, we have learnt about the status of road accidents in India and how VANET can be the key to decrease deaths due to collisions. We have also seen an overview of VANET, along with its implementation and applications. We have simulated VANET through NS2 and the simulation has been discussed. The future is before us, all we need to do is implement it and enjoy the application of it.

References

M. Al-Qutayri, C. Yeun and F. Al-Hawi (2010), Security and privacy of intelligent VANETs. In A. Al-Dahoud (Ed.), *Computational Intelligence and Modern Heuristics*. IntechOpen, London.

B. Howard (2014), Private organization, V2V: What are vehicle-to-vehicle communications and how do they work, February 6, 2014, www.extremetech.com/extreme/176093-v2v-what-are-vehicle-to-vehicle-communications-and-how-does-it-work.

M. Jain and R. Saxena (2017), Overview of VANET: Requirements and its routing protocols, 2017 *International Conference on Communication and Signal Processing (ICCSP)*, Chennai, pp. 1957–1961.

World Health Organization (2015), website Global status report on road safety 2015, www.who.int/violence_injury_prevention/road_safety_status/2015/en/.

12

Big Data Analytics and Hadoop: An Aspiring Expedition for e-Governance Sublimity

Rinkle Rani, Vandana Bhatia, and Himanshu Aggarwal

CONTENTS

12.1 Introduction

The government has a huge amount of data in traditional databases and forums that needs to be organized and migrated into new-age analytics technologies. The government receives data from multiple online and offline channels, thus, the collection of data is an enormous task. Also, sharing data among different departments and across different ministries, while maintaining jurisdictional boundaries, is a big challenge. This data can provide great insights that can deliver opportunities for discovering hidden information and it can enable the government to accomplish predictive analysis and informed decision making across individual, organizational, societal, national, and international levels (Husain and Khan, 2017).

Apart from this, analysis of the data for discovering useful information and its predictive nature provides a better perception of the strategies to be implemented in the future. Determining the useful information from such a large amount of data is a big challenge. The technologies used for Big Data analytics can provide possible solutions to overcome these challenges. They can facilitate government and stakeholders to get faster analysis from both structured as well as unstructured data. Big Data analysis can help government policy makers in taking more corrective decision towards the betterment of society and the nation. The other possible benefits could range from transforming government programs and empowering the citizens to provide transparency and permitting the participation of all people. The various tasks that are needed to be accomplished with the help of Big Data in e-governance are stated in Figure 12.1.

This chapter introduces a framework for the efficient analysis of e-governance using Big Data. The first section of the chapter gives a brief introduction on the sources and impact of Big Data in e-governance. The second section discusses various challenges faced for Big Data analytics for e-governance. The challenges include data collection, data accuracy, data privacy, and quality of service. The third section of this chapter will introduce the proposed framework for Big Data analytics in e-governance. The proposed framework is designed to deal with historical and real-time government data. The steps involved in the framework are data storage, data preprocessing, data analysis, and retrieval of useful information. The details of various Big Data technologies such as Hadoop, Hive, and Spark, which are used in the proposed framework, are given in the fourth section of this chapter. The last section provides a brief summary of the whole chapter.

12.2 Big Data in e-Governance

The government's ability to assist its citizens and address major challenges, including the economy, natural disasters, healthcare, job creation, and terrorism, can be enhanced by using Big Data. Getting insights to the results of predictive analysis can give huge benefits to e-governance. Business organizations have already deployed Big Data analytics. However, the government's activities are different from businesses in terms of goals, mission, and decision making. The main motive of business is to make a profit, whereas for government, the major concern is for sustainable development. While the requirement of taking decisions is limited in businesses, it has a diverse nature in government. Gartner also showed the role of Big Data for government, which is shown in Figure 12.1 (Columbus, 2012). As shown, government data has volume and velocity, as well as variety. It also requires appropriate hardware and services for handling the huge volume, velocity,

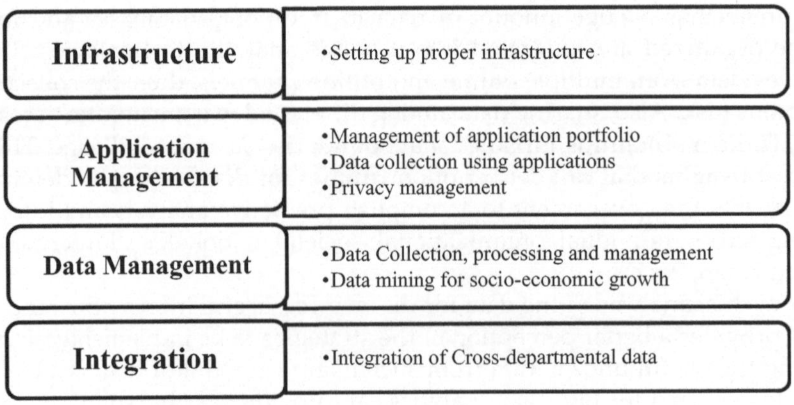

FIGURE 12.1
Tasks involved in the analytics of e-governance.

and variety. Big data will be particularly useful in framing the government's public policy, and thus can improve the development outcomes.

Many countries, such as the United Kingdom, the United States, the European Union (EU) member countries, and many Asian countries, have started Big Data based government programs. The UN's 2012 e-government survey stated that many Asian countries, including South Korea, Singapore, Japan, and India, are participating in providing Big Data based e-governance to citizens. These countries have launched various initiatives based on Big Data and started several projects based on Big Data in e-governance. Big Data can enhance the government's ability to provide facilities to its citizens and address major national and international challenges. Using Big Data can help the government in tracking tax defaulters. Many service queues in government offices can be reduced by serving people online. All such tasks need a solid underlying technology.

Governments of various countries have started many projects based on Big Data. A smart city is all about efficient planning, the right policies, and intelligent decisions that can be taken with the help of Big Data analytics (Malik and Shah, 2017). Keeping a view of the city's problems, plans and policies for a smart city can be designed and implemented (Figure 12.2).

Big Data analytics have an impact on various services provided by the government. By analyzing the large amount of data, the decision-making efficiency of the government can be improved. For example, analyzing more data in the healthcare sector can provide prevention against widespread diseases as it can help in getting to the core of the problem. Also, it can help in efficient supply chain management by analyzing demand from a large group of people.

It can also help in reducing crime rates. Information that is shared publicly combined with data from local authorities and intelligence information from law enforcement offices can help police in spotting criminals with a high degree of accuracy before the occurrence of crime. Sharing data publicly can also help in providing transparency of government functions.

Big Data analytics is also required in the transport industry. With the increase in the use of the Internet, data is generated from online bookings, traffic control, or online route maps (Wang et al., 2015). Data received from airlines also needs Big Data technologies for

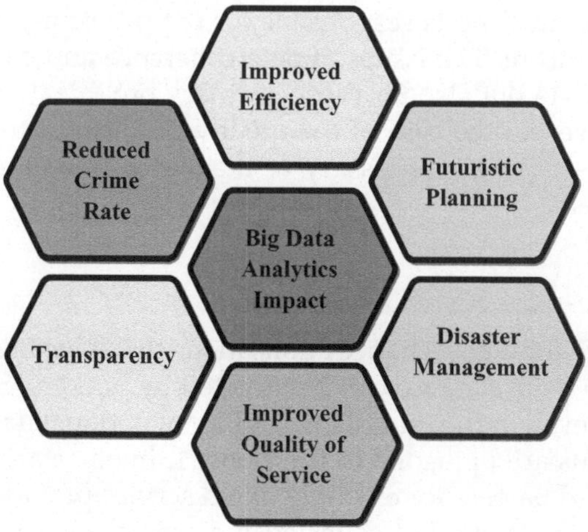

FIGURE 12.2
The impact of Big Data analytics on e-governance.

storage and processing. Governments all around the world are using Big Data analytics with the aim of turning a number of cities into smart cities, where traffic signals can predict traffic volumes and minimize traffic jams, for example, a bus will know about a delayed train on the same route. Geosciences contain a huge amount of time series data, which may also contain high resolution satellite and aerial images. The statistical techniques using Big Data technology can be used for knowledge extraction from such large volumes of data (Song and Di, 2017).

12.3 Challenges of Big Data Analytics for e-Governance

Although Big Data can enhance the decision-making process of government, it comes with many associated challenges. Challenges include issues related to data collection and application management, which involves making policies, legal frameworks and principles, data accuracy management, and protection and integration of cross-departmental data.

12.3.1 Data Collection

The collection of data from various sources is a big challenge in e-governance. Before collecting any data, it is good practice to identify and define the reasons for collecting the data, and the results we hope to achieve. Previously, data collection was manual. Now the data collected is heterogeneous; examples include text, fingerprints, iris recognition data, and images. The meteorological department looks at images continuously to predict climate change. Collection of this huge amount of data requires various tools and techniques. It is also important to collect accurate data.

12.3.2 Data Accuracy

It cannot be guaranteed that source data has a 100 per cent complete data quality, and, what is more, if we discuss who is responsible for the problems, it will make it difficult to disclose data in the future. The issues of data coherence and consistency are common issues not only in Big Data but also for those ordinary organizations that process a large amount of data. However, in the case of the quality problem of the source data, an adequate level of quality assurance is necessary, as the purposes and interests between organizations can be different.

12.3.3 Data Security

Security is a big concern for e-governance applications that have Big Data stores. Some Big Data applications from e-governance can be targeted by hackers. Some advanced persistent threats can also prevail in the case of availability of national data. The databases from government applications are uploaded to the cloud. It invites various security threats as data is accessible to third parties, for example, cloud service providers. Therefore, any gap of confidentiality concerned with data collected and processed by the government in cloud could offer serious implications. Data protection and privacy regulations in e-governance are very important.

12.3.4 Quality of Service

Quality should be maintained in terms of accuracy of data, timeliness delivery of results, and meaningfulness of data. The accuracy in terms of prediction based on data is a major challenge. e-Governance applications contain heterogeneous data from various sources. It also includes real-time data. The processing of data all together for providing efficient predictions to deliver a high quality of service to citizens is a big challenge.

12.4 Big Data Technologies for e-Governance

Big Data frameworks for e-governance should process and store a larger amount of data than the ordinary data handled by a single system. The data can be structured, unstructured, or semi-structured. The data can also be real-time with precise and minute data such as log information that is automatically generated by programs or social networks run by governments or data from mechanical sensors that can help in monitoring the speed of transport. In addition, it is highly possible that the source of generation and the ownership of data becomes uncertain over time. To deal with all the aforementioned problems, a unified solution is required that can handle such a huge amount of data efficiently and can perform multiple tasks with this outsized data.

Apache Hadoop (White, 2012) is one of the well-known Big Data technologies that also has an imperative supporting community for performing various tasks. It is designed for providing superior performance and to reduce the complexity that can be encountered while analyzing and processing large e-governance data using traditional technologies. Hadoop utilizes its parallel cluster processing and native distributed file system for fast processing and the storing of large data respectively. Hadoop ensures fault tolerance by replicating data on servers to prevent data loss.

The power of the Hadoop platform is based on two main sub-components: the Hadoop distributed file system (HDFS) and the MapReduce framework (explained in subsequent sections). In addition, users can add available modules on top of Hadoop according to the objectives of the problem, as well as their application requirements such as performance, reliability, scalability, capacity, and security. The Hadoop community have contributed to enriching its ecosystem with several open source modules such as Pig, Hive, Spark, and so on. Each module has a different functionality. The Big Data technology landscape is given in Figure 12.3. Technologies used to perform different tasks are given in the following subsections:

1. *HDFS*: A distributed file system for Big Data storage that can provide exceptional scalability and fault tolerance. It provides easy access and holds a huge amount of data across various machines in a distributed environment. The files are stored in a redundant manner to avoid possible data loss in the case of failure (Shvachko et al., 2010).
2. *MapReduce*: Data processing in Hadoop is performed using a basic Hadoop component called MapReduce (Dean and Ghemawat, 2004). A MapReduce process consists of two basic steps, Map and Reduce. A MapReduce job splits the input data in chunks that are processed by the map tasks in a distributed environment. The output of the map phase is key-value pairs that are further shuffled such that

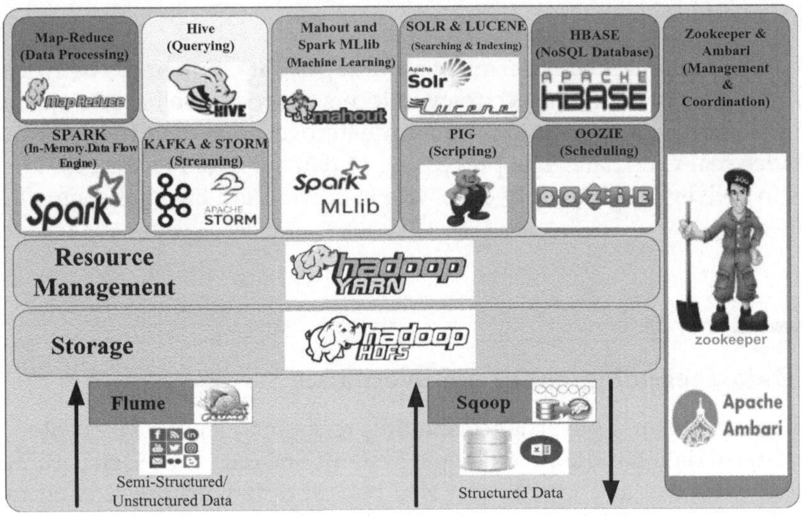

FIGURE 12.3
The Big Data technology landscape.

all the data belonging to one key can be located in the same location. Reducer than performs the final processing to produce a new set of outputs per key and is stored in HDFS.

3. *Hadoop Yarn*: For efficient resource management, Hadoop Yarn (White, 2012) was introduced in Hadoop 2.0. YARN (*Yet Another Resource Negotiator*) allows any distributed program, not only MapReduce, to process the data in a Hadoop cluster.
4. *HBase*: A distributed column-oriented database built on the top of HDFS. HBase is a Hadoop application that is used when real-time read or write random access is required in very large datasets. It stores data in the form of tables that consist of a sole row key and one or more columns defined by qualifiers (Dimiduk et al., 2013).
5. *Spark*: A general-purpose cluster computing engine with Application Programming Interfaces (APIs) in Scala, Python, and Java (Zaharia et al., 2010). It also has libraries for streaming, graph processing (Xin et al., 2013), and machine learning. It offers a functional programming API where the user can manipulate the distributed collections called resilient distributed datasets (RDDs). Every RDD is a collection of Python or Java objects partitioned across a Hadoop cluster. The RDDs can be manipulated using operations such as map, filter, and reduce. It takes functions from the programming language and distributes them to nodes on the cluster.
6. *Hive*: An infrastructure tool like a data warehouse for processing structured data on the top of Hadoop. It is used to summarize, query, and analyze Big Data for getting useful insights. It was created for analysts using strong SQL skills to run queries on the huge volumes of data that Facebook stored in HDFS. Now, Hive is successfully used by several organizations as a scalable, general-purpose data processing platform (Thusoo et al., 2010).
7. *Sqoop*: A tool designed for transferring data between Hadoop and relational database servers. It is used for importing data from relational databases such as Oracle MySQL to Hadoop HDFS and exported back from HDFS to relational databases (Ting and Cecho, 2013).

8. *Flume*: Designed for high-volume ingestion of event-based data into Hadoop. The basic example uses Flume to collect log files from a bank of web servers, and then moving the log events from those files into new aggregated files in HDFS for processing. The usual destination or sink is HDFS. Moreover, Flume is also flexible enough to write to the other systems such as HBase or Solr (Hoffman, 2013).
9. *Lucene*: A widely used open source search library often used to build-up a full-text search engine over the Hadoop cluster. Its powerful components of inverted indexing can help in other platforms such as Flume, Solr, and so on.
10. *Solr*: An open source search platform built upon a Java library Lucene. It is among the most popular search platforms for websites as it can index and search multiple sites and return recommendations for related content based on the search query's taxonomy (Karambelkar, 2015).
11. *Oozie*: A Java web application used to schedule Apache Hadoop jobs. It is a tool for scheduling various Hadoop operations that let the cluster administrators facilitate complex data transformations among many component tasks in Hadoop. It provides more control over jobs in Hadoop and also makes the overall process easier such that those jobs can be repeated at predetermined intervals (Islam et al., 2012).
12. *Kafka*: Generally used for building real-time streaming data pipelines that can reliably gather data between systems or applications. It provides high-throughput, low-latency, fault-tolerant pledged pipelines and is able to process streams of events. It provides reliable and timely responses to support both customer-facing applications and connecting downstream systems with real-time data (Kreps et al., 2011).
13. *Storm*: A distributed real-time computation system that can process large volumes of high-velocity data. It is exceptionally fast and has the ability to process over billions of records per second per node on a Hadoop cluster. The companies harness this speed and combine it with other data access applications in Hadoop for preventing undesirable events or to optimize positive outcomes. Some specific new business opportunities use Storm for real-time customer service management, operational dashboards, data monetization, or cyber security analytics and threat detection (Yang et al., 2013).
14. *Pig*: A scripting language for exploring large datasets over a Hadoop cluster. Pig converts the transformations into a series of MapReduce jobs, but the programmer is mostly unaware of this, which allows the programmer to focus on the data rather than the nature of the execution (Gates and Dai, 2016).
15. *Mahout*: A machine learning library that can implement a number of algorithms such as data clustering, decision trees, latent Dirichlet allocation, regression, and classification. It can mine datasets in parallel by deploying a distributed set of machines (Owen and Owen, 2012).
16. *Spark MLlib*: A distributed machine learning framework on top of the Spark. Several machine learning and statistical algorithms can be implemented using MLlib. It simplifies large-scale machine learning pipelines for easy and efficient analysis of data.
17. *Zookeeper*: Provides a set of tools to build distributed applications that can safely handle partial failures. While writing distributed applications, partial failure can occur. In such cases, a user does not even know about the occurrence of failure (Holmes, 2012).

18. *Ambari*: Enables system administrators to provision, manage, and monitor a Hadoop cluster. It can also integrate Hadoop with the existing enterprise infrastructure (Wadkar and Siddalingaiah, 2014).

12.5 Big Data Framework for e-Governance

The technology and architecture required for implementing e-governance applications should be scalable and shared across all delivery channels. They should accommodate the growing number of user demands. To allow the scalability and accessibility of data, Big Data technologies as well as cloud architecture can be used. The cloud services offer continuous integration with the Big Data frameworks such as MapReduce that fit well in the cloud environment (Yang et al., 2017). By use of both technologies, e-governance applications can mine huge volumes of both real-time and historic data for making better decisions and providing better services.

Apart from providing services, e-governance should also involve the safe management of data and provide good services from the perspective of data. A centered e-governance service should realize Big Data services while protecting personal information and privacy, preventing the monopoly of information, and guaranteeing appropriate data quality. Hence, there is a need to establish a system that can provide such a Big Data infrastructure, as well as services for e-governance through a balance of responsibility and authority.

For dealing with citizens of any country around the world, government policies should be adhered to and implemented in e-governance applications. Infrastructure polies as well as data center polices should be enforced for day-to-day tasks. Data center policies are deployed with respect to application deployment and security.

To accommodate all the prospects for e-governance, there should be a unified framework in which data can be managed, stored, and processed in a secured manner. The framework should involve various technologies, working modules for fulfilling requirements, and getting accurate results. The proposed unified framework for Big Data analytics for e-governance is given in Figure 12.4. In this section, all the prospects required for building a unified framework for e-governance are discussed.

12.5.1 Technology

e-Governance applications deal with a large volume of data over the years. This data needs scalable storage, analysis, and processing. For that, it requires Big Data technology to achieve centralized growth. Also, the handling of all the services, guidelines, and procedures provided by e-governance requires constant monitoring and control over the data and infrastructure. If the monitoring results indicate that an immediate reporting is required, the reporting will be done through procedural processes in accordance with policies and processes. Providing efficient e-governance services is a continuous process and involves technology for data storage and analysis.

e-Governance data is gathered from multiple departments and is stored in a distributed way. It is likely that data from one department can be useful for another department. For example, Municipal Corporation can gain deeper insights about an area when multiple patients suffer from where waterborne disease are most prevalent. Municipal Corporation can use the data from the healthcare sector to locate such areas so that further measures can be taken.

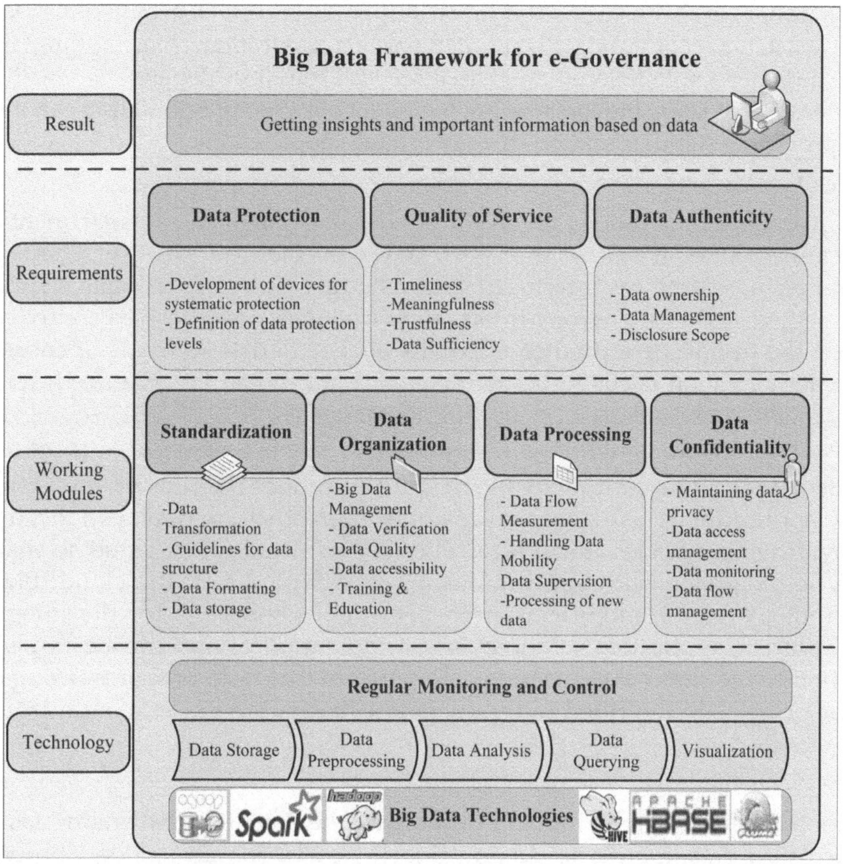

FIGURE 12.4
The Big Data framework for e-governance.

The data gathered also needs preprocessing so that it can be used for analysis. Preprocessing may include data cleaning, feature extraction, removing redundancy, and so on. Further, after preprocessing, data can be analyzed using machine learning algorithms. For that, SparkMLlib and Mahout can be used. For answers to the questions and to get insights about the data, querying data and visualization is executed. Big Data technologies such as Hive, Lucene, and Solr can be used for fast querying and indexing.

12.5.2 Working Modules

Above Big Data technology, there are different modules that work in parallel for providing efficient services for both the government and citizens.

1. *Standardization*

   Migration of technology is a major challenge in every application including e-governance. Shifting to a newer or different version of software is also a challenge. The underlying technology should provide standardization such that it can handle the existing technology and is able to accommodate new technology as well. For easy maintenance, there should be unified guidelines for data structure so that they can be incorporated in various applications. Distributed data storage is also a sub-part of standardization. In various applications, data is stored in relational databases. Relational databases are still the most dependable database in this era of Big Data. Big Data technologies such as Sqoop and Flume can be used for providing standardization in e-governance applications.

2. *Data Organization*

   e-Governance applications revolve around data from various departments such as municipalities, hospitals, transport, and so on. Hence, the organization of data requires more time, resources, effort, and budget. The collected data should also be verified so that any wrong information from any unauthorized source cannot affect the overall performance. Also, the quality of data in terms of correctness and authorization needs to be maintained. Data should be organized in such a way that it can be accessed by multiple departments.

   Big Data technology offers prominent features to create an application such as developing a new municipality. It can also reduce the time of deploying any new application. The e-governance applications that are deployed locally, and providing services at a local level, should be shifted to the cloud so that they can be integrated with applications already deployed in the cloud. Big Data technology over Hadoop can offer tremendous solutions for the integration of different applications. Moreover, various applications can be impeccably shifted to the cloud using Hadoop. To perform this task, proper training needs to be given so that trained individuals can streamline the data organization in the cloud.

3. *Data Processing*

   After successfully gathering and organizing the data, the challenging task is to process the data in order to obtain valuable results. For efficient data processing, the flow of data should be measured continuously. Flow of data here means the timing and sequence of data in which it is required. For efficient processing, there also should be a provision for data mobility. Until now, the applications involved in e-governance have adopted a prototype for gathering the data followed by its analysis. But in this era of social networks and sensors, data is coming continuously. For processing that streaming data, new generation technologies for data mining and knowledge discovery are required. Big Data technologies such as Kafka and Storm deal with this streaming data and can process this new data efficiently. Methods for correlating and integrating the historical data with real-time data are a must in order to provide contextualized information. This whole task needs a suitable supervision of activities that are undertaken for data processing in e-governance.

4. *Data Confidentiality*

   Data from e-governance contains vital government information, hence data should be kept confidential. Data obtained or connected through the web contains private and crucial information, thus it should be prevented from any spurious access. Also, e-governance applications and services need to be examined and every change in the information content should be tracked. By keeping control and by monitoring every activity of government, actions such as corruption in government employees and ministers can be controlled. For ensuring security and transparency in the system, process audits and security audits should be done intermittently. Big Data technologies and cloud computing can help in analyzing the data to detect fraud activities. They can provide a robust defense mechanism to make the system more secure.

Data privacy is another significant security aspect in e-governance. From everyday transactions, the government collects ample information from citizens. Thus, it is imperative to protect the privacy of information of citizens such as personal data and medical and financial data.

12.5.3 Requirements

Some services are a must for e-governance. Those services require many levels of monitoring in terms of quality and protection.

1. *Data Protection*

   For various types of data in e-governance, diverse levels of privacy are required as some data may entail no privacy at all while other data requires a higher level of security. The deployment of Big Data analytics in e-governance requires a strong security mechanism because sensitive data is not only limited to government organizations, but it is also associated with society at large. Government organizations should implement Big Data and cloud-based services in governance, only if they are capable of providing assurances regarding the safety of private and sensitive data.

2. *Quality of Service*

   The services provided by government applications may become unavailable when natural disasters like earthquakes, floods, wars, and internal disturbances occur. Data may also get lost in such circumstances. The underlying technology should provide simple and easy recovery of data. Big Data and cloud technology can dynamically increase the number of sources for maintaining quality of service. Moreover, at the time of high traffic and load, the quality of service should remain intact. The level of future predictions may vary depending on the quality of data. The decision makers may undertake various factors at the same time to make important decisions. There should be criteria for timelessness, sufficiency, and meaningfulness for making decisions. Decision making becomes meaningless if correct timing is missed due to excessive efforts for providing accurate decisions. However, truthfulness should also accompany timeliness for decision making. The meaningfulness in data will be used for analysis of social changes and the behavioral patterns of citizens. Sufficiency of data is also required to measure the amount of data that will be good enough for making an efficient analysis.

3. *Data Authenticity*

   Authentication of information gathered from the data recognizes the actual author of the data. There should be several ways for secure electronic authentication in e-governance. However, many sets of authentication methods are available, which range from software solutions like the use of biometrics and passwords to hardware solutions like the use of smartcards. The storage of this private information is vulnerable to attack by hackers, thus a high level of protection should be provided.

12.5.4 Results

The final results of this framework are the important insights that are gained by analyzing the data. If the results are equipped with proper Big Data analytics for e-governance, it is possible to make decisions for ensuring the appropriate selection of the correct solution. The purpose of Big Data analysis in e-governance is to discover a data rule for taking decisions by exploiting the source data and utilizing it to set up a strategy or to predict a trend.

12.6 Conclusion

In this chapter, the significance of Big Data analytics in e-governance was presented. Further, the impact and sources of Big Data in e-governance were highlighted. The challenges faced while using Big Data technologies for e-governance were discussed. The challenges included data collection, accuracy, authentication, and quality of service. In addition, Big Data technologies such as Hadoop and MapReduce were discussed. Various paradigms that work along with Hadoop for providing different functionality, such as streaming data access, querying, searching, and indexing, were presented. Furthermore, a unified framework was presented that can be used as a base for analyzing technology and risk factors in advance. The Big Data framework for e-governance was presented in four layers consisting of underlying technology, working modules, requirements, and the desired outcomes or results. The goals of e-governance were associated with Big Data and cloud technologies to overcome the difficulties faced by e-governance. Various issues of e-governance that can be solved by Big Data analytics were also discussed. Big Data in e-governance is an inevitable choice for improving the quality of life of citizens.

References

Columbus, Louis. 2012. "Roundup of Big Data Forecasts and Market Estimates." Forbes. www.forbes.com/sites/louiscolumbus/2012/08/16/roundup-of-big-data-forecasts-and-market-estimates-2012/#645c73ed3cdf.

Dean, Jeffrey and Sanjay Ghemawat. 2004. "MapReduce: Simplified data processing on large clusters." In *The Proceedings of the Symposium on Operating Systems Design and Implementation*, 137–49. USENIX. doi:10.1145/1327452.1327492.

Dimiduk, Nick, Amandeep Khurana, Mark Henry Ryan, 2013. *HBase in Action*. Manning: Shelter Island, NY.

Gates, Alan and Daniel Dai. 2016. *Programming Pig: Dataflow Scripting with Hadoop*. O'Reilly Media: Sebastopol, CA.

Hoffman, Steve. 2013. *Apache Flume: Distributed Log Collection for Hadoop*. Packt Publishing Ltd: Birmingham, UK.

Holmes, Alex. 2012. *Hadoop in Practice*. Manning: Shelter Island, NY.

Husain, Mohd Shahid and Neha Khan. 2017. "Big data on E-government." In *Securing Government Information and Data in Developing Countries*, 27–36. IGI Global: Hershey, PA.

Islam, Mohammad, Angelo K. Huang, Mohamed Battisha, Michelle Chiang, Santhosh Srinivasan, Craig Peters, Andreas Neumann, and Alejandro Abdelnur. 2012. "Oozie: Towards a scalable workflow management system for Hadoop." In *The Proceedings of the 1st ACM SIGMOD Workshop on Scalable Workflow Execution Engines and Technologies*, No. 4 Scottsdale, AZ.

Karambelkar, Hrishikesh Vijay. 2015. *Scaling Big Data with Hadoop and Solr*. Packt Publishing Ltd: Birmingham, UK.
Kreps, Jay, Neha Narkhede, Jun Rao, 2011. "Kafka: A distributed messaging system for log processing." In *Proceedings of the NetDB*, 1–7, Athens, Greece.
Malik, Fehda and Munam Ali Shah. 2017. "Smart city: A roadmap towards implementation." In *2017 23rd International Conference on Automation and Computing (ICAC)*, 1–6, Huddersfield, UK.
Owen, Sean and Sean Owen. 2012. *"Mahout in Action."* Manning: Shelter Island, NY.
Shvachko, Konstantin, Hairong Kuang, Sanjay Radia, and Robert Chansler. 2010. "The hadoop distributed file system." In *The Proceedings of IEEE 26th Symposium on Mass Storage Systems and Technologies (MSST)*, 1–10, Washington, DC.
Song, Jia and Liping Di. 2017. "Near-real-time OGC catalogue service for geoscience big data." *ISPRS International Journal of Geo-Information* 6 (11), 337.
Thusoo, Ashish, Joydeep Sen Sarma, Namit Jain, Zheng Shao, Prasad Chakka, Ning Zhang, Suresh Antony, Hao Liu, and Raghotham Murthy. 2010. "Hive-a petabyte scale data warehouse using hadoop." In *2010 IEEE 26th International Conference on Data Engineering (ICDE)*, 996–1005, Long Beach, CA.
Ting, Kathleen and Jarek Jarcec Cecho. 2013. *Apache Sqoop Cookbook*. O'Reilly Media: Sebastopol, CA.
Wadkar, Sameer and Madhu Siddalingaiah. 2014. "Apache Ambari." In *Pro Apache Hadoop*, 399–401. Springer: New York.
Wang, Chao, Xi Li, Xuehai Zhou, Aili Wang, and Nadia Nedjah. 2015. "Soft computing in big data intelligent transportation systems." *Applied Soft Computing* 38, 1099–1108.
White, Tom. 2012. *Hadoop: The Definitive Guide*. O'Reilly Media, Inc.
Xin, Reynold S., Joseph E. Gonzalez, Michael J. Franklin, and Ion Stoica. 2013. "Graphx: A resilient distributed graph system on spark." In *The Proceedings of 1st International Workshop on Graph Data Management Experiences and Systems*, 2, 1–6.
Yang, Chaowei, Qunying Huang, Zhenlong Li, Kai Liu, and Fei Hu. 2017. "Big data and cloud computing: Innovation opportunities and challenges." *International Journal of Digital Earth* 10 (1): 13–53.
Yang, Wenjie, Xingang Liu, Lan Zhang, and Laurence Tianruo Yang. 2013. "Big data real-time processing based on Storm." In *2013 12th IEEE International Conference on Trust, Security and Privacy in Computing and Communications (TrustCom)*, 1784–87, Melbourne, Australia.
Zaharia, Matei, Mosharaf Chowdhury, Michael J. Franklin, Scott Shenker, and Ion Stoica. 2010. "Spark: Cluster computing with working sets." *Hot Cloud* 10 (1–7).

13

Sustainability and Energy Savings: Perspectives through e-Government Practices

Sanjay Kumar Pradhan

CONTENTS

13.1 Introduction

Nature is robust within limits, both chaotic and fragile. Hence, environment conservation and promotion tactics in different parts of the world are guided by information and communication technologies (ICTs) in checking pollution and eliminating pollutants. e-Government practices, with the help of ICTs, while attempting to create green environmental approaches and a sustainable future, look for all aspects of information, precautions, and mitigations measures about the environment, where energy efficiency and energy savings have turned a vital aspect of e-government initiatives and practices. However, the challenges e-government faces today demands for more innovative and pragmatic approaches to enhance the processes and transform administration and service practices. Hence, the emerging e-government steps and innovative approaches reflect how environmental challenges, energy issues, and overall environmental sustainability concerns are taken under e-government mechanisms, apart from having limitations and problems in its operation.

13.2 Contextualizing Sustainability

e-Governance and sustainable development work together and enhance the capacity of public agencies for service delivery through the process of ICT. In this context, technology is the facilitator for delivering affordable, easy, and accessible services that are needed by all sections of society, most particularly by the poor and disadvantaged sections of society. While e-government is an interaction of political arrangement, administrative structure, and civil society, sustainable development is an interaction and interplay of social, economic, and political attributes (Pokorny, 2012). Sustainable here includes three components: social sustainability, environmental sustainability, and economic sustainability. Social sustainability includes accessibility in society for technological choices, e-government services to support public health delivery, e-government services for social and economic development of families, and e-government initiatives for narrowing the digital divide. Environment sustainability includes use of environmentally friendly green ICT equipment for government operations, an alerting messaging service in order to broadcast the weather forecast and any weather conditions that might cause natural disasters, and smart and advanced metering services for judicious water resource management. Economic sustainability includes the use of energy efficient technology and equipment for both government procurement and operations, as seen in India and South Korea, smart work efforts to alleviate traffic issues and environmental pollution, and information and services provided to businesses and people to encourage interaction (Pokorny, 2012, p. 3).

IT, which is largely projected and intended for sustainable development, aims at to be green and sustainable. Green IT refers to the transition to a low-carbon society by limiting and reducing energy consumption in the various IT sectors and devices and using them in an eco-friendly manner. It is expected that with the use of IT, a 15 per cent reduction in the world's carbon emissions is possible by 2020, telecommuting and teleconferencing by 4.61 per cent, energy efficient buildings by 21.54 per cent, smart grid build-up by 30.51 per cent, efficiency increases in manufacturing processes by 12.44 per cent, reduction of paper use by 1.67 per cent, and smart transportation by 29.23 per cent. The United Nations "2030 Agenda for Sustainable Development" encourages governments to ensure responsive, inclusive, participatory, and representative decision making at all the levels of socio-economic and political structures (www.theclimategroup.org). The agenda also acknowledges that partnerships and stakeholders will play a vital role in promoting inclusive development, and the United Nations recognized "the significance and efficacy of e-government in promoting accountability, transparency, efficiency and public service delivery." The survey of the United Nations in 2016 affirmed the fact that there is a shift from a "government-to-you" perspective to "government-with-you" approach (Baum and Mahizhnan, 2014), and thus focusing on collaboration within and outside the government in each country. This shift has a significant and positive impact for progress toward the sustainable development goals (SDGs) at the national and global level. The countries that were surveyed highlighted that there had been considerable increases in developing new tools to drive out poverty, with socio-economic and environmental improvements. Fixed and wireless broadband, mobile Internet, smartphones and tablets, cloud computing, open data, and social media are now understood to be significant enablers of sustainable development. All sustainable development goals can benefit from the application of ICTs so long they deepen, extend, and expand participation opportunities to all, regardless of geographical locations and social status. In short, the UN vision of "End poverty in all of its form everywhere" (Goal, 2015) can directly benefit from the application of e-governance technologies and know-hows that support mutual cooperation and production.

13.3 Extent of Sustainable Development through e-Government

Sustainable development is a holistic need for all sectors of the economy and society. Excess use of natural resources and energy to meet fast expanding requirements has resulted in the rapid depletion of resources to meet the demands of society and the requirements of the people. Recently, a perspective has emerged that states that sustainability should work together with three components: society, the natural environment, and economic performances. Together, these components are known as the "Triple Bottom Line" (TBL) (Dao and Carbo, 2001). However, the overuse of natural resources to meet ever increasing demands has shown a bleak side to the future. The rapid depletion of resources, as well as the negative impacts to fulfill the demands of society, has made societies and the corporate sector realize the importance of sustainability in their own industries and spheres. Attention to the needs of consumers and citizens, alongside those of industrialists, is needed to create sustainable knowledge societies, where ICTs can boost the process (Credé and Mansell, 1998). Sustainable development has four core objectives, which are called the Four Greens. Firstly, Green Savings, which encourages and facilitates families, communities, businesses, and governments to decrease the cost and finance for renewables, recycling, and the reuse of waste. Secondly, Green Opportunities, which promotes clean technology-based industries, ensures jobs and incomes through business development, and market expansion for goods and services that reduces pollution and protects resources. Thirdly, Green Talent, which invests in the assets of education, research, innovation, and entrepreneurial and workforce skills. Fourthly, Green Place, which enhances eco-smart development that presents low-impact, resource-efficient design, multi-transportation, sustainable infrastructure, and green energy (Farid, 2015).

e-Government helps in transformative changes and modernizes government for sustainable development. Environmentalists emphasize the critical role that the government can contribute for innovative platforms, which facilitates innovation, creation, and economic growth by empowering multiple stakeholders in society to cooperate and contribute for value creation. The governance processes, e-participation and e-consultation, which are enabled by new technologies such as electronic and mobile services, open up new ways of interaction and collaboration between governments and public institutions, businesses, and social groups, as well as individuals. Leveraging the Internet and mobile devices, social media helps in improving quality services and access to public facilities and awareness, like e-education and e-health. Furthermore, e-government helps in better transparency, efficiency, accountability, and effectiveness for sustainable development efforts, as well as eliminating red-tapeism and corruption. Secondly, it transforms the lives of the citizens and generates trust between the government and the public, and approaches for equity and equitable services. Thirdly, it improves integration and coordination mechanisms to address and resolve complex and interdependent sustainable goals and developmental issues. Fourthly, e-governance facilitates inclusive and progressive economic growth by creating new jobs and enhancing job opportunities, and thus providing mechanisms for innovative partnerships between government, academia, businesses, NGOs, and the public. Fifthly, e-governance enhances inclusiveness of governance processes, social equity, and responsiveness of government institutions through the fair distribution of welfare entitlements and services to the poor, disabled, vulnerable groups, and those in rural and remote areas. Sixthly, e-government promotes the green economy, green government, disaster prediction, risk management, and the reduction of carbon emissions. And seventhly, e-government can enhance environmentally sustainable business opportunities through green procurement, e-commerce, and online possibilities for job creation (United Nations, 2015 and 2016).

13.4 Some Case Studies of the e-Government Approach for Sustainable Development

In Mozambique, the Service Monitoring System or Monitoria Participativa Maputo (MOPA) is designed to support poor and marginalized sections of society by overcoming the barriers for their entry into urban facilities and services. Under MOPA, Ntxuva is designed to collect information from people through SMSs, a mobile app, web portal, and a voice interface in local and indigenous languages, and it is used to promote access by the less educated and poor sections of society for environmental issues and challenges. The MOPA system is a process of monitoring the quality of solid waste management. The users can send photos, comments, and other clarifications for quick interventions by the urban or local administration for waste management. Accordingly, the Municipal Directorate of Hygiene and Cemeteries manages the information and monitors the operation of waste management.

In the Haiti earthquake of 2010, OpenStreetMap (OSM) mapping was used in the response, and in the Philippines, OSM mapping was used to assess the features and damages caused by typhoon Haiyan. In Indonesia, the humanitarian assistance response was impressive under OSM support and the Humanitarian OpenStreetMap Team (HOT) collaborated with a large number of volunteers, including authorities and students, to collect data under OSM for disaster preparedness and risk management. Thus, the open mapping technologies and services have become significant tools in the context of sustainable development goals of water management and sanitation, industrialization, human settlements, ecosystems, forests, land reclamation, and biodiversity (United Nations, 2015). In Kenya, the people have created public information facilities with the goal of sharing essential environmental, social, and economic resources. In addition to providing useful information to the local government, the public have acquired newly developed professional skills in the field of geographical information systems (GIS) and cartography. In Tanzania, some cities and rural areas have been prone to frequent flooding and drought; houses have been abandoned; and fertile lands have been turned into a breeding ground for diseases. But, these issues have been subjected to resolution through community mapping of OSM technologies. OSM-based maps have helped in identifying disease affected areas, identifying victims, and providing important information on sanitation and hygienic conditions, apart from where there has been afforestation, land upgradation, and reforestation. The Info Ladies project of Bangladesh, created in 2008, talks to farmers about the use of seeds, fertilizers, and insecticides for crops. The Information Network Village (INVIL) of South Korea is a project that established self-sustainable village communities capable of continued growth by creating information network environments and improving the income of residents through e-commerce in agricultural and fishing, and also included mountainous regions that were usually excluded from information networks (Pokorny, 2012, p.14).

In India, Smart Cities Mission (2018), Swachh Bharat Mission, and Gram Swaraj Abhiyan are three significant steps recently taken by the Indian Government for an integrated strategy to resolve the intricacies of energy, environment, and sustainability. Smart Cities Mission is an urban renewal and retrofitting initiative by the Government of India, in association with state governments, to develop selected Indian cities to make them citizen friendly, green, and sustainable. All the data relating to visions and implementation, apart from other things, can be downloaded from a website (www.smartcities.gov.in), which is run by the Ministry of Housing and Urban Affairs. Apart from waste and water management, renewable sources of energy, smart meters, and green and energy efficient buildings, e-government solutions provide public information, engage citizens, resolve grievances, electronic service delivery, and a sustainable environment (http://smartcities.gov.in). To intensify the efforts to have universal sanitation across the country and to put the focus on sanitation, the Prime Minister of India launched the Swachh Bharat Mission (SBM) on October 2, 2014. The Mission Coordinator for SBM is Secretary, Ministry of Drinking Water and Sanitation (MDWS), with two sub-missions: the Swachh Bharat Mission (Gramin) and the Swachh Bharat Mission (Urban). Together, they aim to achieve Swachh Bharat by 2019, as a tribute to Mahatma Gandhi on the 150th anniversary of his birth. The two sub-missions are aimed at cleanliness through solid and liquid waste management activities (Government of India, n.d. and Swachh Bharat Mission-Gramin, 2014). Furthermore, PM Ujjawala Yojana, PM Sahaj Bijli Har Ghar Yojana (Saubhagya), and Ujala Yojana, under the Gram Swaraj Abhiyan of the Indian government, are linked to the www.mygov.in web portal of the Union government, creating awareness among the public about the opportunities of electricity and energy supply to rural areas, so as to minimize pressure on environment and pollution, and ensure rural hygiene (Abhiyan and Gaon, 2018).

13.5 Monitoring Environment and Geography

The ICT applications under e-government facilitate improved access to environmental information for the citizens, government, and institutions. It helps in collating environmental data in a form that will be suitable to different groups of users, allow access to information, and facilitate timely decision support so as to speed up and increase efficiency and effectiveness for environmental monitoring; for example, multimedia public information kiosks, land, air, and water quality monitoring systems, weather warning systems, and environmental emergency management systems for disasters like floods, famine, forest fires, and seismic acts. The specific implementations in this context include geographic information systems (GIS) and global positioning systems (GPS). GIS is a system that includes capture, checking, storage, manipulation, integration, analysis, modelling, and displays of complex spatial data. It helps in solving planning and management issues and formulate a concrete management strategy and policy framework, keeping in mind environmental concerns. The integration of data and information on soils, climate, and terrains from different sources like remote sensing, cartography, and earthbound surveys permit data on potentials and constraints of different areas of occupational activities. Moreover, the application of remote sensing implies that the changes can be observed, integrated, and analyzed with the other data of GIS. This can be explained through deforestation and degradation of the rainforests in Maraca, the riverine island located in the northern parts of the Amazon Basin in South America. Another type of remote sensing device generating input for the GIS is videography, which is an advanced aerial photography system that provides important techniques to provide information on the environment and climate change.

Apart from GIS, GPS is a space-based radio positioning system that ensures 24 hours 3D positioning, time information, and velocity. The global navigation satellite system (GNSS) is an extended GPS system that provides users with accurate information to be used for crucial navigation uses. Allied to the use of GIS is remote sensing that provides a specific perspective to observe large regions, and thus global monitoring is possible from any part of the world. Significantly, satellite remote sensing has been used to estimate atmospheric gases, vapors, aerosol particles, clouds, and precipitation, without moving to different parts of the country for the collection of data.

The role of the United Nations Environment Programme (UNEP) and its Global Resource Information Database (GRID) largely contributes to energy saving and the sustainable environment. The Environmental and Natural Resources Information Networking (ENRIN) of the UNEP is largely supported by a satellite telecommunication system: Mercure. With full Internet connectivity, Mercure provides a high capacity means for delivering environmental data and information for other UNEP initiatives such as GRID.

The Indonesian forestry department has benefitted from two separate initiatives using e-mechanisms. Firstly, a public sector initiative is funded and executed by the Ministry of Forestry to contribute in sustainable forest management. The program includes identifying and coding trees, optimizing forest maintenance, and training in computing using specialized software. Secondly, a private sector initiative includes Forestry Resource Information System (FRIS), introduced by the Forestry Management Association (FMA). The system includes GIS, remote sensing, aerial photography, and digital mapping mechanisms and technologies. In another instance, the Grito de Alerta em Defesa da Floresta Amazonica project was initiated in Brazil with the objective of raising international awareness about the need and significance of protecting the Amazon region against environmental degradation. Since the inception of the program, ICTs have been extensively used as a facilitating tool, which includes video-conferencing, multimedia usages, and home page creation on the Internet ("The potential uses of ICTs for sustainable development," n.d.).

13.6 Energy Saving through e-Governance

Minimization of waste, decomposition, and dematerialization are effective ways in achieving low resource consumption and energy reduction. IT enabled e-government often involves transformation of atoms to the level of bits, which was explored and advocated by the scientist Nicholas Negroponte of the MIT Media Laboratory, Cambridge, United States (Negroponte, 1995). The most significant aspect of e-government is the replacement or substitution of physical products by services and voicemail, and thus replacing machines. For instance, the Swedish IT company, Telia, made a lifecycle comparative analysis of its Telesvar voicemail with the traditional answering machine, and reached the conclusion that voicemail services had reduced waste by up to 20 per cent, with a decrease in greenhouse gas emissions and energy consumption (Negroponte, 1995).

Another instance of e-government for sustainable development includes dematerialization and decomposition of hardware. It is expected that the performance of IT and its equipment will continue to get better without imposing extra demands on materials, resources, and energy; resulting in significant cost and resource savings. However, it is important to note that there still may be rebound effects that could overcome these resource savings. Therefore, e-government through ICTs could help material recycling and the reuse of solid goods through auctions and exchange sites on the Internet, where buyers and owners meet. From the customer side, eBay and other websites have been popular; and from the business perspective, an important industrial secondary market has been established through the Internet. The buyers of industrial products, such as precious metals, are now able to purchase the materials from all over the world through a cost-effective manner and online exchanges (Haghseta, 2003).

The energy intensity, as defined energy consumption relative to gross domestic product, is an indicator that is commonly used to measure progress in energy efficiency. In the United States, energy consumption and intensity has declined steadily since the 1970s, more particularly from the 1990s. Apart from improved energy efficiency in processes and products, a sizeable portion of the recent decrease in energy intensity is largely attributed due to "structural" changes. This refers to the decline in high energy-intensive sectors, and promotion of less energy intensive and energy efficient industries (Romm, 1999). It is important to note that energy intensity serves as an indicator for energy efficiency, rather than energy consumption. In climate change policy, as issued by the George W. Bush (43rd President of the United States) administration, energy intensity was a significant part of the proposal to address the issues related to climate change. But his plan was met with plenty of criticisms from many environmentalists and policy analysts (Revkineeb, 2002), because of the paradox that the energy intensity reductions can occur in spite of an increase in the emission of greenhouse gases due to gains in productivity. Hence, energy intensity reductions are often misinterpreted as an indicator for the improvement of the environment, rather than a mere indicator of economic growth, productivity gains, and such other gains.

In the case of the commercial sector, IT, particularly e-commerce, has had a positive effect on energy conservation by replacing physical stores with virtual stores on the Internet. For tangible goods, there is still a need for warehouses, but inventories are often dramatically reduced and space is allocated more efficiently due to IT advances, thus contributing to increased energy efficiency. Based on a 1998 case study on Amazon.com, it has been estimated that commercial building energy consumption per book sold is up to 16 times higher for a traditional store versus an online store (Romm, 1999). Hence, ICT is working for more efficient supply chain management, inventory reduction, substantial savings in time and materials handling, reduction of warehousing and administrative costs, and minimization of space and transport cost.

Teleworking is an important factor in reducing commercial building use. IT advances have helped and enabled businesses to intensify conveniences and flexibilities to their staff by allowing them to work far away from the office, often from home. For example, companies like IBM and AT&T have executed strategies to ensure alternative workplaces for their staff. These companies count significant cost savings from these steps because of reductions in energy consumption and square footage of commercial buildings and office space (Romm, 1999). Likewise, energy consumption in households needs to be critically assessed to make sure that the commercial energy savings are not offset by increased residential usage. In the residential uses, ICT has contributed a lot to curb electricity consumption, which has been largely successful due to sophisticated control mechanisms used for appliances and lighting. For example, digital energy management control systems and mechanisms have proved successful in cutting energy use with a reasonable rate of payback for businesses and residences.

In the industrial sector, e-government advances can help for more energy efficiency by leading to reduced inventories, better utilization of space and other capacities, and most significantly, supply chains. For example, in 2001, the AG Ford Motor Company, General Motors Corporation, and Daimler Chrysler significantly improved their supply routes and chains by making their purchasing market online and forming one of the world's largest online marketplaces, which is known as Covisint (now OPENTEXT). OPENTEXT allows these automobile makers to quickly share valuable information, such as usage history, inventory levels, use patterns, predictions, receipts, and other such information, to help in eliminating excess entry or register. This type of e-government solution allows industries to monitor and register real consumptions of energy, quick responses, efficient management in manufacturing, and energy utilization. Furthermore, the transportation sector has significant demands for energy and the positive impact of e-government can contribute by reducing energy use by energy efficient transportation substitutes. So the ICT enabled e-government can play a vital role in making transportation system inherently more energy efficient through the application of intelligent traffic systems (Sharma, 2011) and intelligent transportation systems (ITS) (Taming, 2018).

e-Government is an opportunity where education is imparted efficiently and effectively. Internet-based distant education and training are fruitful steps under the IT revolution and e-government. For example, the African Virtual University (AVU), an Internet-based university, provides online education, study materials, classes through video conferencing, and examinations and evaluation of answer sheets. The courses provided by AVU include social science, science, engineering, technology, and business administration (African Virtual University, 2018). If implemented on a wider scale in Africa, distance and e-learning could significantly contribute to sustainable development of the continent and the outcomes could spread across the world. In India, the Indira Gandhi National Open University (IGNOU, 2018) and other institutions have provided online courses and degrees (IGNOU, 2018). Apart from education, other facilities are certified through e-government mechanisms. For example, TARAhaat.com, an Internet portal with a full range of services, has targeted Indian rural villagers on issues like health, sanitation, education, women and children, community services, occupational guidance, e-commerce initiatives, weather conditions, and the weather forecast (http://tarahaat.com). TARAhaat.com has been designed to accommodate a large number of languages, literacy, and levels of understanding. The present communication is available in Hindi and English, but the portal is intended to reach all parts of the country, and thus checks vehicular pollution as the services are provided on the doorstep.

13.7 Challenges and Measures

e-Government initiatives and acts have a visible impact on all stakeholders of society. However, there are some limitations and problems in achieving the objects and reaching to all stakeholders. Firstly, production of IT equipment, such as semiconductors, release dangerous gases (acid fumes) to the atmosphere (Berkhout and Hertin, 2001). Secondly, only 2 per cent of the materials used in the production of computers become parts and the remainder are dumped as waste (Hilty and Ruddy, 2000). Thirdly, the transportation of IT equipment releases a carbon footprint that harms the environment (Choudhury and Veeramani, 2015). Fourthly, use of electricity energy by the ICT equipment while in operation. And fifthly, the danger of an increase in e-wastes (Choudhury and Veeramani, 2015). Sixthly, inequalities or "Information Gap" in the pattern of distribution and dissemination of information and information technology (https://pdfs.semanticscholar.org).

However, there are also avenues to address and resolve these issues, and e-government initiatives mix both energy and environment together to give a better solution to global climate change, energy issues, and sustainability. In many countries, a different matrix is used in measuring e-government for sustainable development: both in developed and developing countries. The priorities and obstacles for e-government implementation are country-specific, and thus, solutions are country-specific. The contribution of e-government for sustainable development can be interpreted through meaningful services, which are accessible and practicable through affordable means. The direct and/or proxy indicators can be utilized for measuring the effectiveness and success of e-government policies and e-services, as well as their impact.

The e-government initiatives focus on critical interventions for developing transformative efficiencies of government organizations and institutions to drive for changes, while avoiding wasteful investment of technologies.

The political will, along with institutional coordination and long-term commitment, is required for dealing with interrelated sustainable development issues and challenges. Strong leadership and commitment at all the levels of government—national, provincial, and local—could be a pivotal force behind the ICT revolution. Nurturing a sense of communication among various agencies is integral for a collaborative and responsive administration to ensure a well-integrated and balanced approach for sustainable development dimensions and challenges. The cooperation across various agencies of the government and civil society can help to address and resolve sustainable development challenges, both targeted and personalized. In addition, consciousness among the people for e-government advantages, and usage and benefits from a sustainable development perspective, will make ICT act more effectively on energy saving and the sustainable environment (Pamlin and Thorslund, 2004).

13.8 Conclusion

The innovation fostered through public and private mechanisms has widely created the level for the success of global sustainability requirements; but, in many cases, ICTs have proven inadequacies and limitations in streamlining sustainable development. Countries have taken steps in facing the challenges and opportunities provided by the emergence of the global IT industry. No growth can be achieved without a conducive environment being set in place by the government or public authorities. Hence, the formulation of a coherent national policy on information establishes norms and regulations, which facilitate competition and investing, and overall, a lasting political solution and stability of the natural environment and energy security. Many countries, particularly developing countries, are facing these issues before they can benefit from the opportunities and benefits offered by e-governance.

References

Abhiyan, G.S. & Gaon, S.S.S. www.mygov.in/, Ministry of Panchayati Raj, Government of India (Accessed on April 1, 2018).

African Virtual University (AVU). www.avu.org/avuweb/en/ (Accessed on March 22, 2018).

Baum, S. & Mahizhnan, A., 2014. Government-with-you: e-Government in Singapore, 2014, www.igi-global.com/chapter/government-with-you/110318 (Accessed on January 10, 2018).

Berkhout, F. & Hertin, J., 2001. Impacts of information and communication technologies on environmental sustainability: Speculations and evidence. Report to the OECD, University of Sussex, UK, http://www.oecd.org/sti/inno/1897156.pdf (Accessed on March 15, 2018).

Choudhury, A.K. & Veeramani, S., 2015. Information technology: Impacts on environment and sustainable development, www.researchgate.net/publication/273130988 (Accessed on March 17, 2018).

Credé, A. & Mansell, R., 1998, Information technology for sustainable development. Knowledge societies—in a nutshell, www.idrc.ca/en/book/knowledge-societies-nutshell-information-technology-sustainable-development (Accessed on March 1, 2018).

Dao, V., Langella, I., & Carbo, J., 2001. From green to sustainability: Information technology and an integrated sustainable framework. *The Journal of Strategic Information Systems*, 20(1), 63–79.

E-Government for Sustainable Development, Report of the Expert Group Meeting.

Farid, S., 2015. The role of technology in the sustainable economic development—The case of Africa, manuscript.advancejournals.org/uploads/.../Manuscript/354.pdf (Accessed on February 22, 2018).

Government of India. https://swachhbharat.mygov.in/ (Accessed on April 1, 2018).

Haghseta, F.S., 2003. Information technology and sustainable development: Understanding linkages in theory and practice. https://gssd.mit.edu/sites/default/files/imce/it_and_sustainable_development.pdf (Accessed on March 1, 2018).

Hilty, L. & Ruddy, T., 2000. Towards a sustainable information society. *Informatik/Informatique*, 4, 2–9. (Accessed on March 15, 2018).

IGNOU., 2018. IGNOU: The People's University. www.ignou.ac.in (Accessed on February 1, 2018).

Negroponte, N., 1995. *Being Digital*. Knopf: New York, NY.

Pamlin, D. & Thorslund, E., 2004. IT and sustainable development-a central issue for the future, www.wsis.ethz.ch/pamlin.pdf (Accessed on February 22, 2018).

Pokorny, G.J., 2012, Using e-Governance to advance sustainable development, UNOSD and National Information Society Agency (NIA), www.unosd.org/content/documents/Using%20e-Gov%20to%20Advance%20Sustainable%20Development_(20121111_Gregory_Pokorny)_Final_Draft.pdf (Accessed on September 10, 2018).

Revkineeb, A.C., February 26, 2002. Climate plan is criticized as a risky bet, *The New York Times*. www.nytimes.com/2002/02/26/science/climate-plan-is-criticized-as-a-risky-bet.html (Accessed on January 15, 2018).

Romm, J., 1999. *The Internet Economy and Global Warming*. The Center for Energy and Climate Solutions: Annandale, VA.

Sharma, A., Chaki, R. and Bhattacharya, U., Applications of wireless sensor network in intelligent traffic system: A review, *2011 3rd International Conference on Electronics Computer Technology*, Kanyakumari, 2011, pp. 53–57.

SMART 2020: Enabling the low carbon economy in the information age, a report by the Climate Group on Behalf of the Global eSustainability Initiative (GeSI), 2008. www.theclimategroup.org/sites/default/files/archive/files/Smart2020Report.pdf (Accessed on January 9, 2018).

Smart Cities Mission, Ministry of Housing and Urban Affairs, Government of India. http://smartcities.gov.in/content/innerpage/what-is-smart-city.php (Accessed on March 22, 2018).

Swachh Bharat Mission-Gramin, 2014. http://swachhbharatmission.gov.in/sbmcms/index.htm Ministry of Drinking Water and Sanitation, Government of India. (Accessed on February 5, 2018).

TARAhaat: Helping People Help Themselves. http://tarahaat.com/Weather.aspx (Accessed on March 28, 2018).

The potential uses of ICTs for sustainable development, n.d. www.sussex.ac.uk/spru/documents/c5 (Accessed on March 18, 2018).

United Nations, 2015. E-Government for Sustainable Development: Report of the Expert Group Meeting, Department of Economic and Social Affairs, Division for Public Administration and Development Management.

14

Building a Smart and Energy Efficient World: An Era of Internet of Things

Rahul Saxena, Monika Jain, and Siddharth Jaidka

CONTENTS

14.1 Role of IoT in Digital Transformation: Advancing e-Governance

In this growing technological world of numerous computing devices, anything that can be seen around us can be put on the network in one sense or other. So the term or phrase *Internet of Things* (IoT) has transformed to *Internet of Everything.* With various technologies coming into play, whether it is wireless sensor networks, cloud computing, or Big Data, everything interconnects to complete the job. As per the *Gartner Inc.* prediction [1] *"8.4 billion connected things will be in use worldwide in 2017, up 31 percent from 2016, and will reach 20.4 billion by 2020. Total spending on endpoints and services will reach almost $2 trillion in 2017."* Table 14.1 shows the capital investment in IoT by big information technology (IT) market players like Google, Apple, Amazon, Microsoft, and so on, and the yearly rise in it.

Therefore, from the above discussion, it is evident that the upcoming generation of technology has a web of interconnected things, and thus, has a big role to play in sociological and economic development. As society and human living is heavily dependent on technological devices and the automated environment, its judicious use is equally important in the conservation of energy. The rest of our discussion in this chapter will be focused on how IoT devices can be used for smart electrical appliances in order to facilitate their ease of use and to save energy.

TABLE 14.1

IoT Units Installed Base by Category (Millions of Units) [1]

Category	2016	2017	2018	2020
Consumer	3,963.0	5,244.3	7,036.3	12,863.0
Business: cross-industry	1,102.1	1,501.0	2,132.6	4,381.4
Business: vertical-specific	1,316.6	1,635.4	2,027.7	3,171.0
Total	**6,381.8**	**8,380.6**	**11,196.6**	**20,415.4**

14.2 Internet of Electrical Energy: IoT as IoE

Certain facts and figures have been compiled from the Cambridge Green Challenge by the Environment and Energy team on the official webpage of the University of Cambridge to find out how much energy one can save from simple actions such as switching off lights and equipment [2]:

- In 2014 to 2015, the University of Cambridge had an expenditure of £16 million (British pounds) on energy. To be precise, the university spends £1,865 every hour.
- Electrical leakage is referred to as energy not being utilized by mobile phone chargers, laptops, and desktops when they are not getting charged, but the energy is still getting consumed as they have been left plugged in. Only 5 per cent of the power taken up by a phone charger is actually used up, while the remaining 95 per cent gets wasted when it is remains plugged in.
- Over 500 pages can be laser printed with the amount of energy wasted when a PC monitor is left on for a night.
- Leaving the fan on for one night wastes enough energy to:
  - keep an LCD TV on for the same duration;
  - provide power to an iPhone for the next 25 years; and
  - keep a laptop on for a year.

There are many such instances where a simple action of switching off the appliance can not only save money and energy but contribute to the nation and our planet as well. Wastage of energy not only harms us economically, but it has adverse effects on our environment too.

14.3 State of the Art

Systems already exist that can control home appliances using Android based phones/tablets. Each system has its unique features. Currently, certain companies are officially registered and are working to provide better home automation system features. The following models describe the work being performed by others.

N. Sriskanthan [3] explained the model for home automation using Bluetooth via PC. Unfortunately, the system lacks the support of mobile technology. Muhammad Izhar Ramli [4] designed a prototype electrical device control system using the web. They also set the server with auto restart if the server condition was down. Hasan [5] developed a telephone and PIC remote-controlled device for controlling a device's pin check algorithm had been introduced when it was with a cable network but not with wireless communication. Amul Jadhav [6] developed an application in a universal XML format that could be easily ported to any other mobile device rather than targeting a single platform. Han et al. [7] proposed an intelligent smart energy-controlled environment for consumers using ZigBee and IEEE 802.15.4 standards for device control and energy management. Hongyu et al. [8] presented a smart home control system with hardware level modifications using the S3C2440 processor hardware platform, which equipped an embedded Linux operating system to design a residential gateway. Experimental results showed that the system had simple wiring, good mobility, and could be used to implement local and remote wireless control of a smart home system. T. Saravanan et al. [9] discussed how to provide better security for home automation and to save energy as well as making a flexible environment for individuals.

A lot of work is already in progress and the subject has a vast scope for improvisation, innovation, and improvement to the proposed systems. The purpose of our study is to have a familiarity with the field of IoT and to explore it by targeting an application with its real-time implications, challenges, and future possibilities to enhance it either in terms of applicability or improvement.

14.4 Architectural Layout to Build an IoT based Electrical Energy Controlling Mechanism

14.4.1 Related Technologies and Components

Before discussing the development and working aspects, we will try to explore the components and the related technologies in brief:

1. *Raspberry Pi*: The Raspberry Pi is a small minicomputer capable of transferring and processing data. It consists of GPIO pins to connect relay circuits and act as an interfacing entity between the hardware circuit and the software environment. As shown in Figure 14.1, the Raspberry Pi module consists of a processor (Broadcom BCM2835 SoC), an ethernet cable port, VGA port, Wi-Fi module, and all those things we need for a computer (Figure 14.1).
2. *Arduino microcontroller*: Basically, a single-board microcontroller and microcontroller kit for building a digital device's interactive system that can control and manage objects in the physical world (Figure 14.2).
3. *NRF24 mini SMD wireless module*: The mini size NRF24 (TW) wireless board, 12×18 mm, original Nordic NRF24L01 compatible, all the same way of use, the only differences with the original one are that the NRF24 can provide higher transmission power up to 7 dBm (0 dBm original) but the same power computation on the same transmission power level (Figure 14.3).
4. *Relay module*: A relay module acts as an instructor to the switches on an electrical board. A relay controls the poles and the contacts are handled by energizing the coil the way the user wants. Commonly open (NO) contacts energizes the circuit once the relay is put into action; the circuit is disconnected once the relay is inactive (Figure 14.4).

FIGURE 14.1
Raspberry Pi 3 B module.

FIGURE 14.2
Arduino nano with ATmega 32.

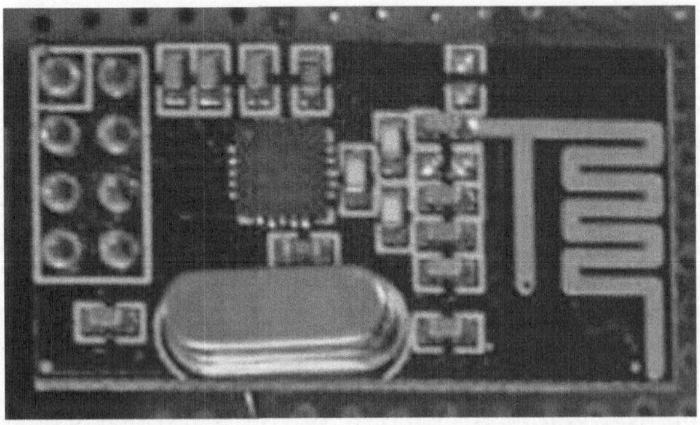

FIGURE 14.3
NRF24L01L long range wireless module (100 m, PA + SMA).

FIGURE 14.4
Relay module.

5. *Raspbian operating system*: The Raspbian operating system is based on software supported by Debian and optimized for the Raspberry Pi hardware. It consists of the set of basic programs and utilities that builds and compiles with the Raspberry Pi files to boot up the system. However, Raspbian provides more than a pure OS: it comes with over 35,000 packages and a pre-compiled software package bundled in a very nice format for simple installation on the Raspberry Pi.

14.4.2 System Interconnection and Working

As shown in Figure 14.5, the relays have been mounted and soldered on the board along with resistors and the NRF 24. To the side, we have the Arduino microcontroller to communicate the message to the relays as per the launch script. The Hi Power link unit is responsible for passing the power to activate the relays.

Figure 14.6 shows a basic layout that shows how different levels of the system are connected and interact. The instructions or the query is passed through the handheld device for accomplishing the required task. Here, the handheld Android device acts as the user interactive medium to the system. The query then reaches to the network router or cloud server from where it is forwarded to the designated IP address allotted by the Raspberry Pi. The Raspberry Pi then transfers the action to the connected relays either through Bluetooth or some other short-range communication protocol. The query passed by the user is an input to the Python script, which guides the Raspberry Pi to actuate the required relay and make the appliance operate in the required mode to which that particular relay is connected. The NRF 24 module has bi channels to read in messages and pass the action. So, the Raspberry Pi first reads in the status by communicating through Arduino about each relay and then passes the required action as guided by the user.

14.4.3 Hardware Implementation

The Raspberry Pi receives the instruction from the user through the application, which it communicates to the Arduino on the board. The Arduino then activates the supply voltage to cut on or off as per the instruction, which then sets the n-p-n transistor into action to operate the relay.

FIGURE 14.5
On board connections for board 1.

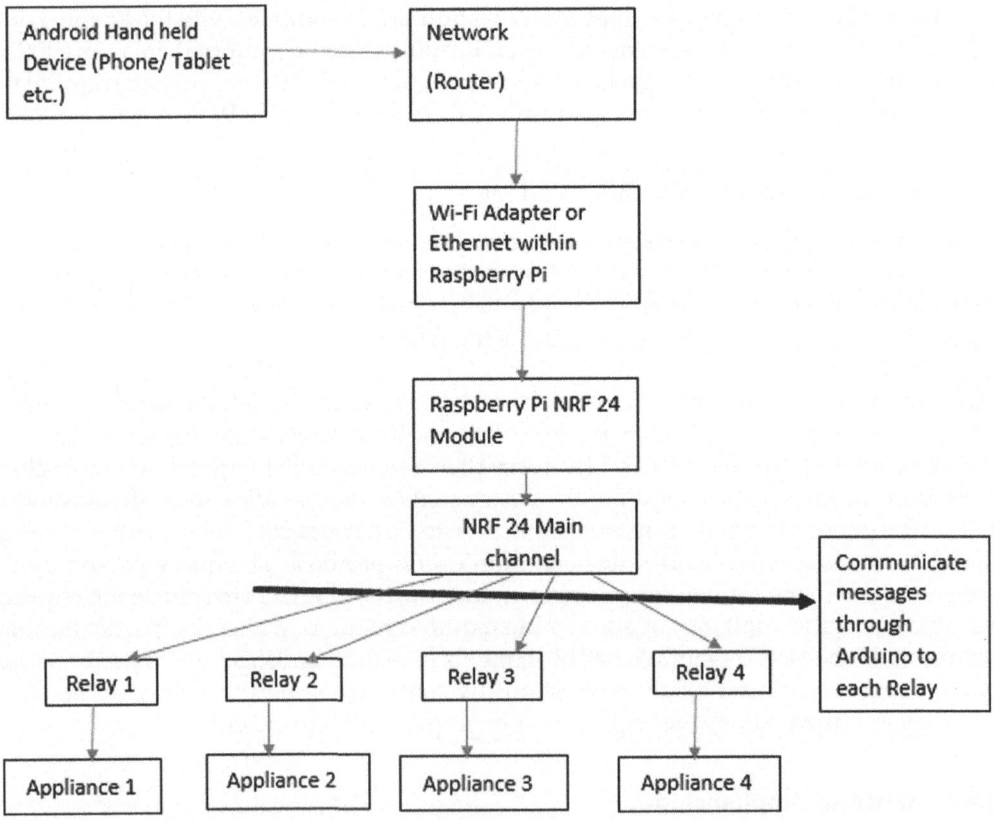

FIGURE 14.6
Block diagram of system interconnection.

Let us consider the load part of the circuit as per Figure 14.7. The hot wire from the mains is connected to at least one terminal. Other terminals of the appliance are connected to the open (NO) contact of the 5 V relay. The remaining neutral wire has a connection to the relay's common contact (COMM). Here, each relay controlling an appliance is of 5 V. So, as shown in Figure 14.6, we have four devices corresponding to the four relays, and thus, we are using a separate power supply unit of 5 V to supply power to all the relays simultaneously [10].

14.4.4 Software Implementation

The previous section discussed how the hardware components are set to function upon receiving the threshold voltage and current. Now, we will discuss how we actually generate the triggers through the software environment in order to facilitate the required activity to happen at the hardware level. To facilitate this, we will require various services and software utilities, which we will look at one by one.

1. *MQTT*: MQTT is a hub and spoke protocol for sending messages among IoT devices. Clients can subscribe or submit messages to a central server, referred to as a broker. One alternative for MQTT messaging on the Raspberry Pi is just to put in mosquitto! One could use the identical mosquitto_pub and mosquitto_sub command line tools to speak with an MQTT server. The other option is to use an MQTT library for the favored language. This service is required to basically establish communication between the devices by placing data on the channels. To start the communication, as soon as the user makes any request, the channel is subscribed through the command *mosquitto_sub*.
2. *OpenHAB*: OpenHAB is a software for integrating unique home automation systems and technology into one single solution that lets in overarching automation regulations and gives uniform user interfaces (Figure 14.8).

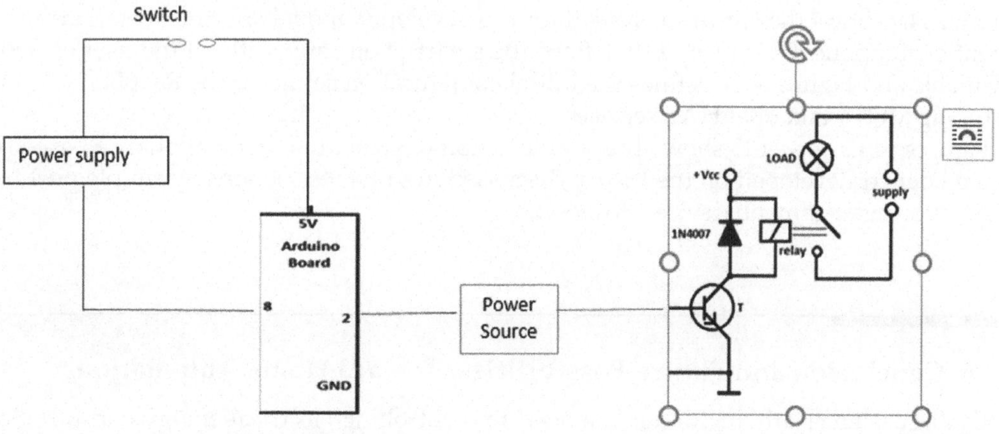

FIGURE 14.7
Electrical interconnection between relay and Arduino.

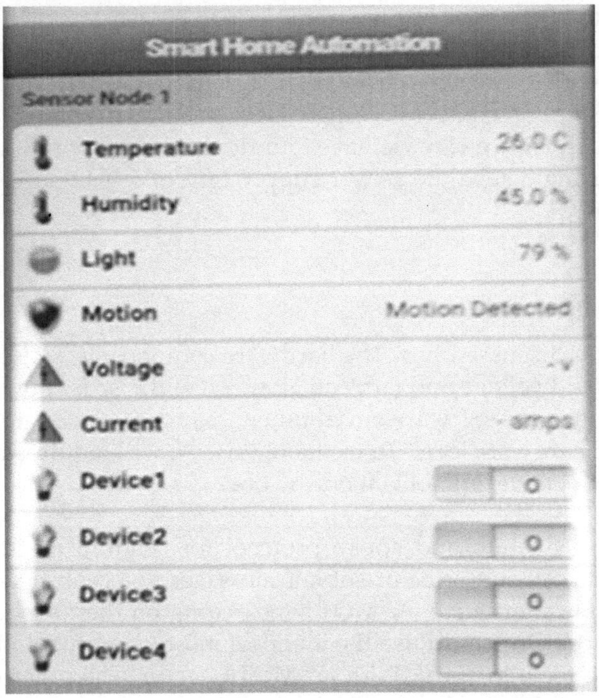

FIGURE 14.8
OpenHAB basic UI.

14.5 Putting the System into Action

14.5.1 The System as a Whole

Figure 14.9 shows the entire subsystem for the developed model and the overall arrangement of components. Figure 14.10 defines the smart phone app with all the user controls available and Figure 14.11 defines the initial configuration setup for the Raspberry Pi initializing MQTT and openHAB services.

Figures 14.12 and 14.13 shows the simple action of switching on an appliance based on the modelled developed on the theory discussed in previous sections by simple pushing the button against menu device 1 to *on state*.

14.6 Conclusion and Future Possibilities: Toward Home Automation

This discussion clearly highlights the need for controlling electrical energy consumption using handheld devices. The concept gives rise to the notion of the smart home and smart city construction, which can help manage energy to its best. The idea has n-dimensions and can be worked out in every domain that we can think about, such as healthcare, agriculture,

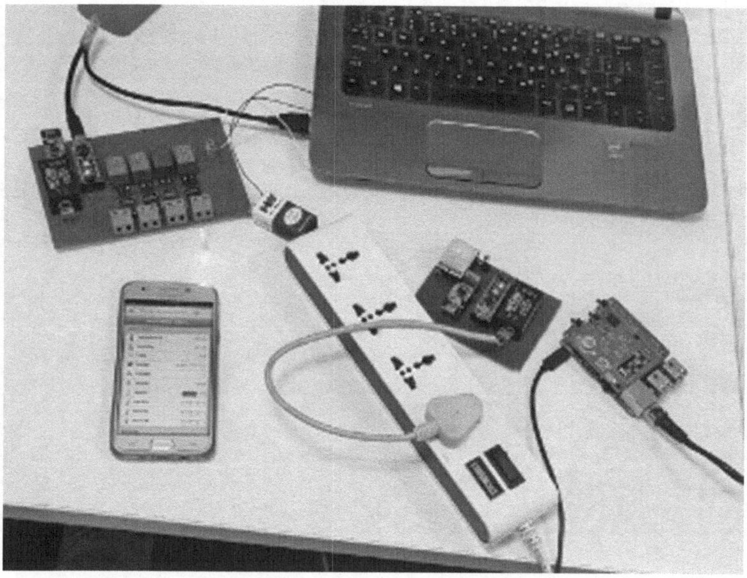

FIGURE 14.9
Overall system setup.

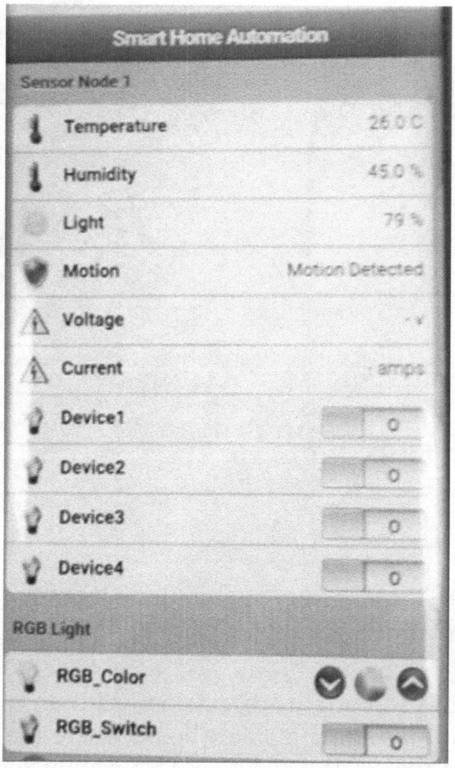

FIGURE 14.10
Smart home app for user control.

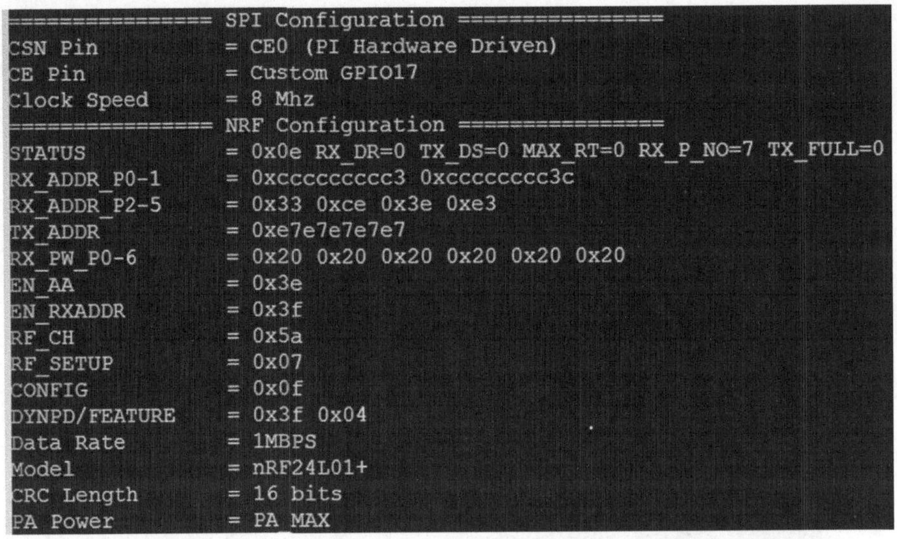
```
================ SPI Configuration ================
CSN Pin          = CE0 (PI Hardware Driven)
CE Pin           = Custom GPIO17
Clock Speed      = 8 Mhz
================ NRF Configuration ================
STATUS           = 0x0e RX_DR=0 TX_DS=0 MAX_RT=0 RX_P_NO=7 TX_FULL=0
RX_ADDR_P0-1     = 0xccccccccc3 0xcccccccc3c
RX_ADDR_P2-5     = 0x33 0xce 0x3e 0xe3
TX_ADDR          = 0xe7e7e7e7e7
RX_PW_P0-6       = 0x20 0x20 0x20 0x20 0x20 0x20
EN_AA            = 0x3e
EN_RXADDR        = 0x3f
RF_CH            = 0x5a
RF_SETUP         = 0x07
CONFIG           = 0x0f
DYNPD/FEATURE    = 0x3f 0x04
Data Rate        = 1MBPS
Model            = nRF24L01+
CRC Length       = 16 bits
PA Power         = PA_MAX
```

FIGURE 14.11
Initial configuration for Raspberry Pi.

FIGURE 14.12
App and hardware status before activating device.

automobile automation, and so on. This discussion has been restricted to the use of IoT devices and technologies in building a smart home where the electrical devices can be controlled and managed using an Android device from anywhere. We had a walkthrough of the components and technologies involved and how the system can be built. The system uses radio wave communication between the components in order to increase the transmission range and prevent interference of the signals, as in the case of Bluetooth, as every

FIGURE 14.13
App and hardware status after activating device.

radio module has bi-channels to read the instructions and transmit the action. The design has certain optimizations, such as instead of using only the Raspberry Pi to control the electrical devices, the design has an Arduino microcontroller to instruct the relays and the Raspberry Pi as the main central hub for communication over the cloud through the user interface. Using the Raspberry Pi to control the devices will certainly add to the cost.

Anything that has been developed always has certain limitations and scope for future enhancements. The model can certainly be further enhanced both at the implementation level as well as the applicability level:

1. The idea can be expanded to help out farmers by developing a wireless sensor-based model for the determination of moisture content in the soil and turning on the sprinklers if needed. Development of an air pollution control management system is another application.
2. A transistor-based relay might not be best for long time use as there will usually be noise within the relay coil. A suitable option could be the use of extra isolation like an opto-isolator or absolutely removing the electromechanical relay and replacing it with a stable nation relay.
3. The proposed model has 5 V relay and thus cannot be used to switch on heavy machines and appliances like AC. For this we require an opto-isolator of at least 20 A current capacity.
4. The model can further be enhanced at application level by adding an additional module to get an estimate of the power consumption by each appliance.

References

1. Gartner Newsroom Press Release, "Gartner Says 8.4 Billion Connected 'Things' Will Be in Use in 2017, Up 31 Percent from 2016", Egham, UK, February, (2017) [Online]. Available: www.gartner.com/newsroom/id/3598917
2. The Cambridge Green Challenge, "Environment and Energy", University of Cambridge, (2015) [Online]. Available: www.environment.admin.cam.ac.uk/facts-figures
3. Sriskanthan, N., Tan, F., & Karande, A. (2002). Bluetooth based home automation system. *Microprocessors and Microsystems*, 26(6), 281–289.
4. Ramli, M. I., Wahab, A., Helmy, M., & Ahmad, N. (2006). Towards smart home: Control electrical devices online, *International Conference on Science and Technology: Application in Industry and Education*, Uganda, pp. 1–7.
5. Erol, Y., Balik, H. H., Inal, S., & Karabulut, D. (2007). Safe and secure PIC based remote control application for intelligent home. *IJCSNS*, 7(5), 179.
6. Jadhav, A., Anand, S., Dhangare, N., & Wagh, K. S. (2012). Universal mobile application development (UMAD) on home automation. *Marathwada Mitra Mandal's Institute of Technology, University of Pune, India Network and Complex Systems*, 2(2): 38–45.
7. Han, D. M. & Lim, J. H. (2010). Smart home energy management system using IEEE 802.15. 4 and ZigBee. *IEEE Transactions on Consumer Electronics*, 56(3): 1403–1410.
8. Zhang, S. Y., Zhu, J., & Xiao, P. P. (2016). Design of smart home control system based on ARM and ZigBee. In *Mechanics and Mechatronics (ICMM2015) Proceedings of the 2015 International Conference on Mechanics and Mechatronics (ICMM2015)*, Hunan, China, pp. 1002–1009.
9. Saravanan, T., Nagarajan, R., Kumar, R., Prakash, V., & Rajkumar, R. (2017). IoT based smart home design for power and security management. *Asian Journal of Applied Science and Technology (AJAST)*, 1(2): 260–264.
10. Electronics Hub "How to Use Relay" [Online]. Available: www.electronicshub.org/use-5v-relay-arduino/

15

Patient Monitoring System using Enhanced EERDT and SIMPLE Routing Protocols in WBAN: An e-Governance Perspective

Jyoti Anand, Deepak Sethi, and Partha Pratim Bhattacharya

CONTENTS

15.1 Introduction to WBAN

Advancements in recent wireless technology, integrated circuits, and autonomous sensing of physiological parameters gave birth to the human monitoring system or the short-range wireless communication network called wireless body area networks (WBANs) [1, 2]. It is also known as a patient monitoring system, which facilitates electronic services like electronic-governance (e-governance). In the health sector, e-governance deals with technical developments of monitoring services of patients. It comprises four main factors: people, resources, processes, and technology. By using information and communication technology, e-governance remotely improves services related to health. For monitoring health-related issues, various tiny, intelligent, low powered, and invasive/non-invasive sensor nodes are placed inside or outside the human body. There is a sink node, which works as a data aggregator and further transmits to the desired location through the Internet, as shown in Figure 15.1. Deployed nodes in WBANs are intended for early detection of various types of life-threatening diseases, for example. cancer and asthma, using different types of sensor nodes like EEGs, ECGs, pulse rate, temperature, and so on [3]. Elderly and disabled individuals mostly benefit through remote check-ups, with doctors prescribing the patient according to sensed information sent by the sink node [4]. Due to the heterogeneous nature of sensor nodes in WBANs, data rates and power requirements are different from other wireless technology discussed in the next section. It follows common network architecture, called star topology [5]. Due to the high mobility nature of WBANs and stringent requirements on reliability and energy efficiency, routing approaches of wireless sensor networks (WSNs) cannot be used [6].

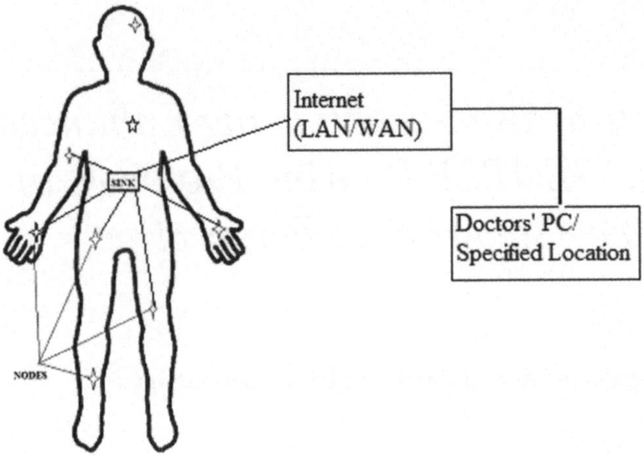

FIGURE 15.1
Deployment of nodes in WBAN.

In this chapter, the requirement of power and data rates and a review of some existing routing algorithms of WBANs are presented in the following sections. Performance of EERDT (energy efficient and reliable data transfer) [7] and SIMPLE (stable increased-throughput multihop link efficiency) [8] routing protocols are enhanced by applying the square root function over the sum of average residual energy of nodes and squaring their cost function. This approach leads to an increased number of packets sent to the base station and the stability period of the network is also increased in both EERDT [7] and SIMPLE [8].

15.2 Requirement of Power and Data in WBAN

As WBAN follows a standard of IEEE 802.15.6, which is based on an ultrawide base band, it means that lower power is enabled and communication is of a limited range [9, 10]. WBAN uses several transmission technologies like Bluetooth (IEEE 802.15.1), Zigbee (IEEE 802.15.4), and WLAN (wireless local area network), and all these technologies work on the same band: 2.4 GHz ISM [11]. Transmission range of WBAN is up to 3 meters according to IEEE 802.15.6 [11]. Requirements of data rates and power in WBANs have been compared with other wireless technology as shown in Figure 15.2. The range of data rates of sensor nodes in WBANs is from 1 Kbit/s to 10 Mbit/s [12].

15.3 Literature Review

Gill R. Tsouri proposed a global routing protocol in [5], with a novel link cost function to increase the lifetime of network in WBANs. To compute the link cost function, Dijkstra's algorithm is used, which helps to balance the energy. In this work, all nodes deplete their

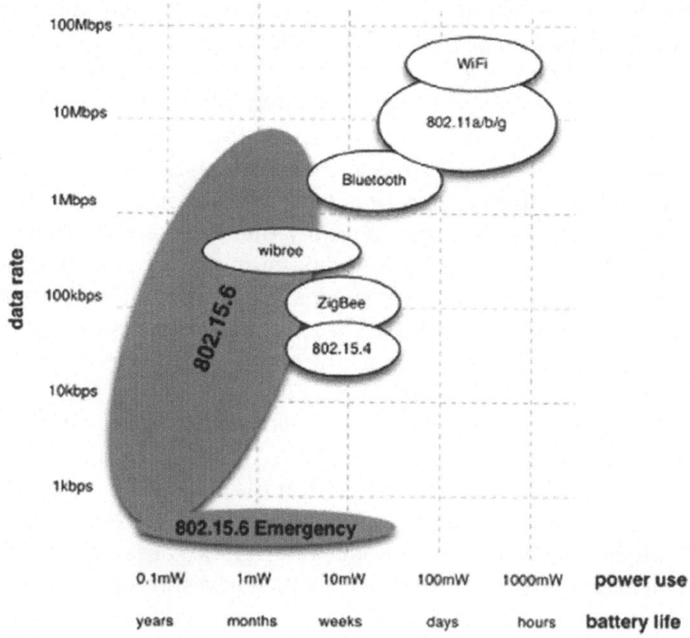

FIGURE 15.2
Data rate and power requirement in WBAN.

energy at the same time due to balancing the energy of nodes in the network. In [7], to reduce the packet loss, hierarchical routing is used, while single hop routing is used to improve the quality of services and directly transmit the critical data to the base station. Cluster head is selected with maximum cost function after the first round. To maximize the stability period and throughput of the network, cost function is evaluated using residual energy of the nodes and threshold value. A reliable, power efficient and high-throughput multihop routing protocol is proposed in [8], in which consumption of energy is at the minimum, and the stability period of the network is increased through multihop topology. A parent node (forwarder) is selected with minimum cost function based on the maximum residual energy of nodes and the minimum distance to the sink. A time slot is assigned to each child node to transmit the sensed data to the forwarder node in its own time. In this way, consumption of energy is minimized and the stability period of the network is increased. In [9], cross-layer optimization performance is investigated based on a real-life example by Samiya and others. The best route is selected to transmit data at the network layer based on the channel state information from the physical layer. Shortest path routing and cooperative multipath routing are the two dynamic routing techniques that are used for reliable data transfer and less packet error rate in WBANs. An extension of SIMPLE [8], which supports the mobility nature of the human body called iMSIMPLE, is proposed in [13] by Nadeem Javaid and others. Linear programming is introduced to reduce the energy consumption and higher data transfer to the forwarder node. At first, energy consumptions of the forwarder and child node is analyzed and then a mathematical linear programming model is used for less energy consumption of nodes in the WBANs. In paper [14], a probabilistic store-forward packet routing protocol is designed using a stochastic link cost that supports human body mobility. The main aim of this algorithm is end-to-end packet delays and end-to-end hop count so that the transmitted energy is minimized. In [15], an energy efficient network coding approach for a cooperative solution is proposed using decode and forward relays sensor nodes. The different messages coming from different sources are combined and generate one message by relay node. And then generated messages are transmitted to the destination, this scheme is called decode and forward-network coding (DF-NC). Here, the relay node works in the half-duplex mode. This approach uses TDMA (time division multiple access) to send the messages at source node, like in SIMPLE [8]. Using this approach, minimum energy is consumed over other existing non-network coding approaches because DF-NC requires only one time slot to forward the message and use direct transmission for WBANs. So, maximum energy is utilized and less time is required to transmit the sensed data from source to destination. In [16], authors N. Javaid and others proposed LAEEBA and COLAEEBA routing protocols to improve the network lifetime and energy consumptions as well as the path loss of network in WBANs. There is a forwarder node in LAEEBA (link aware energy efficient routing for body area), which is selected on the basis of residual energy of the sensor nodes. While COLAEEBA (cooperative link aware energy efficient routing for body area) works on the basis of cooperation, and source nodes are utilized more than one link at the same time. In [17], the authors proposed a dynamic resource allocation scheme to avoid the interferences amongst coexisting WBAN using a table in which activity of nodes interference are updated. The authors also provide a mathematical analysis to validate its efficiency and a probabilistic approach to reduce the interference level. To avoid interferences among WBANs, a complete orthogonal channel is assigned to all sensor nodes in the network, and at the same time, other sensor nodes are allowed to use the whole time slot until all are occupied. Therefore. this proposed scheme is efficient in reusing the channel and maintaining the interference level among sensor nodes in WBANs. In [18], a priority- based energy aware routing is proposed that effectively transfers the information to the sink node while supporting the mobility nature in WBANs. A parent node is selected based on the cost function, considering priority, residual energy, and distance of node. The distance factor helps in packet delivery from child to forwarder node and priority helps to select the best path to forward the critical data. In [19], a cluster-based routing protocol is proposed by the authors to increase the stability of the network and decrease the energy consumption of sensor nodes in WBANs, inspired by the MODLEACH protocol of WSNs. Single hop and multihop communication is used to send the emergency and normal data respectively to the sink node. Threshold value is used to select the cluster head. It will remain cluster head for the next round if the energy of cluster head is greater than threshold value. So, there is no need to select the new cluster head and, in this way, energy is saved. In [20], the authors design an improved routing protocol for effective data transmission and consider even energy consumption called the "Even Energy Consumption and Back Side Routing Protocol" (EECBSR). The main objective behind this routing technique is to increase the lifetime of the network, energy efficiency, and path loss of the node located at the back side of the body. Its aim is to reduce the problems that arise in M-ATTEMPT, such as not supporting mobility, and the operation runs parallel in this work. The authors use the standard deviation function instead of cost function used in SIMPLE [8] and select the minimum standard deviation value for the forwarder node. In this work, to achieve the higher connection probability, sensor nodes are also implanted on the back side of the body.

1. *Research gap*: WBANs have to face many demanding requirements in terms of delivery delay of data packets, low powered sensor nodes, and network lifetime. A lot of routing techniques is proposed to achieve these demanding requirements. From the previously mentioned review of papers, it can be said that not a single

routing protocol is sufficient to meet the basic requirements and quality of services of WBNA. Almost all authors focused on the energy efficient routing technology for WBANs based on a cost-efficient function. The mobility of the human body and the effect of radiation on tissues are the two major concerns of designing an energy efficient routing protocol.

2. *Motivation*: WBAN is a human monitoring system to detect physiological signs in the body in which battery constraints sensor nodes are implanted. Successful transmission of sensed data to the destination is very important. My motivation behind this work is to enhance the work of EERDT [7] and SIMPLE [4] and increase the throughput and network lifetime. A forwarder is selected to transmit the sensed data to the sink node by using a cost-efficient function. This is because if a sensor node directly transmits the sensed data, more energy is consumed and network stability is decreased.

15.4 Enhanced Work of EERDT and SIMPLE

In this work, deployment of nodes all over the body is the same as EERDT [7] and SIMPLE [8]. Eight sensor nodes are deployed on different parts of the body such as the head, palm, chest, arm, leg, knee, as shown in Figure 15.3, which have equal power and computational capabilities. Two sensor nodes, ECG and EEG, directly transmit the sensed data to the sink node, shown as diamond symbol in Figure 15.3. The remaining sensor nodes transmit the sensed data through multihop routing using a forwarder (parent node). There is a sink node, which is placed at the mid part of the body.

1. *Step-by-step process of enhanced EERDT as follows*:
   a. Initially, all sensor nodes are deployed with equal initial energy, i.e., 0.5 J. Node 2 and node 4 are used to transmit the sensitive data. Hence, these two nodes use single hop routing.
   b. After that, a threshold value is used to select the forwarder with maximum cost function, given as follows:

$$\text{Cost\_function}_{\text{eerdt}}(\text{j})=\text{sqrt}\left(\text{AVG\_RE}+\left((\text{AVG\_CF})^2\right)\right) \tag{15.1}$$

   where:

j	is the particular node, for which cost function is to be calculated.
AVG_RE	is the average of residual energy of nodes. And,
AVG_CF	is the average of cost function, i.e., (S(j).E/Eo) used in EERDT [7]. Here, S(j).E is the residual energy of particular node j and Eo is the initial energy of nodes.

   c. Once the forwarder has been selected, the remaining nodes find the distance to the forwarder using Equation (15.2) and to the sink node using Equation (15.3), and transmit the sensed data to the respective forwarder or sink node. After that, energy consumed by sensor nodes is calculated using Equation (15.4).

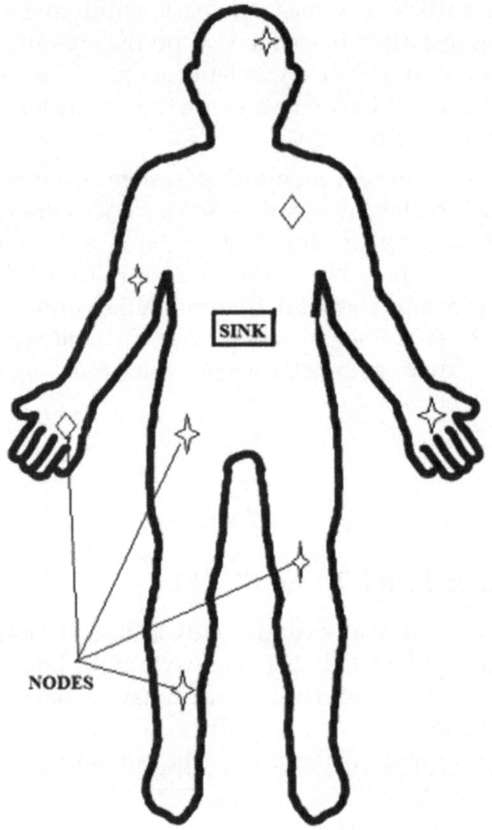

FIGURE 15.3
Node deployment in the human body (enhanced EERDT and enhanced SIMPLE).

$$d_{NF}(j)=\sqrt{((S(j).xd\text{-}S(node\_num).xd)^2)\text{-}(S(j).yd\text{-}S(node\_num).yd)^2)} \quad (15.2)$$

$$d_{NS}(j)=\sqrt{((S(j).xd\text{-}sink.x)^2\text{-}(S(j).yd\text{-}sink.y)^2)} \quad (15.3)$$

$$Trans\_er^*(p)+Amp\_er^*p^*(Min\_dist^2_{(dNF\text{-}dNS)}) \quad (15.4)$$

where:

Trans_er = Energy consumed by transmitter to transmit the data.

Amp_er = Energy consumed by amplifier to amplify the data.

p = Required number of data bits that need to be transferred.

$Min\_dist_{(dNF\text{-}dNS)}$ = Choose minimum distance from node to forwarder or sink node.

d. In the next phase, forwarder node aggregates the data and further transmits to the base station. After that, forwarder node calculates its energy, using Equation (15.5).

$$((Trans\_er+Rcv\_er+Data\_agg)^*p+Amp\_er^*p^*(d^2_{FS})) \quad (15.5)$$

where:

Trans_er = Energy consumed by transmitter to transmit the data.

Rcv_er = Energy consumed by receiver to receive the data.

Data_agg = Energy consumed to aggregate the data.

Amp_er = Energy consumed by amplifier to amplify the data.

p = Required number of data bits that need to be transferred.

d_{FS} = Distance from forwarder to sink node.

e. Once the first round is completed, the forwarder is selected on the basis of cost function, using (15.1) in the next round. After that, sensor nodes transmit the data to the sink node or forwarder and calculate their consumed energy using Equation (15.5).
f. Steps 2 to 5 will be repeated until the all nodes deplete their energy or the number of rounds have been finished.

2. *Step-by-step process of enhanced SIMPLE as follows:*

wAll procedures and network parameters are the same as enhanced EERDT, except cost function and equations of energy consumed by the forwarder node and other sensor nodes. Cost function is estimated using (15.6) and energy consumed by sensor nodes and the forwarder is selected with the maximum value of cost function and evaluated using (15.7) and (15.8) respectively.

$$\text{Cost\_function}_{\text{simple}}(j)=\text{sqrt}(\text{AVG\_RE}+((\text{AVG\_CF})^2)) \tag{15.6}$$

where:

j	is the particular node, for which cost function is to be calculated.
AVG_RE	is the average of residual energy of nodes. And,
AVG_CF	is the average of cost function, i.e., (d(j)/S(j).E) used in SIMPLE [8]. Here, S(j).E is the residual energy of nodes and Eo is the initial energy of nodes.

$$\text{Trans\_er}^*(p)+\text{Amp\_er}^*3.38^*p^*(\text{Min\_dist}^{3.38}_{(\text{dNF-dNS})}) \tag{15.7}$$

where:

Trans_er = Energy consumed by transmitter to transmit the data.

Amp_er = Energy consumed by amplifier to amplify the data.

p = Required number of data bits that need to be transferred.

$\text{Min\_dist}_{(\text{dNF-dNS})}$= Distance from node to forwarder or sink node.

$$\left((\text{Trans\_er}+\text{Rcv\_er}+\text{Data\_agg})^*p+\text{Amp\_er}^*3.38^*p^*\left(d_{FS}^{3.38}\right)\right) \tag{15.8}$$

where:

Trans_er = Energy consumed by transmitter to transmit the data.

Rcv_er = Energy consumed by receiver to receive the data.

Data_agg = Energy consumed to aggregate the data.

Amp_er = Energy consumed by amplifier to amplify the data.

p = Required number of data bits that need to be transferred.

d_{FS} = Distance from forwarder to sink node.

Generally, there are two types of radio model that are used, which are given in Table 15.1. In this work, the first order radio model, named Nordic (nRF2401A) is used because it consumes less energy and performs better as compared with another called Chipcon (CC2420) [13]. All necessary radio models and network parameters to simulate this work are provided in Tables 15.1 and 15.2 respectively.

15.5 Performance Evaluation

To evaluate the performance of enhanced EERDT and SIMPLE, we will use four different criteria:

1. *Residual energy*: To calculate the residual energy of nodes after each round, subtract the initial energy of nodes and energy of nodes after completing the round.
2. *Throughput*: Total number of packets sent to the base station is the throughput of the network.
3. *Number of dead nodes*: If the energy level of node became 0 after a round, then that node is a dead node.
4. *First and all nodes dead*: A very important parameter because it decides the network stability.

TABLE 15.1

Radio Models for WBAN

Radio model	nRF 2401A	CC 2420
Trans_er	16.7 nJ/bit	96.9 nJ/bit
Rcv_er	36.1 nJ/bit	172.8 nJ/bit
Amp_er	1.97 nJ/b	$2.71e^{-7}$J/b

TABLE 15.2

Network Parameters

Parameter	Value
Nodes' initial energy, Eo	0.5 J
Amplifier energy (Amp_er)	1.97 nJ/b
Transmitting energy (Trans_er)	16.7 nJ/bit
Receiving energy (Rcv_er)	36.1 nJ/bit
Data aggregation energy(Data_agg)	5 nJ/bit
Size of data (p)	4000 bits
No. of nodes	8
Tool used for implementation	MATLAB® 7.6

Energy consumption by sensor nodes in the network is shown in Figure 15.4 and actual values of residual energy of nodes are shown in Table 15.3. Enhanced EERDT is more stable because it lost all energy at 14,000 rounds approx. w.r.t. 8000 rounds in enhanced SIMPLE. Figure 15.5 shows data transfer in enhanced EERDT and enhanced SIMPLE. Reliability is increased in both because packet delivery ratio is increased in this work. At 14,000 rounds, 53,450 numbers of packets are sent to the base station, which is far better than enhanced SIMPLE (Table 15.4). After analyzing the number of dead nodes, as given in Table 15.5, not a single node was dead within 2000 rounds. So, the network stability period is increased in enhanced EERDT, as shown in Figure 15.6. Figure 15.7 shows the network lifetime of the network. In enhanced EERDT and SIMPLE, the first node was dead after 4000 and 2000 rounds, respectively. The network lifetime of enhanced EERDT is increased more than enhanced SIMPLE. In enhanced EERDT, the first node is dead after 13,827 rounds, and in enhanced SIMPLE, after 7471 rounds all nodes are dead, as given in Table 15.6.

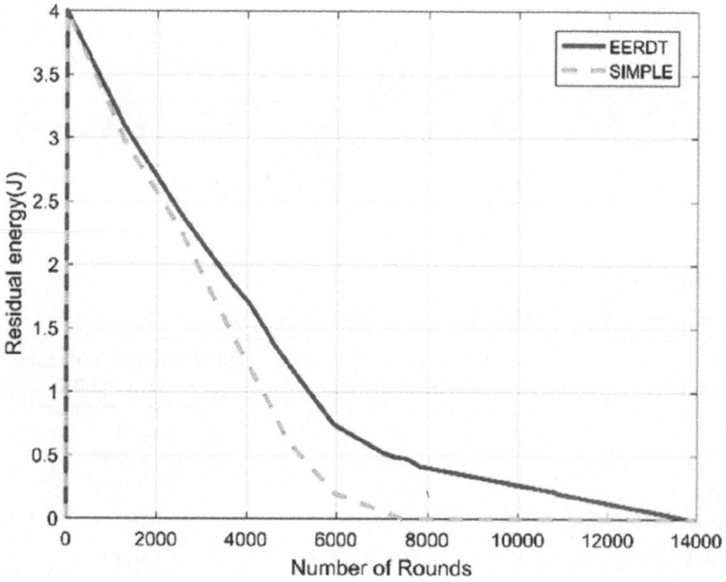

FIGURE 15.4
Residual energy of nodes in enhanced EERDT and SIMPLE.

TABLE 15.3
Comparison of Residual Energy of Nodes

Rounds	EERDT (residual energy)	SIMPLE (residual energy)
1	0	0
2000	2.6985	2.5725
4000	1.7325	1.2407
6000	0.7336	0.1955
8000	0.402	0
10000	0.2659	0
12000	0.1232	0
14000	0	0

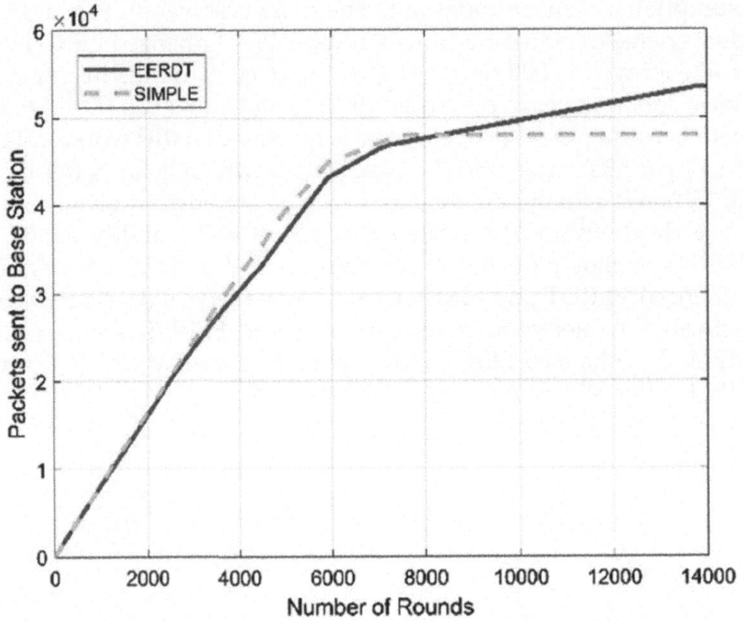

FIGURE 15.5
Throughput of enhanced EERDT and SIMPLE.

TABLE 15.4
Comparison of Number of Packets Sent to the Sink Node

Rounds	EERDT (no. of packets sent to the BS)	SIMPLE (no. of packets sent to the BS)
1	0	0
2000	15,993	16,295
4000	30,216	31,957
6000	43,354	45,015
8000	47,622	47,930
10,000	49,622	47,930
12,000	51,623	47,930
14,000	53,450	47,930

TABLE 15.5
Comparison of Dead Nodes in the Network

Rounds	EERDT (no. of dead nodes)	SIMPLE (no. of dead nodes)
1	0	0
2000	0	0
4000	1	3
6000	3	6
8000	6	8
10,000	6	8
12,000	7	8
14,000	8	8

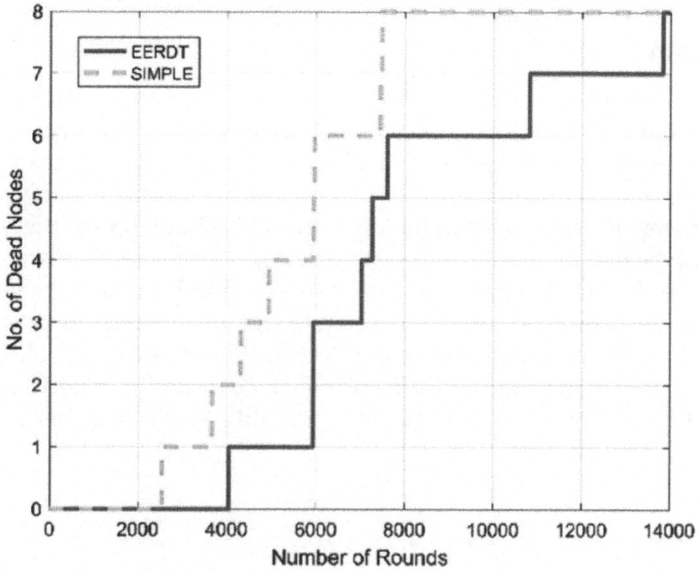

FIGURE 15.6
Number of dead nodes in enhanced EERDT and SIMPLE.

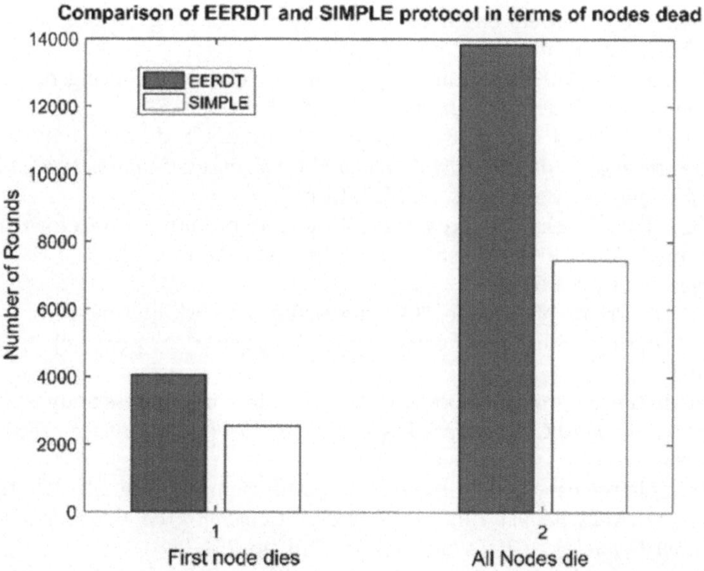

FIGURE 15.7
First and all nodes dead in enhanced EERDT and SIMPLE.

TABLE 15.6
Comparison of the Stability Period

	EERDT	SIMPLE
First dead node	4054	2558
All dead nodes	13,827	7,471

15.6 Conclusion

In this chapter, the work has been enhanced by applying the square root over the sum of average residual energy of nodes and squaring their cost function to select the forwarder with maximum cost function. Enhanced EERDT is more reliable because the residual energy of nodes is more than enhanced SIMPE. The stability period of enhanced EERDT is improved due to fewer dead nodes in the network. This chapter also draws special attention to the role of the patient monitoring system in e-governance services. e-Governance in the health sector is the result of data, communication technology, knowledge, and action. It makes the health monitoring system more reliable and also reduces healthcare cost.

The enhanced work showed that enhanced EERDT and enhanced SIMPLE are more reliable and energy efficient than EERDT and SIMPLE in terms of network stability and throughput. But quality of service like security, mobility, electro-magnetic radiations, and so on, are still a major concern.

References

1. Moulik, S., S. Misra, A. Gaurav, "Cost-effective mapping between wireless body area networks and cloud service providers based on multi-stage bargaining", *IEEE Transactions on Mobile Computing*, May, vol. 16, no. 6, 2017, pp. 1573–1586.
2. Movassaghigilani, S., M. Abolhasan, J. Lipman, "A review of routing protocols in wireless body area networks", *Journal of Networks*, vol. 8, 2013, pp. 559–575.
3. Ullah, F., et al., "Patient data dissemination in wireless body area network: A qualitative analysis", *Proceedings of the Second International Conference on Information and Communication Technology for Competitive Strategies*, ACM, 2016, p. 71.
4. Hoang, D. C., et al., "Thermal energy harvesting from human warmth for wireless body area network in medical healthcare system", *IEEE International Conference on Power Electronics and Drive Systems*, 2009, pp. 1277–1282.
5. Tsouri, G. R., A. Prieto, N. Argade, "On increasing network lifetime in body area networks using global routing with energy consumption balancing", *Sensors*, vol. 12, no. 10, 2012, pp. 13088–130108.
6. Zhou, Y., et al., "Beacon-based opportunistic scheduling in wireless body area network", *IEEE 38th Annual International Conference of Engineering in Medicine and Biology Society (EMBC)*, 2016, pp. 4995–4998.
7. Sethi, D., P. P. Bhattacharya, "A study on energy efficient and reliable data transfer (EERDT) protocol for WBAN", *Second IEEE International Conference on Computational Intelligence & Communication Technology (CICT)*, Ghaziabad, 2016, pp. 254–258.
8. Nadeem, Q., N. Javaid, S. N. Mohammad, M. Y. Khan, S. Sarfraz, M. Gull, "SIMPLE: Stable increased-throughput multi-hop protocol for link efficiency in wireless body area networks", *8th IEEE International Conference on Broadband and Wireless Computing, Communication and Applications (BWCCA'13)* Compiegne, France, 2013, pp. 221–226.
9. Shimly, S.M., D.B. Smith, S. Movassaghi, "Experimentally-based cross-layer optimization across multiple wireless body area networks", CoRR, abs/1701.08605, 2017.
10. Moosavi, H., F.M. Bui, "Optimal relay selection and power control with quality-of-service provisioning in wireless body area networks", *IEEE Transactions on Wireless Communications*, vol. 15, no. 8, 2016, pp. 5497–5510.

11. Movassaghi, S., et al., "Enabling interference- aware and energy efficient coexistence of multiple wireless body area networks with unknown dynamics", *IEEE Access*, vol. 4, 2016, pp. 2935–2951.
12. S. J. Marinkovic, E. M. Popovici, C. Spagnol, S. Faul, W. P. Marnane, "Energy efficient low duty cycle MAC protocol for wireless body area network". *IEEE Transactions on Information Technology*, vol. 13, 2009, pp. 915–925.
13. Javaid, N., A. Ahmad, Q. Nadeem, M. Imran, N. Haider, "iM-SIMPLE: iMproved stable increased-throughput multi-hop link efficient routing protocol for wireless body area networks", *Computers in Human Behaviour*, vol. 51, 2015, pp. 1002–1011.
14. Quwaider, M., S. Biswas, "Probabilistic routing in on-body sensor networks with postural disconnections", *Proceedings of the 7th ACM International Symposium on Mobility Management and Wireless Access*, ACM, 2009, pp. 149–158.
15. Movassaghi, S., M. A. Mahyar, "An energy efficient network coding approach for wireless body area networks", *38th Annual IEEE Conference on Local Computer Networks*, 2013, pp. 468–475.
16. Ahmed, S., N. Javaid, S. Yousaf, A. Ahmad, M. M. Sandhu, Z. A. Khan, N. Alrajeh, M. Imran, "Co-LAEEBA: Cooperative link aware and energy efficient protocol for wireless body area networks", *Computers in Human Behaviour*, vol. 51, 2015, pp. 1205–1215.
17. Movassaghi, S., M. Abolhasan, "Smart spectrum allocation for interference mitigation in wireless body area networks", *International Conference on Communication, IEEE*, 2014, pp. 5688–5693.
18. Talha, S., R. Ahmad, A.K. Kiani, "Priority based energy aware (PEA) routing protocol for WBANs", *82nd Vehicular Technology Conference (VTC Fall), IEEE*, 2015, pp. 1–5.
19. Sharma, R., H.S. Ryait, A.K. Gupta, "Clustering based routing protocol to increase the stability in WBAN", *International Journal of Innovations in Engineering and Technology*, vol. 6, 2015, pp. 119–125.
20. Ha, I., "EECBSR (even energy consumption and back side routing): An improved routing protocol for effective data transmission in wireless body area networks", *International Journal of Distributed Sensor Networks*, vol. 12, no. 7, 2016, pp. 1–11.

16

Routing Protocol Analysis for Internet of Things

Umang and Akanksha Gupta

CONTENTS

16.1 Introduction

The number of Internet users and devices in the world is increasing day by day. It has been estimated that there will be 50 billion connected devices in the world by the year 2020. The Internet of Things (IoT) explores the concept of interconnection and communication between these devices in an intelligent manner.

Stating simply, IoT is basically connecting any kind of device—cell phones, televisions, coffee machines, cars, or any other physical world object—with the Internet, and/or to each other. IoT can be called a large network of connected "things," wherein the network can consist of connections between people and people, people and things or things and things (Figure 16.1).

Conceptualization of this approach with appropriate implementation in the real world is also an important aspect. The devices and objects to be interconnected are provided with built-in sensors (connected to an IoT platform) that integrate the data collected from these devices, analyzed, and then share the useful information extracted (ignoring any unrequired information in the process) with various applications that address specific needs. This information can be used to identify patterns, make recommendations, and detect potential problems before they occur.

Today, there are various real-life applications like smart alarm clocks, smart vehicular systems, smart homes, smart cities, and consequently, a smart world. A few applications along with appropriate processes are mentioned below:

Case Example 1: A smart alarm clock integrates with IoT, and collects data about the metro schedule, the weather outside, traffic conditions, and so on. It analyzes this data to recommend the right time and mode of transport to take in order to reach the office in time and wake you up accordingly. It could also be connected to the toaster and the water heater in order to get everything ready even before you wake up.

Processes used in the smart clock in real-life scenarios are as follows:

1. Scan all sensors present in connected devices
2. Data collection from connected devices
3. Set time (select HH:MM:SS format)
4. Get time
5. Set alarm
6. Off alarm
7. Initiate service
8. Select service
9. Get service
10. Off service

Case Example 2: There are various online vehicular systems such as the UberGoogle system. This system provides automatic dispatch service to the customer that will match a trip request with respect to the requested source and destination generated by the customer. This service will take a request and match a trip request to the best available automatic transport unit. If any driver is not willing to process and execute the request, then the request may be cancelled by the driver and will be automatically allocated to the next driver. Research by Google is successfully trying to implement driverless cars, however, research is still ongoing.

Case Example 3: The Health Care System in the "Missing Towel Problem" (Towel Tracking Module):

Scenario Explanation: As a patient enters the hospital, either the patient will take treatment from the outpatient department (OPD) or the patient will go to the emergency room. Accordingly, the patient may be moved to a general ward, an intensive care unit, or operating theatre based on the health status. Initially, a radio frequency identification (RFID) tag will be assigned to each new patient: "RFID ID ISSUED." There is need to monitor the status of patient health, which can be compared as well as evaluated in order to get health improvement based on an hourly, daily, and weekly basis. Thereafter, Generate Alarm Status will be set to OK. A Yellow Alarm

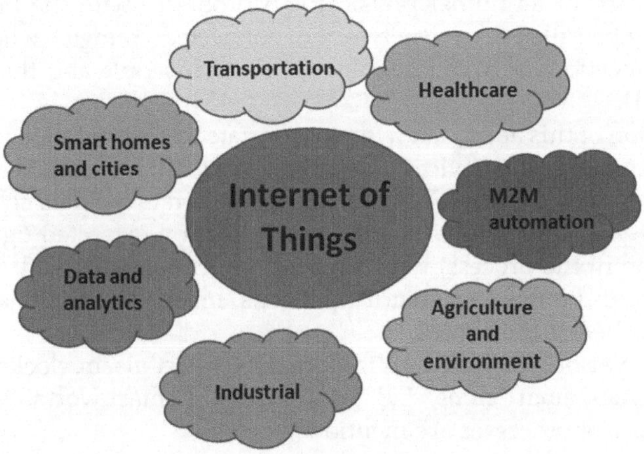

FIGURE 16.1
IoT applications in different areas.

will be generated at the instrument table (Count Towel: Status_1). And a Orange Alarm will be generated as the operation starts and it will calculate Towel Status_2 with Towel Status_1. It will generate a Yellow Alarm during the operation time at intervals of every five seconds and compare Status_3 with Status_2 and Status_1. In case of any mismatch or inconsistency, a Red Alarm will be generated. A Green Alarm will be generated at the end of the operation if all counting status are ok, otherwise it will be a Red Alarm. Then Immediate Take Action On. Check towel status before stitching of the patient, if any inconsistencies are found, then put it in Alarm Container and the doctor and the team should receive a penalty. If a number of such happenings from the team increases, then their certification of practice should be cancelled by the health organization. After successful completion of the operation, at the time of discharge, the RFID Tag will be returned "RFID TAG RETURNED" by the patient.

Step-by-Step Process:

1. Source of stimulus: Towel as a component that has been integrated by the RFID sensor tag (which is composed of a digital device called tag including an antenna and an IC-chip with a unique identification code, and a radio scanner device) will extract physical information along with connectivity and send to the server) allotted to the patient.
2. Stimulus: A component towel will send the signal and share its status as it is used, in use, or not used.
3. Environment: Normal operation.
4. Artifact: Database (cloud server).
5. Response: Track the towels issued to patient and in case of missing status "GENERATE ALARM."
6. Response measure: The system must be available and give a response at every 30 second interval. To maintain consistency in towel status, check the number of towels at the instrument table in the operating theatre and check the number of towels before operation "START" at regular 2-minute periods. Check the number of towels "In Operation Progress" every 1 minute and calculate status every 30 seconds and calculate status in case of comparative evaluation based on monotonically decreasing time analysis of the number of towels. RFID data will send the information from the cloud server and connectivity needs to be maintained with the operating theater. The updated information received from sensors must be checked with the alarm status periodically in intervals of 30 seconds so that data can be tracked.

The issue related to security and privacy of personal data in the above discussed system may degrade the performance of the system. In addition to this, automation of devices also makes it difficult to secure private information on the IoT platform. Data management also plays an important role in managing communications between devices, as an enormous amount of data is being constantly produced, which needs to be transmitted and/or analyzed from time to time in order to keep the applications working at the right pace. Storing this data efficiently so that it is readily available and easily accessible is also a concern. Delayed request response by the underlying server also raises potential concerns. Such IoT devices require a higher amount of power supply and hence they can be expensive and more difficult to realize. Portable devices require batteries, which might be needed to be replaced from time to time. Even though various mobile devices have now been optimized for lower power consumption, the cost of running enormous amounts of such devices, in terms of energy requirements, remains high.

16.2 Routing Protocols in IoT

Routing protocols such as Ad Hoc On-Demand Distance Vector (AODV), Dynamic Source Routing (DSR), and Optimized Link State Routing (OLSR) can be deployed with IoT, but before that, let us consider the IoT network stack and how it differs from the traditional network stack of the TCP/IP protocol suite and the Internet. Figure 16.2 illustrates the stated comparison. In the IoT smart devices stack, the IEEE 802.15.4 data link and physical layers have been optimized for energy efficiency and the ability to be deployed on cheap devices. In the network layer, the size of the maximum transmission unit (MTU) has been kept at a mere 127 bytes, conflicting with the minimal MTU of 1280 bytes of the IPv6. This limitation has led to the demand for an adaptation layer: 6LoWPAN—"IPv6 over Low Power Wireless Personal Area Networks" operating in the 2.4 GHz frequency range with 250 kbps transfer rate. Here, IPv6 headers are compressed and the packets exceeding the new 127-byte MTU are fragmented.

The fragments thus produced can be reassembled by all border routers that connect a 6LoWPAN network to the Internet (Figure 16.3).

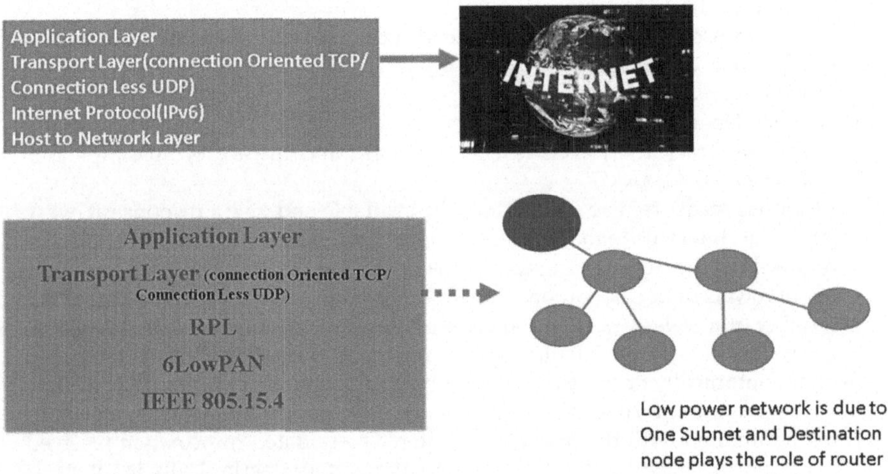

FIGURE 16.2
IPv6 on low power and lossy networks.

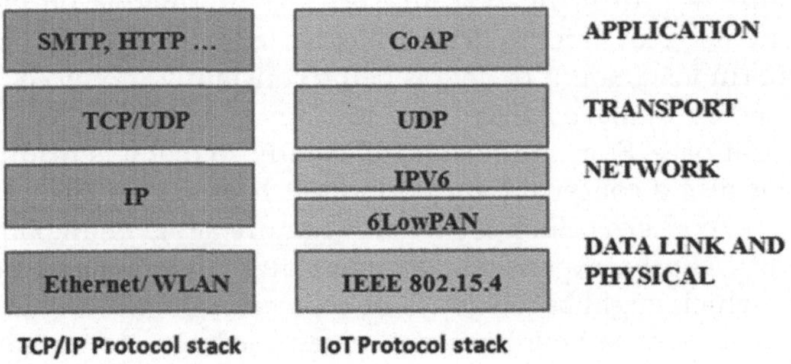

FIGURE 16.3
Comparison between traditional and IoT protocol stacks.

Figure 16.2 presents a comparison between the TCP/IP protocol stack and the IoT protocol stack. Further, there is need to consider and understand the concept of a few protocols that are deployed with IoT in today's scenario.

16.2.1 RPL

RPL stands for the routing protocol for low power and lossy networks. It is a distance-vector routing protocol developed by the IETF "Routing Over Low power and Lossy (ROLL) networks" working group. It works on the principle that the network has a *sink node* having more computing power and resources than the other nodes of the network. The protocol operates by constructing a destination oriented acyclic graph (DODAG) with its root as the sink node. All traffic is routed toward this sink node from all other leaf nodes. A DODAG information object (DIO) message is emitted by each node in the DODAG, containing information about its identity and rank in the DODAG proactively making RPL a proactive protocol. RPL can provide support for potentially constrained and lossy link layers, and is usually used with devices with limited resources, like home, industries, and transportation applications. Its ability to build network routes in a quick manner and an effective adaptation of the network topology makes it an ideal choice for 6LowPAN devices.

16.2.2 CORPL

Cognitive Routing Protocol for Low-Power and Lossy Networks (CORPL) is a protocol used for cognitive networks. The cognitive RPL is an extension of the RPL designed for cognitive networks and uses the RPL DODAG topology generation with two modifications. DODAG is built in the same way as RPL but here, instead of forwarding the packet to only one pre-decided node, each node maintains a forwarding set. This protocol forwards the concerned packet by using opportunistic forwarding, that is, it chooses multiple nodes from the forwarder set and then analyzes the network and routes toward the selected nodes for the best way to forward to the next hop. The node then updates its neighbor with the changes using DIO messages. Based on the updated information, each node then dynamically updates its neighbor priorities in order to construct the forwarder set [1].

16.2.3 CARP

Channel aware routing protocol (CARP) is used for underwater communication and so can be used in conjunction with IoT as it supports light weight packets. Link quality is calculated using historical information about the successful data transmissions gathered from neighboring sensors, which is then used to select the forwarding nodes. In CARP, the network is first initialized and then data is forwarded. For initialization, the sink node broadcasts a HELLO packet to all other nodes in the network. After the broadcast, the packet is routed from the sensor node to the sink node in a hop-by-hop fashion. The route toward each hop is determined independently.

This protocol does not support reusing historic data. Therefore, the CARP data forwarding technique is not beneficial to an application that requires sensor data only when it changes significantly. Energy-efficient common address redundancy protocol (E-CARP) is an enhancement to CARP and it allows the sink node to save historic information in terms of previously received sensor data. When new data is needed, a ping packet is sent to the sensor nodes by E-CARP, which is replied with the data from the sensor nodes. Thus, E-CARP is able to reduce the communication overhead drastically [2].

The three protocols, although based on similar grounds, have a few differences in the supported technologies. The RPL and CORPL protocols support different server technologies; there is no support by the CARP protocol. Also, storage management is performed by the RPL and CARP protocol only. Data management is supported by all three, whereas no security is provided by any of the three protocols.

16.2.3.1 Working of the RPL

This section undergoes the detailed analysis of the working of the RPL protocol for IoT. But before that, the working of a low power lossy network on which the RPL protocol works on needs to be understood.

According to RFC 7228:

> *A low power and lossy network is composed of many embedded devices with limited power, memory, and processing resources interconnected by a variety of links, such as IEEE 802.15.4 or low-power Wi-Fi. There is a wide scope of application areas for LLNs, including industrial monitoring, building automation (heating, ventilation, and air conditioning (HVAC), lighting, access control, fire), connected home, health care, environmental monitoring, urban sensor networks, energy management, assets tracking, and refrigeration.*

RPL is a distance routing protocol because it works upon calculating distances from each node in the network to the other nodes in the network. It is an intra-domain routing protocol, which time to time indicates changes in the topology of the neighbors of the network routers. Distance-vector protocols calculate the direction, that is, the next hop address and the exit interface, as well as the distance, which is the measure of the cost to reach a certain node. Between any two nodes, the route that comes out to have the least cost is said to have the minimum distance. Hence, each node in the network maintains a vector of minimum distance calculated to each and every other node of the network, and using this table, the cost of reaching any destination in the network can be found out using the various route metrics available.

RPL also supports source routing by allowing a packet sender to partially or fully specify the route of the packet in the network. It enables a network node to obtain all the possible routes towards a host.

RPL organizes a topology as a DODAG, which is a directed acyclic graph, having a single root node with no outgoing edges. All other nodes are directed toward the root node. The rank of a node defines the node's individual position relative to other nodes with respect to the DODAG root (Figure 16.4).

An objective function (OF) in the RPL (OF) defines how the RPL nodes select and optimize routes within an RPL instance. The OF also helps in translating one or more metrics into a rank for each node and also aids in selecting parents for each child node.

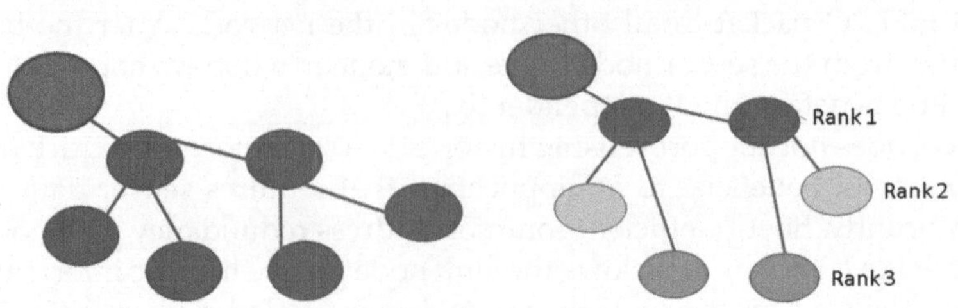

FIGURE 16.4
Rank of nodes in DODAG.

An RPL instance is a set of one or more DODAGs that share an RPLInstanceID. An RPLInstanceID is a unique identifier within a network. DODAGs with the same RPLInstanceID share the same OF used to compute the position of node in the DODAG (Figure 16.5).

The RPL has a self-monitoring capability using triple timer mechanisms. Hence, as soon as the network becomes stable, the frequency of control packets is reduced, further reducing the control overhead.

The traffic flows supported by RPL are:

- Multipoint to point (MP2P)
- Point to multipoint (P2MP)
- Point to point (P2P—non-storing) (Figure 16.6)

The network topology is constructed and thereby controlled by three types of control messages;

- DODAG information object (DIO)
- DODAG information solicitation (DIS)
- Destination advertisement object (DAO)

This set of messages belongs to a type of ICMP message control group. First, the leaf nodes construct the DIO message for upward routing construction toward the sink node. This scenario depicts a MP2P communication, which is dominant in most of the RPL applications. The sink node broadcasts the DIOs and the nodes that receive the DIO

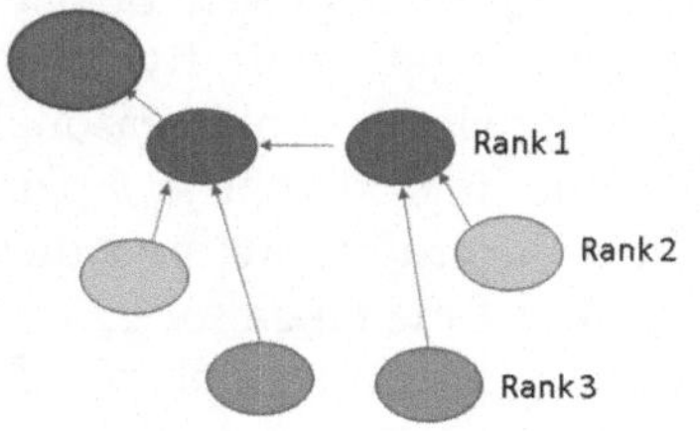

FIGURE 16.5
An RPL instance.

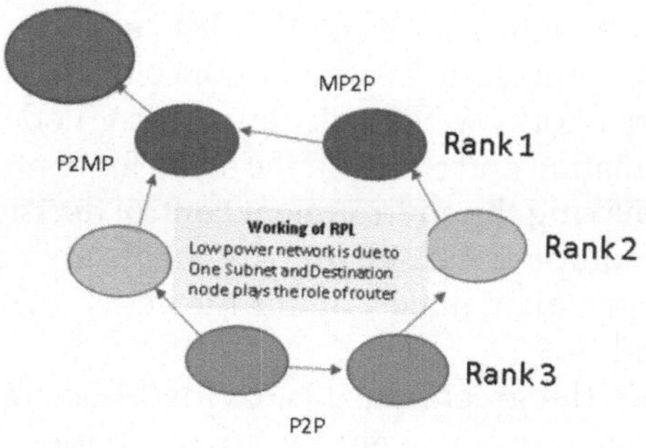

FIGURE 16.6
Traffic flows in RPL.

message directly from the sink node become its neighbors. These neighbor nodes then set the sink node as their parent, and then rebroadcast the DIOs to further nodes in the network. Repetition of this step by all the subsequent nodes will lead to the construction of the DODAG by handling these DIOs and building parent sets for each node. Next, the DIS message solicits the DIO message for immediate response to any kind of inconsistency in the network.

There are two ways in which the RPL works, that is, storing LLN and non-storing LLN. Storing is fully stateful, wherein each non-root and each non-leaf node has to maintain all its routing information and so traffic is directed as far as the common parent. In comparison to this, the non-storing LLN uses source routing, that is, it sends all traffic toward the root. Thereby, the root uses its available routing information to further divert the traffic toward other nodes. The DAO message can be used for P2P and P2MP route construction. If it is a storing LLN, the selected parent receives the DAO message from the selected node. Whereas, in case of a non-storing LLN, the DODAG root receives the DAO message from the node. A destination acknowledgement message (DAO-ACK) could be sent back to the node (if requested) that generated the DAO message by the destination node.

However, RPL has a few limitations as cited by [3], including diversification of OFs, high energy consumption, and proximity to attacks that could lead to failures in authentication, maintenance of routing information, and attacks on the integrity or availability of the network operations [4].

16.3 Analysis of the Greenhouse Environment System

Greenhouse environment systems are places used for plant growth and monitoring by constant surveillance of temperature, light, humidity, carbon dioxide level, and so on. It avoids crop damage due to changing weather and seasonal changes and hence creates a safe and sound environment for budding of crops and plants, which increases economic efficiency [5]. The factors affecting the crop growth need constant analysis and monitoring in order to increase plant quality, time taken for growth, and financial effectiveness. Such a system is complex to handle and requires optimized control, real-time monitoring, and information processing. It also poses convenience problems and is quite high maintenance. A number of developed countries have had high growth and progress in greenhouse management systems and control by adopting the developments in the field of IoT.

As greenhouse monitoring requires manual intervention for keeping track of the irrigation process, temperature, light, and humidity, IoT technology could be deployed for automating the majority of processes. The greenhouse environment monitoring system, based on wireless sensor networks (WSNs), deploys sensor nodes at the monitoring center that collect essential information and transmit the same for control purposes [6]. This data, when analyzed, helps in making the environment control decisions that are further transmitted to the controlling equipment inside the greenhouse. Regulating the environment based on the analyzed information makes up for the best growth environment for plants and crops (Figures 16.7 and 16.8).

As visible in Figure 16.7, the greenhouse is divided into multiple measurement and control areas, each managed respectively by a base station. Many sensor nodes are placed in each of the measurement areas (also called a virtual grid) and hence from a cluster of nodes, having a sink node serving as the root (selected through an algorithm)

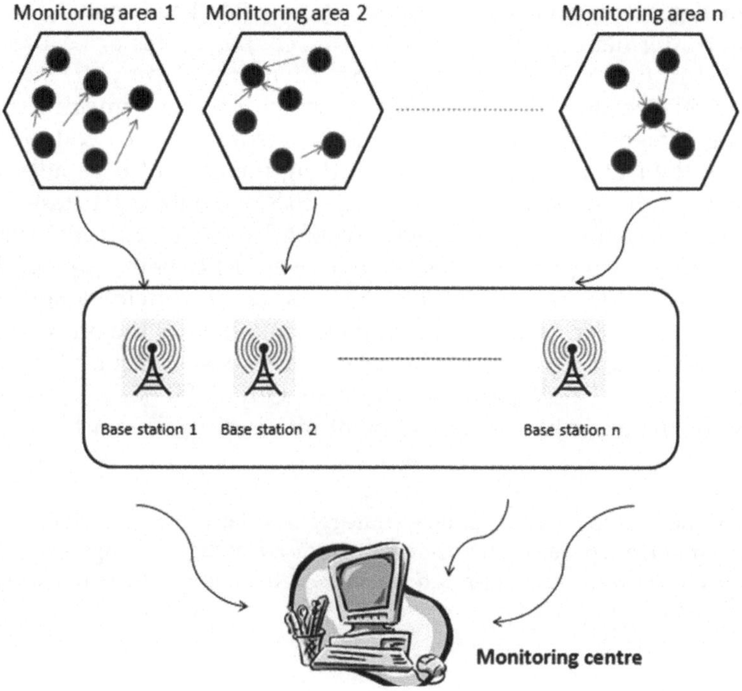

FIGURE 16.7
Block diagram of a greenhouse monitoring system.

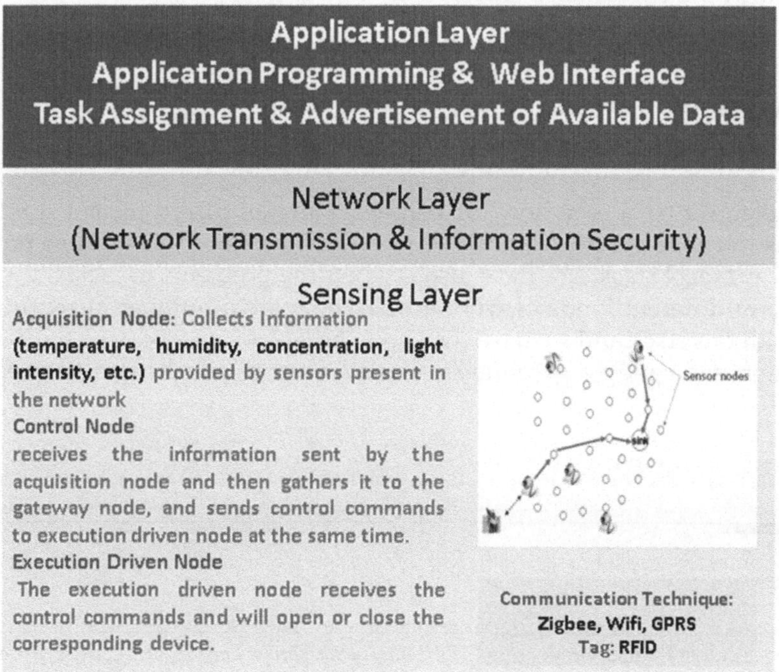

FIGURE 16.8
Layer design of main components of a greenhouse system.

and other sensor/control nodes as members of the grid. The sensor nodes of the grid collect relevant information for analysis and the control nodes are capable of altering the in-house environment based on the information provided by the base station. The information is relayed onto the base stations, which further transmits it to and from the monitoring center. The monitoring center is responsible for collecting all sensor data, analyzing the factors, and then transmitting the control parameters back to the virtual grids through the base stations. Figure 16.8 presents layer design of the main components of the system. For implementation of IoT over such an environment involving WSN, the RPL routing protocol can be deployed. RPL, being a proactive, distance routing protocol over low power and lossy networks, can provide a flexible and easily to deploy mechanism over various WSN applications, such as the one discussed above. To overcome the resource constraints in terms of sensor nodes and unreliable wireless links, in the case of single-path RPL protocol, Quynh [3] has proposed a multipath RPL protocol for the greenhouse environment monitoring system [7][8]. According to Quynh:

> RPL is designed based on a single route strategy. Especially in case of RPL, we develop RPL-based multipath protocols for overcome the disadvantages of single-path approach and the results show that our approaches achieve better energy efficiency, load balance, end-to-end delay and packet delivery rate compared to traditional solution of single-path RPL.

Hence, it can be observed that based on the real-life deployment and scale of the greenhouse network grids, IoT in conjunction with the multipath RPL protocol can be used for better performance in terms of the rate of delivery of the packets, time delay, and errors [9] as compared with the traditional single route strategy.

16.4 Conclusion

In this chapter, we have seen how IoT concepts can be utilized for automating various applications. We have seen the contrast between the traditional networking protocol stack and the IoT protocol stack. We have also studied the problems associated with deployment of IoT in different kinds of work areas. There are a number of routing protocols available with this stack and we have seen how the RPL protocol can be the best fit for the application of automating a greenhouse environment by adopting a multipath routing approach.

References

1. A. Aijaz and A. Aghvami, "Cognitive machine-to-machine communications for Internet-of-things: A protocol stack perspective," *IEEE Internet of Things Journal*, vol. 2, no. 2, pp. 103–112, 2015.
2. Z. Zhou, B. Yao, R. Xing, L. Shu, and S. Bu, "E-CARP: An energy efficient routing protocol for UWSNs in the Internet of underwater things," *IEEE Sensors Journal*, vol. 16, pp. 4072–4082, no. 99, 2015.

3. T. N. Quynh, N. L. Manh, and K. N. Nguyen, "Multipath RPL protocols for greenhouse environment monitoring system based on Internet of things," *Proceeding International Conference on Electrical Engineering/Electronics, Computer, Telecom. and Information Technology (ECTI-CON)*, Hua Hin, June, pp. 1–6, 2015.
4. T. Tsao, R. Alexander, M. Dohler, V. Daza, A. Lozano, and M. Richardson, "A security threat analysis for the routing protocol for low-power and lossy networks (RPLs)," Internet Engineering Task Force, https://tools.ietf.org/html/rfc7416. Accessed September 2017.
5. L. Yanzheng, T. Guanghui, and L. Shirong. "The problem of the control system for Greenhouse Climate," *Journal of Chinese Agricultural Science Bulletin*, 23, pp. 154–157, 2007.
6. M. Arun Kumar, Alagumeenaakshi, "RPL optimization for precise green house management using wireless sensor network," *As Conference Proceedings in the 2014 International Conference on Green Computing Communication and Electrical Engineering (ICGCCEE)*, Coimbatore, pp. 16, 2014.
7. Y. Song, J. Ma, X. Zhang, and Y. Feng, "Design of wireless sensor network -based Greenhouse Environment monitoring and automatic control system," *Journal of Networks*, vol. 7, pp. 838–844, 2012.
8. S. Umang, B. V. R. Reddy, and M. N. Hoda "Enhanced intrusion detection system for malicious node detection in ad hoc routing protocol using minimal energy consumption," *Communications IET*, vol. 4, no. 17, pp. 2084–2094, 2010.
9. L. Shi-hua, C. Zhong-fei, L. Fu-juan, W. Zhi-song, and Z. Xin-yuan, "Design and research of intelligent greenhouse monitoring system based on Internet of Things," *International Conference on Computer Science and Electronic Technology (CSET 2016)*, pp. 76–79, 2016.

17

Soft Computing-Based Simulated Model for Enhancing the Applicability of e-Governance

Minakshi Kalra, Dilbag Singh, and Vijay Kumar

CONTENTS

17.1 Introduction

During the last ten years, e-governance applications were based on traditional information technology (IT) or information and communication technology (ICT) systems using the Internet [1]. With the new trends of Web 2.0 and e-governance 2.0, e-governance developers have moved to rich Internet applications [2]. ICT is an emerging computing paradigm that provides a variety of services in such a way that has not been experienced before. e-Governance as an ICT service (SaaS) can be one among them [3]. Availability and affordability of government related services to the public is an important factor for sustainable development [4]. The importance of good governance, especially in developing countries such as India, is increasing because of the pressure to chase the developed world, that is, global competitiveness [5]. Typically, infrastructure availability is different in developing countries than in developed countries, for example, a low quality of education and fewer possibilities to have computers, the Internet, or mobile phones in rural areas because of long distances and high costs [6].

The uses of ICT in the e-governance domain have many benefits. In the existing system in government organizations, it is very difficult to exchange information between different suborganizations [7]. For instance, data from the election commission cannot be easily shared with the police and defense sections. When a situation arises, it has to go through levels of bureaucracy and authorization, and a lot of paperwork, to finally acquire the required information, which wastes a huge amount of resources and time [8]. One good objective of the thesis is to provide an e-governance model that will allow this information to be shared easily, reliably, and with the appropriate security attached to it without any such hassle [9]. For instance, if a traffic police wants to know the personal information of a driver, he will just provide the registration number of the driver and his personal information will be forwarded from the road transport officer (RTO) or election commission to the police officer [10].

17.2 Problems and Challenges in Providing e-Governance Services

India has started adopting e-governance applications by paying attention to its benefits to the population [11,12]. The primary objective behind this is to improve the efficiency of government policies and provide them to its end users [13–15]. Recently, the Indian government has started exploring and monitoring historical information to recognize significant features so that e-governance can be improved and delivered to its users in an efficient manner [16,17].

1. *Data mining in e-governance*: Data mining techniques play a significant role in improving the performance of various policies associated with e-governance applications [18]. Various data mining techniques have been used by various researchers to improve the accuracy of e-governance applications [19]. Data mining techniques utilize historical information of existing government policies and its impact to end users. Afterwards, it processes this data by using various preprocessing techniques of data mining to monitor and select potential features of the data [20]. Figure 17.1 shows the cycle of data mining techniques that can be used for building and improving e-governance applications.
2. *Soft computing tools used in e-governance*: Soft computing techniques also play an efficient role in designing an efficient e-governance tool [21]. As previously known, data mining techniques for e-governance suffer from over/under fitting issues (i.e., efficient tuning of input parameters for given data mining technique(s)). Therefore, many researchers have started using fuzzy logic, artificial neural networks, genetic algorithms, and so on, to enhance the performance of data mining technique. These techniques will be described in subsequent sections.
3. *Fuzzy logic*: Fuzzy sets are used to handle the uncertainty and impreciseness in the decision support or prediction system. Based on the fuzzy set and their relations, some mathematical forms can be derived in order to calculate the impreciseness, vagueness, or amount of fuzziness in the system. The logic is designed in such a way that it reduces the impreciseness but also minimizes the information loss [22]. Figure 17.2 shows the diagrammatic flow of fuzzy logic.

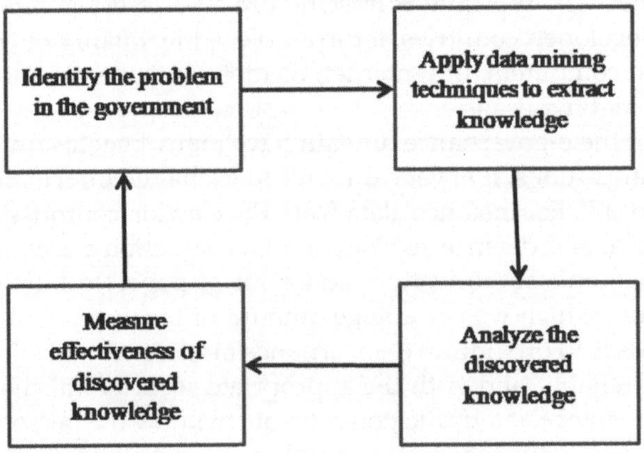

FIGURE 17.1
The data mining cycle.

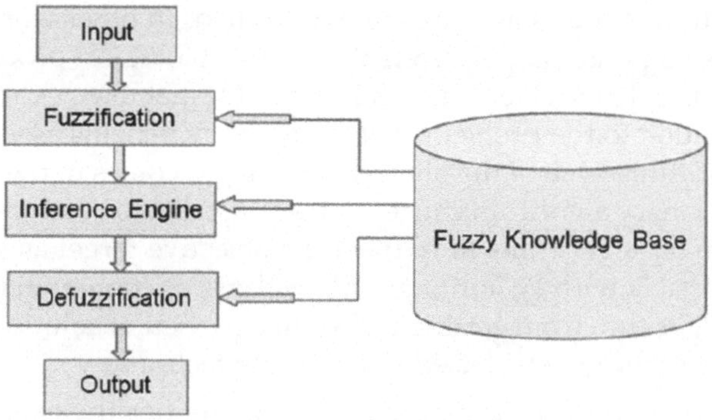

FIGURE 17.2
Layout of fuzzy logic.

4. *Neural network*: Neural networks and so-called artificial neural networks also play a significant role while designing neuron-based data mining techniques [23]. A neural network utilizes layers-based networks (i.e., feed forward, feed backward, or hybrid) to iteratively optimize the neural weights to efficiently recognize the mining rule. Neural networks consist of three layers: input, hidden, and output layers. Figure 17.3 shows a layout of a neural network.
5. *Evolutionary algorithms*: An evolutionary algorithm is considered as a component of evolutionary computation in artificial intelligence. An evolutionary algorithm functions through the selection process in which the least fit members of the population set are eliminated, whereas the fit members are allowed to survive

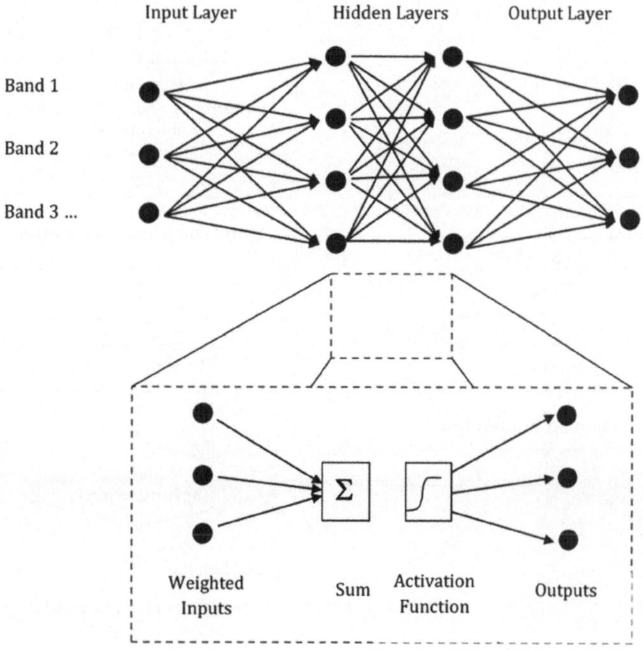

FIGURE 17.3
The diagrammatic flow of a neural network.

and continue until better solutions are determined. In other words, evolutionary algorithms are computer applications that mimic biological processes in order to solve complex problems. Over time, the successful members evolve to present the optimized solution to the problem. There are many benefits associated with evolutionary algorithms. One of the biggest advantages comes in the flexibility gains, as most evolutionary algorithm concepts are adaptable to even complex problems. Most evolutionary algorithms fit to meet the objective target as well. Better optimization is possible with evolutionary algorithms, as the population of solutions prevents the algorithm from getting locked in a particular solution [24]. Figure 17.4 shows the flow of the genetic based data mining technique.

6. *e-Governance areas associated with soft computing*: As per the existing literature, it has been observed that soft computing techniques play a significant role in implementing e-governance strategies. Subsequent sections describe various applications of soft computing techniques in the field of e-governance.
7. *Performance evaluation*: Governments make several promises prior to elections, it is therefore necessary to evaluate the level of fulfilment of these promises and make recommendations. An important area in which fuzzy-set theory can be applied is performance evaluation. Fuzzy logic models provide a reasonable solution to these common situations, which may easily be converted into human linguistic forms and subjective constructs [25].
8. *Information security*: It is observed that e-governance applications suffer from several vulnerabilities and threats. Therefore, providing the security to these applications becomes a challenging issue. Recently, many soft computing

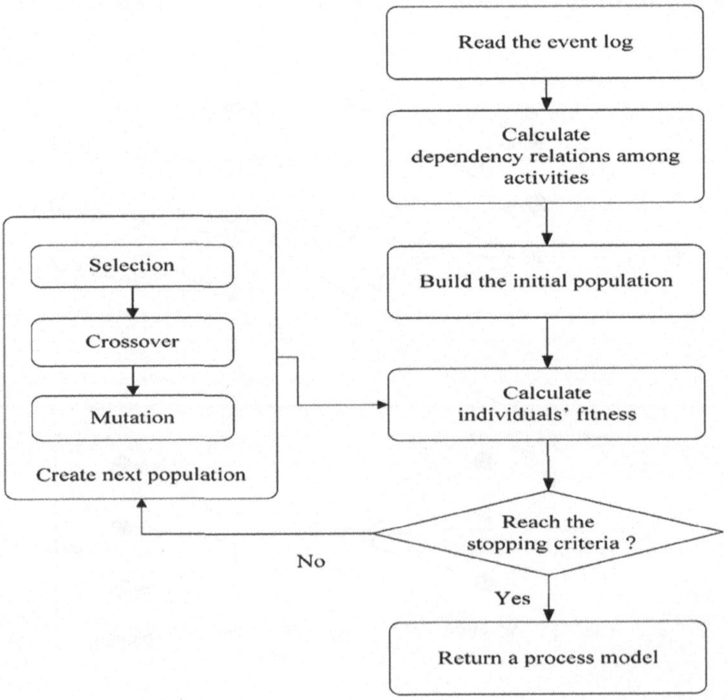

FIGURE 17.4
The flow of the genetic based data mining technique.

based data mining techniques have been designed to improve the security of e-governance applications such as malicious detection, unauthorized access prevention, and so on [26].

9. *Crime data mining for a police information system*: In today's world, crime rate is increasing. Therefore, it becomes a challenging task for governmental organization to reduce the crime rate. Data mining techniques are used to implement the crime analysis tool successfully [27] and by considering the data mining techniques, government organizations can trace a criminal person based upon certain features and his/her activities in society.
10. *Insurance fraud detection*: Insurance fraud is when a person or entity makes false insurance claims in order to obtain compensation for which they are not entitled. The total cost of insurance fraud is estimated to be more than 40 billion dollars. Therefore, for governmental organizations, it becomes a challenging problem to detect these fraud claims. This problem can be successfully solved by considering various soft computing-based fraud insurance claim detectors [28].
11. *Smart city*: Generally, smart cities providing the best of the amenities to local people in an urban setup is quite challenging. In the Indian context, the role of e-governance is essential and logical for building smart cities. To successfully implement e-governance policies, it becomes more significant to classify the different types of people in that area. However, it is hard to classify these people into different groups because individuals may be classified into more than one group. It causes a redundancy problem that becomes a critical issue for building smart cities. Therefore, soft computing-based machine learning techniques are used to categorize individuals in a more efficient way [29].

17.3 Future Research Directions

Many techniques have been implemented by governmental organizations to improve e-governance applications for its end users. However, it still suffers from various challenges. As known, data mining techniques play a significant role in improving the efficiency of various e-governance applications. However, the majority of data mining techniques suffer from various issues such as:

1. *Parameter tuning:* Many data mining techniques are from parameter tuning issues. An efficient tuning of these parameters has an ability to improve the accuracy of data mining-based e-governance applications. Generally, tuning is done manually by considering the hit and trail approaches, which is time consuming and far from an optimal solution. Therefore, in the near future, one can design an efficient meta-heuristic based data mining technique to enhance the results.
2. *Computational speed*: Neural network and evolutionally based data mining techniques outperform existing data mining techniques. However, these techniques are computationally intensive in nature. Therefore, designing an efficient computationally faster technique is still an open area of research.
3. *Ensemble of data mining techniques*: Ensemble based data mining techniques perform significantly better than existing techniques. However, it is mostly done by

considering an averaging or voting system. Therefore, in the future, one can utilize meta-heuristic techniques to design a novel ensemble approach to improve the performance of e-governance applications.

4. *Feature selection*: Feature selection techniques play a significant role while designing a novel e-governance tool. Therefore, in the future, various feature extraction techniques can be explored and implemented in designing soft computing-based e-governance applications.

17.4 Conclusion

Government agencies can benefit from this study as they could know the extent of website implementation and compliance with the guidelines. It is expected that this investigation can add to the body of literature on the subject and provide a baseline for evaluation in subsequent studies. After extensive investigations, it is very clear that there are few studies addressing e-government accessibility or usability testing in the Indian context. This study provides empirical evidence and the outcomes enrich the empirical findings in an Indian e-government setting. This research will attract both researchers and decision makers because it will contribute significantly and enrich the body of knowledge about the usability of e-government websites.

This study is important because it fills the gap in the research on website usability studies based on design analysis. It can serve to build a research agenda for research scholars in the e-government context. Hence, website usability is important both to the owner of the website who needs to deliver services in an effective way and to the visitor of the website who needs to access the website in an effective, efficient, and easy way. As India followed other nations in developing e-government websites, it is important to improve the effectiveness and efficiency of e-government websites. This improvement will allow a better use of limited public resources to accomplish more significant needs.

The findings of this study could assist government leaders to design strategies to increase citizens' adoption rates by making improvements in the design of e-government websites. The results of this study will help government organizations introduce websites that can be accessible to users with impairments or disabilities and allow them to get the maximum benefits of online services and provide them with an opportunity to participate in the virtual world. In short, this research work presents a set of approaches that aims to evaluate the usability of e-government websites through effectiveness, efficiency, and satisfaction. It also serves as a benchmark on the current status of e-government websites. The value of this work will be an increase in the number of usable and accessible e-governance websites to the public.

References

1. Bhattacharya, K. and T. Suri "The curious case of e-Governance." *IEEE Internet Computing*, vol. 21, no. 1, pp. 62–67, 2017.
2. Gudgel, J. E., "e-Governance in Antarctica: Internet technology's role in administering a global commons." *IEEE Internet Computing*, vol. 10, no. 6, pp. 64–68, 2006.

3. Sen, S., D. Marijan, C. Ieva, A. Grime, and A. Sander, "Modeling and verifying combinatorial interactions to test data intensive systems: Experience at the norwegian customs directorate." *IEEE Transactions on Reliability*, vol. 66, no. 1, pp. 3–16, 2017.
4. Martinez-Balleste, A., P. A. Perez-Martinez, and A. Solanas, "The pursuit of citizens' privacy: A privacy-aware smart city is possible." *IEEE Communications Magazine*, vol. 51, no. 6, pp. 136–141, 2013.
5. Liu, S. and J. D. Hwang, "Challenges to transforming IT win the US government." *IT Professional*, vol. 5, no. 3, pp. 10–15, 2003.
6. Niesten, E., A. Jolink, A. B. L. de Sousa Jabbour, M. Chappin, and R. Lozano. "Sustainable collaboration: The impact of governance and institutions on sustainable performance." *Journal of Cleaner Production*, vol. 155, pp. 1–6, 2017.
7. Hashmi G., Khanna P., Sharma P. "e-Governance an Ease or Difficult to Chase in Lucknow, Uttar Pradesh." In: Saeed K., Chaki N., Pati B., Bakshi S., Mohapatra D. (eds) *Progress in Advanced Computing and Intelligent Engineering. Advances in Intelligent Systems and Computing*, vol 564. Springer, Singapore, 2018.
8. Alloghani, M. A. M. A., A. Hussain, D. Al-Jumeily, A. J. Aljaaf, and J. Mustafina. "Gamification in e-Governance: Development of an online gamified system to enhance government entities services delivery and promote public's awareness." In *Proceedings of the 5th International Conference on Information and Education Technology*, pp. 176–181. ACM New York, 2017.
9. Mukherjee, F. "GIS use by an urban local body as part of e-Governance in India." *Cartography and Geographic Information Science*, vol. 45, pp. 1–14, 2018.
10. Liu, L., J. Ju, and Y. Feng. "An extensible framework for collaborative e-Governance platform workflow modeling using data flow analysis." *Information Technology for Development*, vol. 23, no. 3, pp. 415–437, 2017.
11. Kumar, T. "e-Governance and decentralisation—Study of an Indian District." *Journal of Rural Development*, vol. 36, no. 1, pp. 61–82, 2017.
12. Singh, H., A. K. Kar, and P. VigneswaraIlavarasan. "Assessment of e-Governance projects: an integrated framework and its validation." In *Proceedings of the Special Collection on e-Government Innovations in India*, pp. 124–133. ACM New York, 2017.
13. Agnihotri, N. and A. K. Sharma. "Big data analysis and its need for effective e-Governance." *International Journal of Innovations and Advancement in Computer Science*, vol. 4, pp. 219–224, 2015.
14. Paramashivaiah, P. and B. K. Suresh. "e-Governance: Issues and challenges in India." *OIDA International Journal of Sustainable Development*, vol. 9, no. 8, pp. 11–16, 2016.
15. Meijer, A. "e-Governance innovation: Barriers and strategies." *Government Information Quarterly*, vol. 32, no. 2, pp. 198–206, 2015.
16. Gupta, R., I. P. S. Sethi, V. Gupta, A. P. Maurya, and R. Rajamanickam. "e-Transformation in Indian telecom sector through m-governance." In *Proceedings of the 10th International Conference on Theory and Practice of Electronic Governance*, pp. 266–271. ACM, 2017.
17. Gilmore, A. and C. D'Souza. "Service excellence in e-Governance issues: An Indian case study." *JOAAG*, vol. 1, no. 1, 1–14, 2006.
18. Sajja, P. S. and R. Akerkar. "Knowledge-based systems for development." *Advanced Knowledge based Systems: Model, Application & Research*, vol. 1, pp. 1–11, 2010.
19. Khot, S., P. Ghildiyal, P. Dubey, M. Patil, and P. Matere. "Big data mining approach to e-Governance: Mining Census data for enhanced citizen centric policy making." *International Journal of Engineering and Computer Science*, vol. 6, no. 12, pp. 22312–22314, 2017.
20. Sarkar, A., S. Karforma, and J. K. Mandal, "Object oriented modelling of idea using GA based efficient key generation for e-Governance security (OOMIG)." *International Journal of Distributed and Parallel Systems (IJDPS)*, vol. 3, no. 2, pp. 171–183, 2012.
21. Mitra, S., S. K. Pal, and P. Mitra. "Data mining in soft computing framework: A survey." *IEEE Transactions on Neural Networks*, vol. 13, no. 1, pp. 3–14, 2002.
22. Gupta, R., S. K. Muttoo, and S. K. Pal. "BAT algorithm for improving fuzzy c-means clustering for location allocation of rural kiosks in developing countries under e-Governance." *Egyptian Computer Society Journal*, vol. 40, no. 2, pp. 613–616, 2016.

23. Sinha, B., S. Chandra, and M. Garg. "Development of ontology from Indian agricultural e-Governance data using IndoWordNet: A semantic web approach." *Journal of Knowledge Management*, vol.19, no. 1, pp. 25–44, 2015.
24. Mukhopadhyay, A., U. Maulik, S. Bandyopadhyay, and C. A. Coello Coello. "Survey of multi-objective evolutionary algorithms for data mining: Part II." *IEEE Transactions on Evolutionary Computation*, vol. 18, no. 1, pp. 20–35, 2014.
25. Gupta, M., B. Chandra, and M. P. Gupta. "Crime data mining for Indian police information system." *Proceedings of the 2008 Computer Society of India*, pp. 1–10, 2008.
26. Gupta, R., S. K. Muttoo, and S. K. Pal. "Development of e-Governance in an Emerging Economy Like India: Assessment and Way Ahead for Key Components." In *Proceedings of the 10th International Conference on Theory and Practice of Electronic Governance*, pp. 613–616. ACM New York, 2017.
27. Mathur, S. and U. S. Modani. "Smart City-a Gateway for Artificial Intelligence in India." In *Electrical, Electronics and Computer Science (SCEECS), 2016 IEEE Students' Conference*, pp. 1–3. IEEE Bhopal, India, 2016.
28. Panicker, S. and R. Srivastava. "Emerging role of data analytics in combating financial frauds: The era of big data in India." In *Proceedings of the 10th International Conference on Theory and Practice of Electronic Governance*, pp. 167–173. ACM New York, 2017.
29. Meijer, A. and M. P. R. Bolívar. "Governing the smart city: A review of the literature on smart urban governance." *International Review of Administrative Sciences*, vol. 82, no. 2, pp. 392–408, 2016.

18

Strengthening Agriculture through Energy Efficient WSN for Drip Irrigation in Deserts

Ranjana Thalore, Raunak Monir, and Partha Pratim Bhattacharya

CONTENTS

18.1 Introduction

A wireless sensor network (WSN) [1] comprises many nodes with the ability of sensing, computation, and wireless communication. WSNs are being used in a broad variety of significant institutions [2–5] such as the military, agriculture, healthcare, and industrial process monitoring.

Wireless transmission permits the deployment of sensors in unapproachable, critical, and dangerous locations. WSN has several advantages including a small size, easy installation, cost-effectiveness, and low power consumption. Currently, agriculture faces many challenges [6], while humans depend on water and agriculture for existence, precision agriculture monitoring is critical, and demand is rapidly rising for remote controlling in agriculture and environmental monitoring. However, the research on the application of WSN for agriculture has been limited.

The applicability of WSN technology in agriculture can be broadly categorized into three areas: (i) fertilizer control; (ii) irrigation management; and (iii) pest management. The various types of sensors that can be interfaced with the motes are environmental temperature, solar radiation, relative humidity, wind speed and direction, rainfall, soil temperature and moisture, soil pH, and leaf wetness. These sensor readings can be aligned with a decision support system that assists the management of resources.

Traditional irrigation techniques [7] normally wet a plant's stem and the lower leaves. The entire soil surface is soaked and frequently remains wet long after irrigation is finished. Such a condition advances infections by leaf mold fungi. These techniques expend a lot of water, yet the region between edit columns stays dry and only gets wet from accidental precipitation.

The drip irrigation technique gradually directs a small amount of water to the root zone of the plant. Water is provided regularly to keep up the ideal soil dampness condition. The appropriate utilization of water assets avoids dampness in the plant. A drip irrigation system based on WSN is a control system with constant inputs, which screens and controls every exercise of the system. A typical system incorporates a conveyance system, channels, weight controllers, valve or checks, chemical injectors, estimating instruments, and controllers. The WSN structure introduced in the field may assemble different physical parameters identified with the water system. The information is sent to the central server wirelessly through the nodes and gateways. In light of the information, the central server creates important control activities, which are directed to the individual controllers through control transports empowering usage of closed-loop automation of the drip irrigation system. The essential element is to turn on and off the motor distantly. The device guarantees that all the faults are tested, and at exactly that point, the motor is started.

To adequately utilize this promising technology, the difficulties related with arranging and overseeing information securing, proficiently dissecting the gathered information, putting away information for future investigations, and showing information to the end client must be overcome.

18.2 Application of WSN in e-Governance

Advanced government, e-government, and e-administration are words that have turned out to be equivalent with the utilization of data and corresponding innovations in government organizations. So, a versatile foundation is required for building these administrations. Distributed computing is one approach for making an adaptable foundation. Distributed computing [8] is a piece of software engineering that empowers web administrations to manage clients by means of exceptionally adaptable processing limits. It is a highly adaptable and controlled PC system that has applications for end-clients. Information and administrations are situated in a shared, dynamic, and adaptable arrangement of assets in view of innovations of virtualization and versatile application conditions. For upgrading e-government administrations, there is a requirement for sending virtual servers and storing information in a distributed computing condition. Information can be gained from a wide range of sources. WSNs can be utilized for gathering this information because they display appropriated systems that comprise various sensor hubs. Sensors are spatially appropriated and they are utilized for measurements, for example, temperature, moistness, sound levels, weight, condition factors, and so forth. WSNs are adaptable and their design and reason can be effortlessly changed. This chapter depicts conceivable uses of WSNs for making e-taxpayer supported organizations more effective, and some answers for incorporating WSNs in e-government. Some e-government regions that can use WSNs incorporate regions of open transport, issuing individual reports, reporting on regular dangers, and so on. This chapter gives a model of utilizing WSNs for outlining and sending in e-taxpayer driven organizations. A distributed computing system is utilized for building up this model.

The innovation of WSNs shows spatially conveyed and independent sensors remotely connected that are utilized for observing and gathering information of physical or natural conditions, for example, temperature, sound, vibration, weight, development, and poisons.

The innovation of WSNs can be extremely valuable in numerous application zones, for example, conditioning, pharmaceutical, military, horticulture, stock checking, interruption location in gas pipes, movement, machine breakdown, and numerous others. For gathering information, WSNs utilize sensor hubs that as segments have a microcontroller, outer memory, handset, control source, and at least one sensor. Wireless sensors are furnished with a radio handset and an arrangement of transducers through which they get data about the conditions. These sensors, in an extensive sensor field, can naturally sort out themselves to speak with each other and with other sink hubs. A remote client can add charges into the WSN by means of the sink to allocate information gathering, handling and exchange errands to the sensors, and accepting gathered information through the sink. Sensors are controlled by batteries, typically a few standard 'AA' standard batteries that can be supplanted upon termination. Battery estimate, as a rule, decides the span of the sensor, so existing equipment measurement is around a couple of cubic centimeters. Sensors are devices that send an experimental effect to a modification in a physical condition. Keeping in mind the end goal is to connect with the sensor equipment, software engineers can utilize distinctive working systems, for example, TinyOS, Contiki, Mantis, Nano-RK, and LiteOS.

18.3 Need of WSNs in Agriculture

About 20 per cent of earth's land mass is deficient in water or rainfall. However, these deserts offer many natural advantages to farmers such as multiple growing seasons, longer periods of sunshine, and a lower number of invasive animals and diseases. If available farming techniques are combined with modern techniques, these advantages may eliminate the traditional disadvantages that have caused desert farming to suffer (high soil salinity and lack of water). The success of modern desert agriculture completely depends on the fact that researchers and farmers work together to adjust to the challenges of change.

In order to develop an efficient plantation management system, the availability of accurate data (soil properties, physicochemical parameters, agronomic data, atmospheric data, etc.) is a foremost requirement. This data must be collected preferably on a daily or hourly basis. Manual decision making and laboratory analysis of these parameters takes a long time and by the time results are available, farm conditions might change, leading to an inappropriate decision. In order to enhance agricultural productivity and quality, quick decision making is needed at the farm level. The drip irrigation method is a good transport method to water crops. It utilizes a PVC pipe with tools for dripping water and low-volume showers, Laser Soaker Line, drip tape, or Porous Pipe systems. The systems are easy to introduce as they do not need trenching and shears for cutting. An opening punch is required for introducing a producer into the polyethylene hose. The drip irrigation method can keep up dampness intensities in the root zone of the plants, staying away from excessively wet/excessively dry swings, which can happen in overhead watering. These systems can be controlled physically or by the utilization of a programmed clock in combination with a tensiometer and can be utilized to apply manure straight to the base of plants. With the improvement of cutting-edge innovation, checking of physical and natural parameters (soil dampness, soil temperature, soil pH, leaf temperature, relative mugginess, air temperature, precipitation, vapor weight, and daylight hours) is conceivable through a WSN.

As the small sensors batteries are usually impractical to recharge from the technical and economic point of view, one of the most critical issues related to WSNs is to guarantee the unattended operation of the network for a long period. Research on WSN is gaining tremendous importance due to an ever-widening range of applications: disaster and environmental monitoring, wildlife habitat monitoring, intrusion detection, and security surveillance are some areas where sensor networks can be used. The transfer of information between the sensor nodes and a sink node in an efficient manner is a challenging task that many researchers are currently focusing on.

Out of many applications of sensor networks, the potential impact is huge in the area of environmental monitoring. Sensors allow monitoring an area of interest at a low cost and without human presence. The sensor nodes used in environmental monitoring collect data using sensors integrated into each node and send this information to a central device called a base station. The base station acts as a gateway by allowing access to the collected data via the Internet.

The technical requirements of a WSN applied to environmental monitoring include:

1. *Autonomy*: Batteries must have the capacity to control the nodes for the entire network lifetime. As the radio transceiver represents a large portion of the power utilization in a node, the network needs to decrease information movement as much as possible and the number of bounces required communicating something specific.
2. *Robustness*: In this use, human maintenance is normally troublesome in view of the harshness of the landscape. Hence, it is vital to plan strong programming and equipment that can be adjusted to any episode.
3. *Flexibility*: The network must have the capacity to include, move, or expel nodes to meet application needs. The network should naturally distinguish the progression, arranging communication in consequence.

WSNs have been generally examined for environmental monitoring. In such monitoring applications, naturally distinguishing occasions are fundamental, for example, in identifying vehicles or backwoods fires. As of now, the ordinary occasion location technique depends on choices made at the sensor node(s) in view of predefined information limits for typical conditions. The justification for such limit based methodologies is that when occasions happen, there will be noticeable changes in ecological information. Accordingly, an occasion can be caught once the watched sensory information surpasses the predefined edges.

4. *Specific Benefits of Drip Irrigation*:
   - Water saving, as only the areas around the plant's root zone are irrigated.
   - Plant appearance is enhanced, as they suffer less stress from variations in soil moisture.
   - Constant moisture increases plant growth.
   - Slow application rate prevents additional surface water build-up and reduces evaporation.
   - The low application rate and the use of automatic timers result in precise water control.
   - The growth of weeds is decreased because areas between plants are not irrigated.
   - The system can be designed for use in all types of terrain and soil conditions.

- The low flow rate of the system allows irrigation of larger areas.
- Drip irrigation systems are normally installed at considerably lower costs than those of an underground sprinkler, bubbler, or shrub spray system.
- Chemicals and nutrients can be fed directly to the plant in controlled quantities through the use of fertilizer dispensers.
- The hydraulic design of a sprinkler system is more than adequate, leading to easy conversion to drip irrigation.
- The drip system is cost-effective with native landscapes in dry weather conditions.

18.4 Literature Review

In the field of agriculture, the most vital part is to initially get data about the productivity and dampness of the soil. In the wake of estimating these two factors, an agriculturist can begin the sowing of seeds [9], giving a brief outline of various methods to quantify soil ripeness to check the efficiency of the product. Two devices are utilized to quantify the constituents (potassium, phosphorus, nitrogen) of the soil. In the wake of estimating productivity, an arrangement of programmed drip irrigation through the chip is proposed to quantify the dampness of the soil.

WSN technologies are currently progressively implementing precision agriculture monitoring [10]. The various benefits of WSN in agriculture include high performance, low power consumption, increase in the production efficiency while decreasing cost, and collected distributed data.

In the most recent decades, a remotely monitored embedded system for irrigation purposes has turned into another need for a farmer to spare his or her energy, time, and cash.

An automated irrigation system [11] was created to enhance a water plan for rural yields. The system comprises a circulated wireless network of temperature and soil dampness sensors that are put in the roots of plants. The automated system was tried in a field for 136 days and water reserve funds of up to 90 per cent contrasted with conventional irrigation practices of the farming area were accomplished.

Efficient water management [12] is a noteworthy worry in numerous cropping systems in semi-arid and dry zones. Dispersed in-field sensor-based irrigation systems give a potential answer to help site-particular irrigation administration, which enables farmers to boost their profitability while sparing water. The work portrays points of interest of the outline and instrumentation of a WSN, variable rate irrigation, and programming for continuous in-field detecting and control of linear-move irrigation systems.

18.5 Simulation Overview

Using QualNet Network Simulator 6.1, it was possible to design a scenario for analysis purpose by taking 100 m × 100 m of a land area and placing 100 nodes randomly in a 2-dimensional plane. The sink node was considered to be node number 70 and using the traffic generator, 20 applications were used for this terrestrial wireless communication. The antenna in the sensor nodes was taken to be omnidirectional and contained a battery of 200 mAhr in each. It is a software-based simulation hence no real sensors were used in this experiment. The simulation was conducted for 1000 seconds after setting up the necessary parameters and 4 different routing protocols were used to conduct a batch experiment. The simulation was conducted in total eight times, as we wanted to compare both the sink node being static or using a random waypoint being mobile (Figure 18.1).

Table 18.1 shows a list of parameters that were assumed for this simulation. Hence, the outcome of the experiment is discussed below including a graphical presentation. The parameters taken into consideration are throughput, delay, and network lifetime because they help us to analyze the performance of the network designed using a particular scenario. Comparison of simulation work using four different routing protocols has been conducted to analyze the necessary parameters. The graphs are discussed below.

Figure 18.2 shows the performance of Dynamic Source Routing (DSR) to be better than the rest in the case of the sink node being static or mobile. Dynamic MANET On-Demand (DYMO) being the second best is also a suitable routing protocol for this scenario. Ad Hoc On-Demand

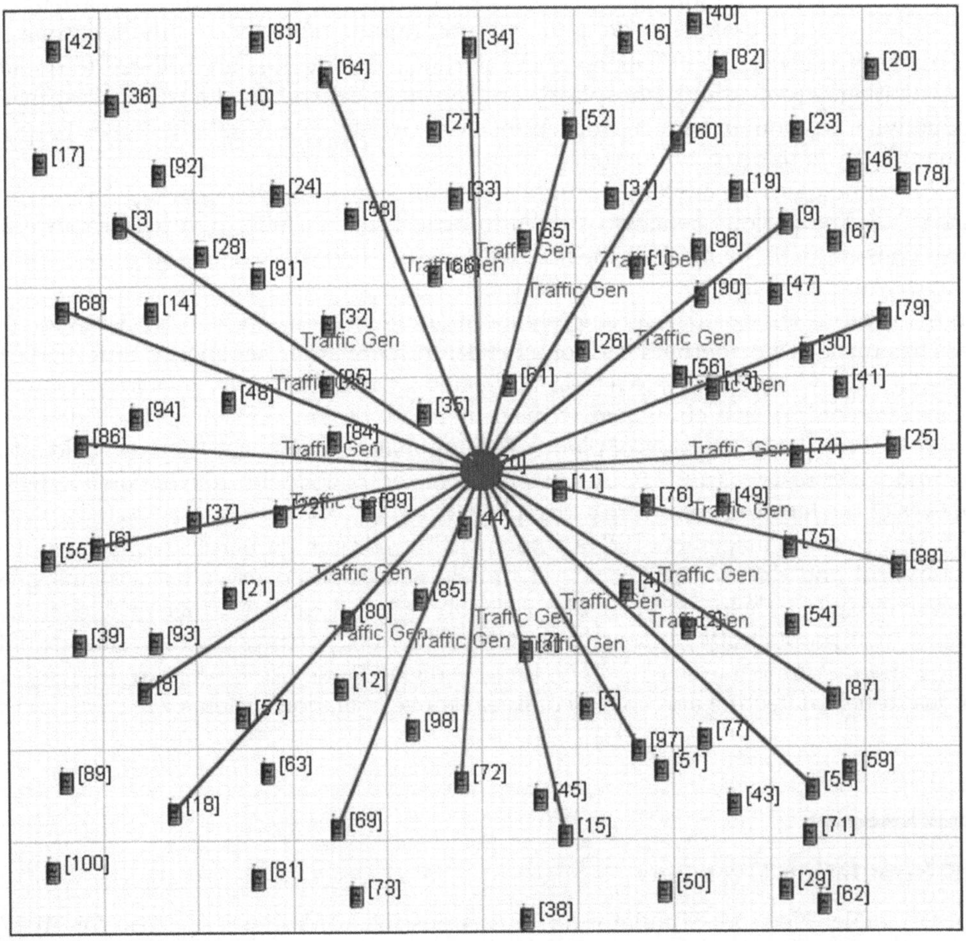

FIGURE 18.1
Network design scenario.

TABLE 18.1
Simulation Parameter for WSN

Parameter(s)	Value(s)
Deployment strategy	Random
Total number of nodes	100
Terrain in 2D	100 m × 100 m
Number of PAN coordinators	1
Communication protocol	IEEE 802.15.4
Simulation time (sec.)	1000
Channel frequencies (zig bee)	2.4 GHz
Routing protocol	DYMO, AODV, DSR & ZRP
Traffic type	TRAFFIC-GEN
Packet size (bytes)	50
Wireless propagation model	Two-ray ground propagation
Battery capacity (mAhr)	200
Transmission range (m)	10
Antenna type	Omnidirectional
Energy model	Generic
Transmit circuitry power consumption (mW)	24.75
Receive circuitry power consumption (mW)	13.5
Sleep circuitry power consumption (mW)	0.005
Idle circuitry power consumption (mW)	13.5

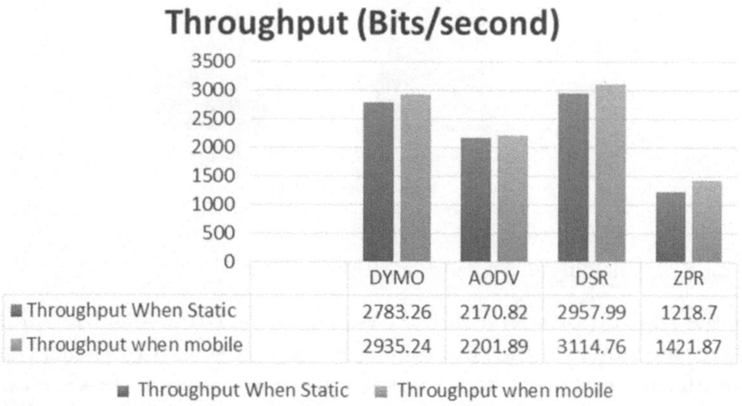

FIGURE 18.2
Throughput in bits/second.

Distance Vector (AODV) is an old technique and hence does not perform as well. Zone Routing Protocol (ZRP), as a hybrid protocol, has the worst performance amongst them all.

Figure 18.3 shows the least delay in ZRP when the sink node is static. However, DYMO is comparatively better than the rest in the case of delay because it almost stays the same when the sink node is either static or mobile. DSR has a comparatively high delay, still, it is a suitable routing protocol for consideration. However, AODV has the highest delay and thus is not advisable for use in this scenario.

Figure 18.4 shows the total residual energy left within the nodes after completion of the 1000 second simulation. The graph shows the average value of the nodes when DYMO was

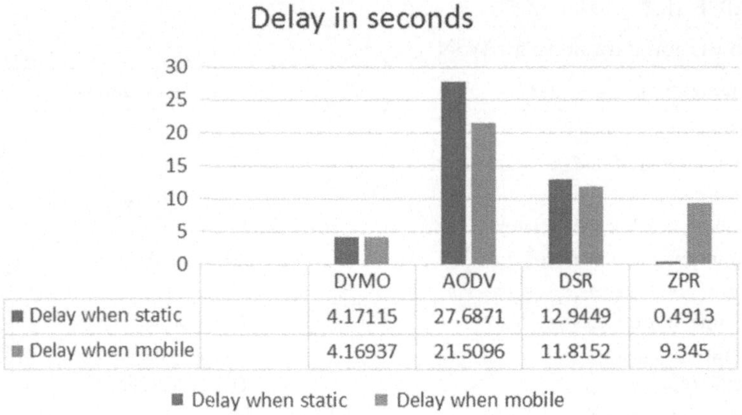

FIGURE 18.3
Delay in seconds.

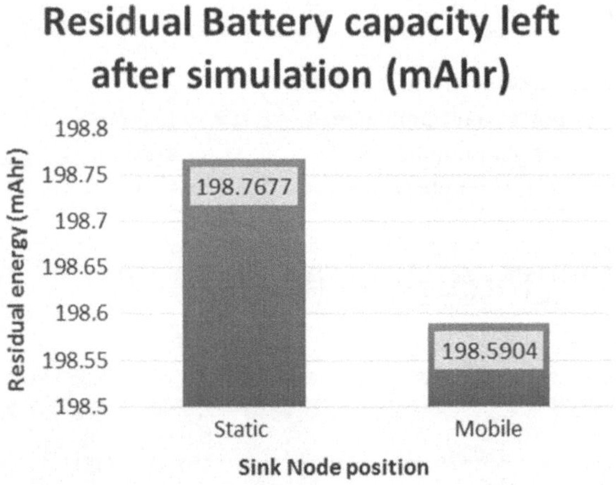

FIGURE 18.4
Residual battery capacity remaining after simulation (mAhr).

considered as the routing protocol. In the case of all the protocols, the value happens to be approximately the same for the sink node when either static or mobile. Using the given value, network lifetime of sensor nodes when static was found to be 45.08 hours, while in the case of mobility, it was found to be 39.41 hours. It clearly shows how mobility can result in more consumption of battery power during simulation.

Thus, it can be said that both DSR and DYMO routing protocols were found to be suitable for use in this scenario with the sink node being either static or mobile. The network lifetime calculation suggests increasing the input value of the battery for a longer lifetime of the network.

18.6 Future Road Maps

A WSN based drip irrigation system efficiently uses water and causes healthy and fast growth in plants. A small amount is lost to evaporation, while pavements and areas between the plants remain dry. The method also reduces the growth of weeds and allows cultivation during and immediately after an irrigation cycle. A large area is allowed to be watered from a small water source because drip irrigation uses water slower than other irrigation methods. The biggest saving for the home gardener is time: one can now garden on a larger scale, and with an automatic timer, the gardener can travel or deal successfully with a busy schedule while the garden or landscape flourishes.

Acknowledgments

The authors want to thank the editors, Dr. Puneet Kumar and Dr. V. K. Jain, for motivating us to write this chapter.

References

1. Zhao, F. and L.J. Guibas. *Wireless Sensor Networks: An Information Processing Approach.* Morgan Kaufmann, New York (2004).
2. He, D., N. Kumar, J. Chen, C.-C. Lee, N. Chilamkurti, and S.-S. Yeov. "Robust anonymous authentication protocol for health-care applications using wireless medical sensor networks". *Multimedia Systems* 21.1 (2015): 49–60.
3. Xu, G., W. Shen, and X. Wang. "Applications of wireless sensor networks in marine environment monitoring: A survey". *Sensors* 14.9 (2014): 16932–16954.
4. Abbasi, A. Z., N. Islam, and Z. A. Shaikh. "A review of wireless sensors and networks' applications in agriculture". *Computer Standards and Interfaces* 36.2 (2014): 263–270.
5. Rashid, B. and M.H. Rehmani. "Applications of wireless sensor networks for urban areas: A survey". *Journal of Network and Computer Applications* 60 (2016): 192–219.
6. Ioan, I. and C. V. Rădulescu. "New challenges for agriculture within the context of climate change". *Theoretical and Applied Economics* 22.4 (2015): 253–262.
7. Keraita, B. and O. O. Cofie. Irrigation and soil fertility management practices. In Drechsel, Pay; Keraita, B. (Eds.) *Irrigated Urban Vegetable Production in Ghana: Characteristics, Benefits and Risk Mitigation.* International Water Management Institute (IWMI), Colombo, Sri Lanka, pp. 74–88 (2014).
8. Khan, S.U., A. Y. Zomaya, and A. Abbas. Handbook of Large-Scale Distributed Computing in Smart Healthcare. Springer, London (2017).
9. Rashid Hussain, J. L. S. and Anshulgangwar, Md. R., "Control of irrigation automatically by using WIRELESS SENSOR NETWORK", *International Journal of Soft Computing and Engineering (IJSCE),* 3.1 (2013): 324–328
10. Singh, S. and N. Sharma, "Research paper on drip irrigation management using wireless sensors", *IRACST – International Journal of Computer Networks and Wireless Communications (IJCNWC),* 2.4 (2012): 461–464.
11. Gutierrez, J., J.F. Villa-Medina, A. Nieto-Garibay, and M.A. Porta-Gandara, "Automated irrigation system using a wireless sensor network and GPRS module", *IEEE Transactions on Instrumentation and Measurement* 63.1 (2014): 166–176.
12. Kim, Y., R. G. Evans and W.M. Iversen, "Remote sensing and control of an irrigation system using a distributed wireless sensor network", in *IEEE Transactions on Instrumentation and Measurement,* 57.7 (2008): 1379–1387.

Index